A black school, a white school
and their season of dreams

First and Long

Greg Borowski

Badger Books Inc.
Oregon, Wisconsin

© Copyright 2004 by Greg Borowski
All Rights Reserved.
Published by Badger Books Inc.
Edited by Pat Reardon
Printed in the U.S.A.
All photos used by permission.
Cover photo of Shorewood senior Drew O'Malley carried off the field by Messmer juniors Petrell Mallett and Rob Wyatt by Benny Sieu, *Milwaukee Journal Sentinel*
Hardcover: ISBN 1-932542-02-7
Softcover: ISBN 1-932542-03-5
This work is based, in part, on an article that appeared in the Nov. 25, 2001 edition of the Milwaukee Journal Sentinel.

Badger Books Inc./Waubesa Press
P.O. Box 192
Oregon, WI 53575
Toll-free phone: (800) 928-2372
Fax: (608) 835-3638
Email: books@badgerbooks.com
Web site: www.badgerbooks.com

Library of Congress Cataloging-in-Publication Data

Borowski, Greg.
   First and long : a black school, a white school, and their season of dreams / by Greg Borowski.
      p. cm.
   ISBN 1-932542-02-7 — ISBN 1-932542-03-5
   1. Football—Wisconsin—Milwaukee. 2. Messmer High School (Milwaukee, Wis.)—Football. 3. Shorewood High School (Shorewood, Wis.)—Football. 4. School sports—Wisconsin—Milwaukee. I. Title.

GV959.53.M55B67 2004
796.332'62'0977595—dc22   2003028015

For my father,
who would have loved this team.

Contents

Foreword

My connection to the Shorewood-Messmer football team is that the current coach, Ron Davies, was my classmate, roommate and teammate at the University of St. Thomas in St. Paul, Minnesota, a long, long time ago.

When Coach Davies told me he was taking the job at Shorewood-Messmer for the 2002 season, I thought he was being overly pessimistic about the problems facing him and his staff. Now, having read Greg Borowski's excellent book, I can't imagine what Ron was thinking when he took the job!

Talk about challenges.

My father once said, "The most important element in the character makeup of a man who is successful is that of mental toughness." Coach Jim Trost, his assistant coaches, and the players from the 2001 team, as depicted in this book, had the quality of mental toughness in abundance. Unfortunately, that's about all they had. But it was enough to get them through a very difficult year.

This book is a great read.

It's a testament to the value of high school athletics. High school football, in particular, teaches young men, in their most formative years, the qualities of mental toughness, commitment and sacrifice. And it tears down racial, social and economic barriers.

Read this book and see if you agree.

— **Vince Lombardi Jr.**

Acknowledgments

Some people believed in this story from the start. Others only came to believe later. As a first-time author, I am indebted to them all.

Thanks to Lonnie Herman, who got the publishing process started, telling me to write the book I wanted to write, and to Marv Balousek and the folks at Badger Books, who got it finished, after several detours and dead ends. Along the way, many friends and strangers helped navigate the publishing world, opening many doors. Among them: Mike Ruby at the *Milwaukee Journal Sentinel*; William Elliott at Marquette University; Br. Bob Smith at Messmer High School; Kate Huston at the Milwaukee Public Library; Steve Rushin of *Sports Illustrated*; author and radio host Charles Sykes; Peter Collier of Encounter Books and Mildred Puechner, who happens to be my aunt.

It was midway through the 2001 season, as I was following the team for an anticipated feature story for the *Journal Sentinel* — a time when most of the editors were struggling to see the story I saw — that one of the parents, Robert Wyatt Sr., suggested, perhaps unintentionally, that it may really be a book. He was a frequent sideline partner at the games and practices, greeting me every day with a handshake and "Another day, another page." Thanks to George Stanley, managing editor of the paper, for a focused edit that rescued the article, which went on to be named the top sports story of the year by the Milwaukee Press Club, and to other editors for allowing a City Hall reporter to moonlight one fall as a high school sports writer. Annette Griswold and Sherman Williams helped arrange for the use of the photos, shot during the season by photographer Benny Sieu. Michael Tucker, a Messmer teacher and high-school classmate, provided some additional photos. College classmate John Saller took my headshot for the cover. Ron Smith, a classmate and now a colleague, gave it a final copy edit.

Of course, the project would not have been possible without the cooperation and patience of the administrators at the two schools, including Br. Bob Smith, Jeff Monday and Joy Bretsch at Messmer and Rick Monroe and Cindy Wilburth at Shorewood. There were surely times when they questioned the wisdom of allowing a reporter to witness such a trying season. Likewise, thanks to Coach Jim Trost and the rest of the Shorewood-Messmer coaching staff, who let me blend in as best I could. From the start, Trost said I could see it all — "The good, the bad and the ugly" — and never wavered, though many others would have pulled the plug. Coach Ron Davies, who took over for season two, graciously let me to finish what I started, allowing me to talk with players as I followed the second year for the book's Epilogue. Many parents and guardians, notably Sandra Tomlinson and Mark and Mary Wallner, offered insight into the players, the communities and the team.

The players, though, are the true stars of this book and of the landmark season. Many put up with repeated interviews, prying questions and the near-constant presence of a reporter during a period that tested them all. Many quit the team, but it is my belief all passed an important test. From the top of the roster to the bottom, they are better people than players and will surely go on to even greater success.

As the newspaper article turned into a book project, and many long nights and weekends at the computer, the Shorewood-Messmer team provided a perfect model of commitment, perseverance and dedication to the belief that something good comes out of hard work. My hope is they see themselves in these pages — and see the season as the triumph it was — as they move on to bigger things and greater success.

Finally, many people offered support during the writing process or thoughts on early drafts, including my mother, MaryAnne, sister, Amy, and two brothers, Mark and David. My colleague, friend and fellow author Tom Kertscher helped sharpen the story in parts and smooth it out in others — providing valuable thoughts at a critical time in the process. They all believed in this book from the start and at the finish, never wavering in the confidence it would be published someday, even when I did.

— *Greg Borowski*

Winning isn't everything,
it's the only thing.

The greatest accomplishment
is not in never falling, but in rising
again after you fall.

— *Vince Lombardi, football coach*

Chapter 1
"Red and blue make purple."

It was the first day of football practice and the afternoon sun was blinding. The temperature topped 95 degrees, the hottest day yet in a brutal and unrelenting heat wave, and stepping outside, even from the stale air of the basement locker room, was like walking into an oven. It took a moment to steady yourself, to get your bearings.

Coach Jim Trost walked through the locker room, where the stragglers were still lacing up new cleats, and out to the practice field. He carried four footballs under his arms and had a practice plan rolled up in the back pocket of his red shorts.

He stopped and squinted into the sun.

There were maybe three dozen kids waiting. A few leaned against the fence, under a circle of shade from a single tree. Others slapped hands and joked with old friends or just took a silent measure of the competition. The practice field doubled as the softball diamond in the spring and out near second base, a hose snaked across the dry grass and was slipped through the handle of a shovel that was staked in the dirt. The nozzle sent the water sailing wildly through the air, wiggling and shimmying in the slight breeze, a small puddle forming at the base, the water not soaking into the hardened ground.

There were more kids than most anyone could remember for a football practice at Shorewood High School, a mostly white public school in one of Milwaukee's more affluent suburbs. A year earlier, the team started with 22

players, finished with 17 and had so few freshmen that all
but the sophomores had to play the freshman game Thursday night, then suit up for varsity on Friday. This year,
Shorewood had combined its program with Messmer High
School, a largely black Catholic school scarcely a mile down
Capitol Drive, whose students were mainly central city
residents, many from low-income families. It was the first
football partnership in the state of Wisconsin to involve a
private school and a public school. Of the two-dozen or so
like it in the country, it was the only one to mix city kids
and suburban kids, black and white.

In Milwaukee, a community so racially divided it has
been labeled "hyper-segregated," that alone was enough
for some observers to label the effort a success. But not the
coaches. Or the players. They wanted success on the field.
Desperately wanted it. Not next year, or the year after.

Now.

Trost dropped the footballs and blew his whistle, a
sharp, insistent blast.

"Let's go, let's go, let's go," he yelled.

Already, after a summer of weightlifting and workouts,
there was brash talk among the players of a conference
championship — and Trost did little to discourage it. If
not a championship, then a long-awaited playoff berth, or
at least a stop to the perpetual losing at Shorewood. Since
the 1988 season, when the team finished 3-6, Shorewood
had won four games and lost 104. When the team broke a
63-game losing streak in 1996, it was featured on ESPN.
The arrangement with Messmer, which had been without
a team since 1983, meant an influx of gifted athletes, but
mostly ones whose only exposure to football was in front
of a television or in pickup games on the street or playground.

To be sure, it was not a typical recipe for success, adding inexperienced players to a bad team. But high school
is about possibilities, not limitations; horizons not fences.

The dream was theirs.

"All right," Trost yelled again. "Bring it in. Run, run, run. Let's go."

Jim Trost, 33, never wanted to do much more in life than coach football. Indeed, when he finished playing in high school, some 15 years before, and classmates from St. Patrick's on the northwest side of Chicago were going off to college or the military, Trost took a job as an assistant at the high school and began coaching the team at nearby St. Bartholomew Elementary School, where he had gone to school and where his family went to church. They practically filled a row of pews, back when the 12 kids — Rick, Mary, Tim, Jackie, Chris, Terry, Tommy, Jerry, Jimmy, Geralyn, Kim and Danny — were growing up and everyone was still at home or not too far away.

Of course, Trost would have played college football if he had the chance, would have kept playing in a heartbeat. Given anything to keep playing. But for his first time in organized sports, back to the day in the seventh grade when Trost first pulled on his St. Bart's jersey, reality got in the way of a dream. Trost stood a mere 5'3" and, back then, weighed about 135 pounds. At St. Pat's, an all-boys school with more than 1,100 students, Trost played fullback and defensive tackle — two power positions — on guts and desire more than strength or size, winning raves and notice in the Chicago newspapers. Copies of the articles still get sent out with his resume. But no college would take him, not at that size. And Trost had no interest in college without football, so he went back to St. Bart's, tucked in the working-class neighborhood where he grew up. It was the kind of neighborhood that had a bit of dirt under its fingernails and was proud to admit it. The sort of neighborhood where some of the kids would end up on the wrong side of the law, and others would become the cops who arrested them.

Now, in his third season at Shorewood, his second as

head coach, married with three young children and living in rural Hartford, Wisconsin, so far from the streets of Chicago that sometimes even he could not believe it, Jim Trost had filled out and carried a slight gut. He was balding, with the hair that remained cut bristle short. He wore wire-rim glasses, which he sometimes lifted to his forehead, a whistle dangling around his neck and two watches on his left wrist, just in case one stopped.

And, as always, he was eager to start practice.

Players jogged over. Some knelt on the brittle grass. Others stood, arms folded. Some wore navy blue shirts, a mistake on such a hot day, but they were Messmer shirts, and Messmer was their school. It was a statement. Others wore Shorewood football shirts, old and faded. Some were muscular and fit, others out of shape, bellies hanging over their shorts. A couple could only be described as scrawny. Some were white, but most were black. Although there were a few exceptions on both sides, in a community where race seems to infuse nearly everything, the football partnership could easily be reduced to the simplest of views: Messmer was black and Shorewood was white.

Trost paced, waited for everyone to settle in.

The day before, at a team meeting, he had talked with the players about the season, the history involved, how it was about more than football, it was about the journey, being part of something bigger, a team. Yes, they were from two schools. And, yes, they went home each night to different worlds, worlds the other could barely fathom. But for a few hours each day and under the lights every Friday, they would be one. They had to be one, or it would never work. The season would test them all, coaches and players alike, on the field and off. The test was this: Could they line up side by side and see not Shorewood red or Messmer blue, not a stranger or a race, but a teammate, a brother, a friend.

Now 33 players, each a jumble of nerves and excitement, surrounded Trost.

One, the star running back, was playing for a college scholarship, but his success would depend as much on his new and untested teammates as himself. Another, the fullback, was playing high school football for the first time, though a bad knee already threatened his dream season. One, the quarterback, was seeking redemption at a new school where he didn't feel welcome. Another, the would-be quarterback, didn't know the spot he had been promised in the spring was now earmarked for someone else. There were seniors from Messmer playing football for the first time and seniors from Shorewood starting their final season. There were kids from perfect homes and kids from broken homes, kids who had tried drugs and one who had sold them. There was a wide receiver who longed to play in college, a wide receiver who had never caught an official pass and a wide receiver — so short he stood in front so he could see Trost — who had dreamed of playing on this field ever since he was a boy watching wide-eyed from the stands.

For some, the dream would come true. For others, it would surely die.

For all there was promise.

Trost had barely slept the night before. Neither had some of the players.

It was Aug. 7, 2001.

"First practice," Trost said. "Let's make it a good one."

He paused a beat.

"Helmets on."

After a series of stretching exercises, the team split into five groups, rotating from station to station for drills. At each, the newcomers followed the lead of the returning players. They had to shuffle between orange cones, hips low. They had to drop to the ground, roll, and in an elaborate human weave, jump up and over the next guy. They crawled between heavy padded bags, then high-stepped over them, the whistles and shouts from coaches blending together and echoing against the nearby buildings.

"Down down, good job, that's it, dig dig dig, don't look for the cones, drop your butt, no hopping, work the knees, c'mon, faster, digdigdig, shoulders squared, downdowndown, keep your feet moving, good job, excellent job."

Mark Moore was the star running back, and he looked the part, from his chiseled arms to his powerful legs to the earrings that gleamed in the dim light of the locker room. He practically rippled when he walked. Mark was a senior at Shorewood, his shoulder was strong after off-season surgery and the colleges were calling.

This was the year.

His year.

Mark had written "No. 22, The Heat" on a piece of athletic tape and pasted it above his locker and no one, not even the new players from Messmer, had to ask who that was. He thought about writing "The Quiet Storm," but it didn't have the same ring to it.

Mark was black, a Milwaukee resident who attended Shorewood under a program aimed at reducing segregation that opened a limited number of slots in suburban schools to city residents. For elementary and middle school, Mark had gone to Blessed Trinity, a Catholic school in Milwaukee, along with his two brothers, twin Matthew and younger Micah, who was two grades behind. But for high school, their mother — who was an administrator in the Milwaukee Public Schools system — sent them all to Shorewood. Mark knew little about Shorewood when he caught the Capitol Drive bus to school on that first day. Though Shorewood was only about five miles away, from the west side of Milwaukee it seemed like a distant and exciting place, so much bigger than Blessed Trinity, where there was only a classroom or two for each grade and you saw the same people all day long. So much more happening, so much more to do.

Education, of course, came first. Mark's mother insisted it be that way, with designs on her three boys going to college. But football, that was important, too, at least for Mark. At one of the first practices, Mark asked a coach if Shorewood was any kind of football powerhouse. "You don't know much about Shorewood football, do you?" came the unvarnished response. After missing his freshman year to an injury, torn ligaments in the shoulder, suffered when making an arm tackle on the first play of the first game, Mark started on varsity as a sophomore and Trost quickly designed an offensive scheme that took advantage of his speed to the outside.

Then Mark's mother died. Cancer.

And then there was the tailspin.

Nancy Moore had raised Mark and his two brothers mostly alone. She and their father were divorced in 1989 when the twins were three and Micah was one. Her death in January of 2000, by all accounts, came hard and came fast. For a time afterward, the coaches said, Mark appeared lost. His grades suffered and that fall he was ineligible for the first three games of his junior season. Matthew, meanwhile, left Shorewood after being arrested and pleading guilty to possessing cocaine and intending to sell marijuana at the school, according to the police report. Football, the coaches thought, had kept Mark going, kept him focused and on the right path. So had Leslie, a senior track star, whom Mark had started dating the previous spring. The grades, finally, came together and once Mark returned to the field he notched 641 yards in five games, good enough for a second-team all-conference selection. He was easily the best player on a team that after a 38-game losing streak managed to win one game, a 51-19 triumph over Brown Deer on October 13, 2000 — Mark's 17th birthday and the day he and Leslie officially started dating.

Sandra Tomlinson, an aunt to the boys, was appointed guardian for all three. Tomlinson, a no-nonsense woman, had lived in the other half of the duplex from the time the boys were born. When the boys were small, she would sometimes take them to the recreational program she ran during the summer for the Milwaukee Public Schools. Indeed, it was one summer day, when Mark was six or seven, that he got his first football. He spotted it on the roof of a building at a park and his aunt helped boost him up to get it. Mark played with that ball for years, until it finally wore out and burst. Tomlinson came to all of Mark's games, just as she had with her sister, before her sister became too sick to make it. Now she often toted along a video camera so she could capture the moments before they were lost and so Mark and Micah would have tapes to watch someday. She saw it as her duty to see the boys were raised the way their mother, her older sister, would have wanted.

Of all the players on the team, Mark had the most at stake. He needed a football team, first of all, and without the partnership with Messmer, which brought much needed bodies, there wouldn't have been one. And, in order to have an eye-popping season, the kind that would keep the scouts talking and the coaches interested, the kind that would let him fulfill his dream of playing in college, Mark needed a strong line to open holes, a quarterback who could take some of the pressure off and a rock-solid blocker. That's where Nathan Shorter came in.

Nate, a Messmer junior, was the fullback.

Nate had never played high school football before and was now too old for the Athletes For Youth league, where his team lost in the championship game the year before. The league, which focused on central city kids, was for those who didn't have high school teams to play on — or lacked the grades to be eligible. The league was founded

in 1969, two years after the Milwaukee riots, by Green
Bay Packers great Willie Davis. At Messmer, Nate had been
asking about football from the time he was a freshman,
even before the first day of school. At the fall extra-cur-
ricular fair, where the football table amounted to an empty
chair and a sign-up sheet, Nate was always among the first
to sign. With no chance at football, Nate helped start the
weightlifting club and became its most dedicated member. At the beginning, he could bench press 135 pounds
about 10 times. Now, at a burly 6'1" and 290 pounds, he
could lift more than 400 pounds.

Nate was big from a baby, arriving at 9.13 pounds and
more than 20 inches long. As a baby, when a football,
truck and basketball were placed in front of him, Nate
always went for the football. After church on fall Sundays,
Nate would sit with his father, a high school football player
himself back in Mississippi, and watch the Dallas Cowboys. It was the glory days of Troy Aikman and Emmitt
Smith and Michael Irvin, but Nate always liked lineman
Charles Haley best. The first football he remembers ever
getting came at about age seven — a Cowboys ball under
the Christmas tree. Once the presents were all unwrapped,
Nate called his friends and everyone gathered in a vacant
lot where they played football — tackle — for hours in
the snow, until ice was stuck to sweaters and hats.

Nate, though, had given up on football at Messmer,
which had been without a team since the school closed
briefly in 1984. There were always, it seemed, promises
and more promises: We're working on it. Give us some
more time. There were always promises, but no results.
Nate had considered transferring to Vincent High School,
a public school in Milwaukee, whose team was favored to
win the City Conference and whose coach had come to
watch him in the championship game of the recreation
league. Instead, back in the spring, at the end of a prayer
assembly in the auditorium, Joy Bretsch, the Messmer

athletic director, stepped to the podium and, as excitement rippled through the students, she announced the partnership with Shorewood, pulled out a football and called Nate to the stage. He would be Messmer's honorary captain. When Nate reached the top step, Bretsch tossed him the ball. Nate caught it and held it in the air to screams and shouts and applause.

For a big guy, Nate was surprisingly quick on his feet, quick and powerful. He had been nicknamed "Diesel" during summer camp. The coaches dreamed of Nate rumbling through the line, like a steamroller, Mark slicing through behind him. The two, Nate and Mark, were at the center of the talk about Shorewood-Messmer football from the beginning. They were the best players, the dream backfield and the two with the brightest football futures. So when students from the two schools who were interested in playing met for the first time, at a meeting in the "S" Room in the basement of Shorewood's gymnasium building, everyone at Shorewood already had heard about big Nate Shorter, and everyone at Messmer knew about Mark Moore, the stud.

At the meeting, Shorewood players in one group, Messmer players in another, each side casually sizing the other up, Nate and Mark finally met.

Looks good, Mark thought.

They shook hands.

He's ripped, Nate thought.

In the spring, the players gathered several times a week at Messmer to lift weights. Messmer had a new weight room, part of its recent gymnasium addition. Shorewood had a weight room, too, but it was open to the community as a fitness center, so it was awkward to bring in a bunch of kids and coaches. Indeed, when more than 30 players, most of them black, showed up at Shorewood for a special agility camp, Trost was asked to shift it to nearby

Estabrook Park. At Messmer the players would run through the quiet hallways getting in shape. It was at once a solitary and a group pursuit, their commitment tested with each trip up the three flights of stairs and with each set of weight-room repetitions, arms shaking and bodies straining to do one more lift. Sometimes they would play tag football in the gym, the bleachers pushed back and glass backboards lifted, shoes squeaking on the shiny new floor.

Trost would usually quarterback one team, making up the plays as he went along. He was at home in the spot, laughing at missed passes and trash talking when his team scored. Trost was competitive, always had been. He had been exposed to sports before he even knew what they were. From the time Trost learned to talk, his older brothers trained him on the names of Chicago sports figures. They would say "Dick." Trost would respond, "Butkus." One time they even took Trost to a downtown department store so they could meet Chicago Blackhawks great Tony Esposito and show off little Jimmy's skills. "Tony," they said. "Eschpazhito," he replied.

As a boy, Trost sometimes would bike with friends the three miles to Wrigley Field on opening day, where they'd sign up to lift the seats back into the folded position after the game. They would work all the way from one end of the stadium to the other, where they would be given a ticket for the next home game so they could come do it again.

The boys played football and basketball and baseball, even street hockey. They all were going to be professional athletes when they grew up, of course, and they would all play for the hometown team — the dream varying only by what sport was in season. They called themselves the Melrose Monsters, after their street, or the 21st Century Kids, after the nearby bowling alley, not a gang so much as a bunch of jocks. Some summer days, they would complete elaborate triple headers. If there weren't enough guys

Milwaukee Journal Sentinel photo by Benny Sieu

Shorewood senior Evan Rivera runs onto the field through a gauntlet of teammates as he is introduced at a home game. Throughout the long early-season practices, the team dreamed of moments like this.

for a baseball game, they gathered at a nearby playground to play Fastpitch, in which a box was painted on the wall and a batter squared off against a pitcher, the lines on the asphalt determining whether a hit was a single, double, triple or home run. Even today, when Trost goes home to visit his parents, he and a couple of his brothers sometimes jump the playground fence and match up again. The only difference: Less taunting from the winner.

As small as he was, Trost always had to play harder than the others to get ahead. With seven brothers and four sisters, it was that way in life, too. Trost's father, Christ, worked three jobs — candy salesman, bus driver, laundry attendant — so his wife, Carol, could stay home and the kids could go to private schools, the boys to St. Pat's and the girls to Notre Dame or Good Counsel high schools. Their neighborhood was a modest one, houses squeezed an arm's-reach apart, most with porches or front stoops, ideal for chatting on lazy summer evenings. At the Trost household, when Christ came home, on most nights he would give each of the kids $2 to spend at Nick's hot dog stand, just down the street, where after paying $1.25 for a soda, dog and fries, there was still 75 cents to live on tomorrow.

As the Trost family grew, they built an addition on the back of the house that ate into an already small backyard. They later added a second floor to the addition for nine bedrooms in all. Before the new space, the kids would sometimes sleep on the dining room floor on hot summer nights, an air conditioner rattling in the window and a blanket over the doorway to keep the chill air in. They'd watch reruns of *The Honeymooners*, which came on at 9 p.m. and 9:30 p.m., on WGN, Channel 9, their giggles often prompting Dad to shout for quiet from the other room: "You kids, you always laugh at the same jokes."

Indeed, sometimes Trost — Jimmy — would be on TV himself. When he was four, his parents had lined up a contract for him with a modeling agency, which would call when it needed a kid to round out a family in a commercial. He was in a Kentucky Fried Chicken commercial, no lines just a big grin at the "Finger Lickin' Good" part. And he did the opening sequence for the *Hallmark Hall of Fame* specials — the kid who knocked over the stack of saucers during the intro before the movie. The gigs netted $40 or more an hour, the money split between savings and helping the family. It all lasted until age 12, when Trost got too embarrassed by his mother coming to pick him up at school and accompany him on the bus downtown. No more modeling.

Eventually, Trost's father got a candy delivery route and, as the boys got older, they went on the daily runs in the summer or when they weren't in school, loading and unloading boxes. Still, it wasn't enough, so in high school, Jim Trost was on a work-study program, which meant he did cleaning and odd jobs around the school. St. Pat's was about two miles west of Trost's home, with Hansen Stadium, where the Shamrocks played their home football games, about two miles to the south of the school. For those years, Trost's whole world fell within that triangle. There was one time, and only one time, that Trost's father made it to one of his football games — the last game of Trost's senior year, when the team had made the playoffs for the first time ever. But Christ Trost was the one to get Jim out of bed in time for practice and, on days when he was dragging and grumbling, would demand that he get up and follow through on the commitment he had made. There would not be any quitting of something that had been started. Never.

When they played those pickup games in the gym, players from the two schools mixing for the first time, many of the Messmer players readily lumped Trost in with the Shorewood side. He was white, after all. He lived in the suburbs. And he seemed far removed from a past that tracked closer to that of the Messmer players.

In the pickup games, Trost would often face off at quarterback against George Lasley, who would be a senior at Messmer in the fall.

George was born to a mother who was on drugs. And his father had left before George could even register a memory of him, off to Missouri and a new life, complete with a new pair of children. George was sent to foster care with an older sister, until an aunt agreed to take them in. A cousin, Rickie Lee, became like a brother and along with George helped take care of a great-great-aunt — their "auntie." She lived a few blocks away in a neighborhood where ramshackle houses sat uncomfortably with ones where flowers were planted, almost in defiance, out front. There was a rambling cemetery across the street, its headstones worn and uneven. When his "auntie" couldn't make it to services, George would sometimes be sent to church to pick up extra bulletins. Off he would go, bouncing a basketball along the way.

Even as a boy, George knew which house in the neighborhood belonged to his father's parents, who he had never met. Sometimes he would walk past the house and see the people on the porch, all foreign to him, as if they weren't his family at all. He would wonder if the people recognized him, the way he recognized them, or if they would always be so close and so far away, familiar yet foreign, at the same time. As a freshman at Milwaukee's Bay View High School, George turned to dealing drugs himself, until he was caught, arrested right in school. That was the bottom. George had transferred to Messmer, where by all accounts he was excelling as a student and a leader. He had an unruly Afro that was frequently reined in with cornrows and soft, quiet eyes that masked a hard, steely determination. It was the result of seeing the sharp edges of life, from getting beat up on the playground as a boy to having basketball games at the park interrupted by gunfire from over where the adults were drinking and throwing dice.

Ever since he was a kid, whenever George and his cousin and their friends would play football in the street, George was the quarterback. It was the same in the workouts in the Messmer gym. George liked the idea of calling the plays, being in control, at the center of the action. He had a confidence about him that anyone could see.

Trost had put him down as the starting quarterback for the fall.

Of all the matchups and pairings between players from the two schools, the unlikeliest was Martin Wallner and Maurice Ragsdale. Marty, who was going to be a sophomore at Shorewood, was white. Maurice, who was going to be a senior at Messmer, was black. Marty lived in a tidy house on a tree-lined street with his father, mother and a younger brother, Jack, who adored him. A sister was away at college. Maurice, an only child, lived in a rented, one-bedroom house with his mother. She often worked nights, so Maurice came home to a dark and empty house. He had never met his father.

Marty, short and skinny, had sleepy eyes and a quiet, polite demeanor. Sometimes he would blend into the group so well that one would forget he was there. Maurice, tall and lanky, was always cracking jokes, talking in funny voices or bopping to music that sometimes only he seemed to hear. He was frenetic. Hard to miss.

When Marty was four, maybe five, his dad would get on his hands and knees in the living room and, as Marty tried to run past, pretend to tackle him, always telling Marty to keep his feet moving, never stop moving the feet. When Marty was eight, maybe nine, they would go for walks on the long streets of Shorewood, brother Jack riding in a stroller. Marty would race down the sidewalk and his dad would throw a football to him, over and over, Marty's small feet pounding the pavement. Now, at 5'5" and about 115 pounds, Marty looked more like a candidate for water boy than wide receiver. But Marty had always wanted to play football. Not just varsity football — Shorewood football. In high school, his father had been the team manager for several years, but his uncles played and Marty had heard all the stories. Now he wanted his own. At a larger school, or one with a more successful program, he never would have had a chance.

Maurice, meanwhile, had never played organized football before, never even tossed a football around much as a kid. Basketball was his game, the city game. One summer, Maurice wore out four pairs of shoes playing on the blacktop. He always played hard, never backed down. You couldn't, not on the playground, where you had to win to keep playing and it didn't take long for word to get around if you were a crybaby or sissy. Maurice hardly ever called fouls. He had long sideburns and seemed to wear a perpetual grin, though it could slide into a scowl at a moment's turn, matching the shadow behind his usually bright eyes — at once, somehow, both happy and sad.

One day, during a game in the Messmer gym, the two found themselves paired against each other. On one series, Marty would be the receiver and Maurice the cornerback. When the ball was turned over, they'd switch and Marty would cover Maurice. They kept their thoughts to themselves, but it didn't take long for each to come to respect the other.

Man, he's fast, Marty thought.

Dude has some moves, Maurice thought.

Once school let out, some of the players had jobs or other summer commitments. But there was a core group of players, maybe fifteen, who regularly worked out in the weight room at Messmer under the watchful eye of the coaches. The weight room was often hot. It was humid and sticky and some players had jobs to get to, so they quickly went from station to station, the machines and weights clanking in a steady metallic rhythm. Squats. Curls. Bench press.

This was the investment being made for the fall. Every day, every lift and every drop of sweat was like putting money in the bank, to be withdrawn when the season began. Football games, coaches say, are won in the off-season, not from August to November.

Before players left, there was always a stop in front of Trost for power-cleans.

The exercise involved a set of free weights on the floor. The player had to snatch the bar to his waist, then in almost the same motion, curl it to his chest, then reverse everything and do it again. Power-cleans were all about football. They required power and quickness, strength and coordination. The back had to be straight. There had to be a good pop from the legs. A snap of the arms. An absolute explosion of power.

At the start of the summer, some of the players did power-cleans with only the bar, a mere 45 pounds, as they struggled just to get the maneuver right. But day to day, week to week, the players got stronger, quicker, sturdier. By the end of the summer, some couldn't believe how little they were able to do at the start.

Pertrell Mallett, who would be a junior at Messmer in the fall, was a poster boy for progress. He was tall with broad shoulders and a muscular frame. His smile came easy and when he wore glasses, he appeared particularly studious. Pertrell was inconsistent. He would come one day, miss the next, resurface a week later. But at 6'2 and 195, he could storm through the power cleans, and by late July had made it up to 140 pounds.

When Pertrell would lift, Trost would sometimes sit on a stationary bicycle and lean forward, arms across the handlebars, feet peddling, watching and counting, peddling a bit harder as he encouraged Pertrell to lift faster, yes, again, c'mon, again. And most every afternoon, when Trost got into his car and drove home to Hartford, he'd shake his head and marvel at the amount of talent, raw talent, that was walking the halls at Messmer.

We're gonna win some games, he thought. *Without a doubt.*

As the summer went on, the number of core players grew, including some transfer students. To attend Shorewood, a student's family would have to move into Shorewood. But Messmer was a viable option, particularly with the state's school voucher program, which allowed low-income families to choose private schools at no cost. The program was available to any Milwaukee student who qualified based on family income, but on a practical level that meant mostly black families. Aided by the program, Messmer had become one of the fastest-growing schools in the state, topping 500 students. There was a waiting list for freshmen and sophomores, but Messmer had more flexibility in accepting new students at the higher grades, since some students invariably washed out.

By rule, football coaches cannot recruit players. But no one could stop the players from talking to friends. And Mark Moore, excited about the potential for the fall, tried to track down Rob Wyatt, whom he had played with on a grade-school team. Rob, a year behind Mark, was finishing his sophomore year at Marshall High School, a public school in Milwaukee where the football team had finished 4-6. Rob, at 5'10" and 245 pounds, was a lineman, offense and defense. Another big body for up front. Mark tried to find Rob through a mutual friend, but they didn't connect until one day in late April or early May when Mark went to the Target store on the city's west side, looking for a copy of the football movie *Varsity Blues* and bumped into Rob, who was working there. Rob didn't know much about the partnership or about Messmer. But the Marshall coach had left, and he was thinking about transferring anyway. The new team sounded promising.

"You should come," Mark said.

"I might," said Rob.

Rob found the video in the back room, where he had a stash of football movies set aside, in case he wanted to get them for himself come pay day.

Could make for a good team, Rob thought.

If Rob came, so would Ronell Halbert, a lanky wide receiver. Ronell was Rob's nephew, but at just two weeks apart in age, the two were more like brothers. Wherever one went, the other did, too. As boys, they would sometimes set up obstacle courses in Rob's backyard, or play games where one tried to get past the other without being tackled. A cousin, Willie Wyatt, had played for the University of Alabama in the late 1980s, kicked around the NFL for a year, and wound up with the Tampa Bay Storm in the Arena Football League. Whenever his team was in

Milwaukee to play the Mustangs, tickets would be left at the box office, and Rob's father would pile everyone into the van to go downtown and watch Cousin Willie, big number 55, mixing it up on the line. Afterward, the boys would wait for him outside the locker room or at the front row of the stands, wanting — desperately — to be like that someday.

Ronell also had played on the grade-school team, though he was considerably smaller than Rob and had to hang around the team for a time before he was invited to play — a trick his grandfather told him to try. Of the two, Rob was more reserved, often chuckling and smiling through a gap in his teeth, while Ronell joked and strutted around the locker room. Both went to a summer football camp at the University of Wisconsin in Madison, where they met Nate Shorter, who like Rob worked out with the linemen. That helped seal it. The two came to the weight sessions and the summer camp workouts, which were conducted at Shorewood by a coach from North Division High School. The cost was only $10, intentionally low so anyone could afford it. After the last session of summer camp, when it came time to claim a locker, Rob Wyatt wrote "Big Dub" on his, while Ronell wrote "Lil 'Nel, a.k.a. Showtime."

Dave O'Harrow was the next target.

The quarterback.

Dave had played at Marshall with the two, though he was a senior at Milwaukee School of Languages. The school had a football arrangement with Marshall, a partnership made easier by the fact both were part of the Milwaukee Public Schools system. He came off as reserved, moody. He had a bone dry sense of humor, but it was well guarded. On the Marshall team, Dave was a backup quarterback but hadn't played much as a junior. He clashed with the coach and one day — told he would have to sit out a game — got so mad he punched his locker, broke his hand, end of season. Dave had also played on the grade-school team, the Cardinals, which was coached by his father, Mike. One year, the team went undefeated and won the league championship. The boys called it the Golden Season.

Mark Moore and Rob Wyatt called Dave over the summer, finally convincing him to come and at least meet the guys. He did and basically felt comfortable, though he called his father several times in Pennsylvania, where the rest of the family was vacationing, uncertain if the move was the right thing. Like Rob and Ronell, Dave would have to transfer to Messmer. But while Rob and Ronell were black and would fit in, Dave was white. In a senior class of about 75 at Messmer, there was only one other white guy. Dave thought about it. He went back and forth. Called his father again. "Pray over it," his father said. "See if you feel comfortable with the team and coaches."

Dave thought some more, before arriving for the last camp session.

At the end, when the players chose sides for the regular pickup game, Dave quarterbacked both ways. Trost was in the stands, pacing in the front row, though he wasn't allowed to do any coaching for another 12 days. Several of the other coaches were also there. Dave floated passes over defenders, feathered them through coverage.

Afterward, as the players changed in the locker room, Trost walked through. He was headed home, but just had to say something and stopped.

"I'm the most excited about a season as I've been in my life," Trost told them. "We will be a team. You mark my words: You'll never forget this year. You'll never forget the experiences you go through. You young men will make history."

Everyone stopped changing and packing their bags and listened. The lockers, 29 of them, were battleship gray, as dreary as the walls and the speckled tile floor. With the number of players expected, the team would have to double up in lockers for the first time in years and many had already written out names and nicknames on tape to claim lockers — "Blake/Redhot," "Holley, J.," "C. Albano," "Trey Dog," " Shorter," "White Boy," "Blanke 55," "Drew" and "J-Dub."

Coach Stanley Smith, an assistant, warned the group to come ready to work.

"You'll hate the practices," he said. "But for those two hours Friday night, you will play like a god and love the practices."

This might just work, Dave thought.

As the group broke up, he took a roll of athletic tape, pasted a strip above a locker and wrote out "O'Harrow, #11" in black letters.

He was coming, too.

Nobody felt like gods, though, on the first day of practice, the sun beating down, the small splotch of shade offering no relief, the water breaks not coming fast enough or lasting nearly long enough and everyone spent, coaches and players, just weary and spent. The first days of practice were conducted without pads. By rule, no hitting was allowed until Friday. But the players had to wear helmets, so they could get used to running with eight extra pounds on their head. It left many of them woozy.

Trost had the entire practice planned out down to the minute on a printed schedule he distributed to the coaches and kept rolled up in his back pocket. With about two-thirds of the players from Messmer, the coaches focused on the basics, stuff other teams would not have given a thought. To work on tackling, the coaches lined up the team in two rows, with one set of players on their knees — the tacklers — and the other standing across from them, arms raised in the air, a live version of tackling dummies. In each attempt, the tacklers thrust their arms up, catching the player around the hips or waist, their heads crossing the partner's stomach.

Coach Smith, who would work with the linebackers, demonstrated. He went so hard into one player, the player staggered backwards.

Several players watched, miming the thrust up motion, then waited for the call.

"Ready, hit."

No one staggered backwards.

"You don't want to hug him, you want to hit him," admonished Coach Joe Trawitzki, the defensive coordinator.

Trawitzki was a poster-perfect image of the throwback defensive lineman, lumbering across the field, pawing at his balding head in frustration, ready to spit nails.

Again.

"Ready, hit."

This time, a few wobbled a bit in place.

"Helmet across the ball," Coach Trawitzki said, then pointed to a player. "If he keeps his head down, he'll break his neck, which is bad — and miss the tackle, which is worse."

Again.

The team soon broke into groups — linemen with Coach Trawitzki and Coach Steve Hoagland; linebackers with Trost and Coach Smith; defensive backs with Coach Jim Carroll. The staff was a young one, almost all in their 20s, except Coach Luke Groser, 58, who had been at Shorewood for 30 years and was helping out with the varsity until the freshman team started practice. Coach Herb Larsen, a Messmer teacher, had been added to the staff so there would be a familiar face for the Messmer players. He hadn't coached before, but played in high school and would also work with the linemen.

The linebackers, 10 of them, were put in the proper stance, on the balls of their feet, arms bent, hands steady, ready to go. They were told to hold the stance for 30 seconds. As Trost checked one of his watches, legs shook and wobbled. Faces strained.

"You guys are the cornerstone," Coach Smith barked as he walked between them. He was the only black coach on the staff, muscular and fit, a walking motivational speech. "No one is tougher than linebackers."

Again.

Nearby, the defensive linemen were in their own stances, bursting up when a coach snapped the ball, running a few steps, then lining up again.

"Watch the ball, you're offsides," Coach Hoagland shouted.

Hoagland was huge. At the team meeting the day before, he introduced himself by announcing his height, 6'7", and weight, 300 pounds, to answer the two most obvious questions. At 23, he was beginning to lose some of his hair. He had played at Lakeland College, a Division 3 school in Wisconsin, but had never coached before. Trost had recruited him a few weeks before while in a class at Cardinal Stritch University, where both were working on master's degrees in education

Again.

The defensive backs, meanwhile, were practicing running backwards and changing directions, keeping an eye on the quarterback. Feet were tangled and slow. Shirts were already stained with sweat and sticking to stomachs.

"Keep your head on a swivel," said Coach Carroll.

Carroll was intense. Focused. He got married during the season last year, but had yet to schedule a honeymoon. Carroll was a first-year English teacher at a Milwaukee public high school and was always talking and instructing. At times, his comments were dry, at times sarcastic, often delivered with a disappointed scowl and a sharp clap of his hands.

"C'mon."

Again.

Each of the helmets had a strip of athletic tape across the front with the player's name written out in magic marker. It was a standard practice, but also necessary with so many new faces.

At one point, Coach Groser walked up to Justin Moore, a Messmer senior who was working out with the linemen and had been a bit wobbly in his stance. Justin had a sturdy enough build, though wasn't nearly as well defined as Mark Moore or Nate Shorter, or even Rob Wyatt. But Justin was eager to play. He had written his nickname — J-Flex — on his helmet. Groser looked it over and a perplexed look crossed his face. Flex waited, unsure what the pronouncement would be, what he had done wrong.

"You're Felix," Groser said, a statement not a question.

Justin shook his head.

"Oh," Groser said. "Flex."

Groser continued past, to check on the other linemen, commit more names to memory. Of all the coaches at Shorewood, in any sport, Groser was one of the best liked by the players. At the end of the last season, when Trost asked players to write out comments on all the coaches, many had simply listed one word for Groser, repeating his trademark declaration of approval whenever good work was taking place: "Quality." Groser had worked with the varsity the year before, but had the perfect blend of crusty credibility and a teacher's patience — as the economics instructor he was one teacher every student at Shorewood had to have before graduation — to work with the freshmen.

Groser, tall and with a face that brought to mind a hawk, had been a coach longer than any of the players — or even the coaches — had been alive. He was responsible for washing the uniforms, keeping track of the equipment and calling the newspaper with the statistics after each game. Groser would often say he wanted to be cremated when he died, his ashes spread on the football field. The location, though, should remain a secret, he'd joke, lest any of his former players find out and some night come take a leak on that spot.

Flex lined up again.

"Good job," Groser said and called out over his shoulder to reinforce it: "Quality."

At the end of the afternoon session, the coaches lined the team up as they would be on defense. A series of cones were set up at 10-yard intervals down each sideline. This was the pursuit drill. A running back would get the football and take off toward the sideline, zipping around the cone and then up the field. Each defender, depending on his position, had a designated cone to run to. It was all about angles, cutting off the runner before he made it past them and into the end zone. In the drill, each defender had to get to the cone before the runner did and shout out "Hit."

The starting defense went first, with Marty Wallner, one of the smallest and fastest on the team, getting the ball at running back. He raced to the sideline, as the defenders ran toward the cones.

"Hit."

"Hit."

"Hit."

The words echoed down the line, as the last defenders reached their spot, most after Marty had already sped past it.

"Hit."

"Hit."

Trost shook his head.

The players jogged back and were told to line up and do it again. This was like game conditions. You had to hustle back and be ready for the next snap. No time to rest. Clock ticking. But instead of running, some walked back, hands on their hips. They weren't in game shape. It was hot as hell. And they were mad to be made to do it over again.

"Somebody is going to have to run after practice," Coach Smith declared.

He was looking at George Lasley, the Messmer senior, in at linebacker.

"Who?" George asked in bewilderment. "George?"

"Yeah."

"Why?" Louder.

"You're not in shape," Smith said. "What did you do all summer?"

"Nothing but Cheetos and girls," George replied, with a grin.

"Not a good mix," said Smith.

They lined up again.

Now Smith looked at Dave O'Harrow, who was doubled over in the secondary, where he was in at safety.

"Don't worry," Smith said. "We ain't gonna get our pretty-boy quarterback hurt."

The exchange was brief. For most, it passed without any notice — as quick as the flash of realization by George that he was no longer the chosen quarterback.

Whistle. The runner took off. So did the defense, legs heavy and slow, players fighting cramps in the heat.

"Hit. Hit. Hit. Hit."

"C'mon," Trost yelled. "Get there."

"Hit."

"Hit."

"Hit."

A lot had changed for the team since the spring, since the get-acquainted session at Shorewood and the pickup games at Messmer, starting with the quarterback spot.

George had been out of town most of the summer, attending a college enrichment program at the University of Wisconsin in Madison, about 80 miles away, so he missed all of the workouts. On June 15, he had celebrated his 18th birthday by himself. The day was significant not because he was now an adult — as if it took a date to make it so — but because it meant he was off probation for the drug arrest. Since the case was handled in children's court, his record, officially anyway, was clean again. A fresh start. But in the meantime, the new guy, a white guy, was in at quarterback.

If anything, the trust that had been built between George and Trost during the spring workouts had been all but lost the day before, at the end of the team's organizational meeting. Trost had told the team the season would be a long journey. And George, sitting in front, raised his hand. "With a long journey, we can't go without God," he said. "Want to pray before we do?" Trost paused just long enough to do the calculation that organized prayer plus public school didn't add up, and brushed past. George seethed.

Fuck you, he thought.

There was a host of other problems facing the team, some obvious, others lurking beneath the surface.

One was numbers. Several returning Shorewood players didn't come out for the team. Some quit because they didn't like Trost. Others didn't like the idea of the extra competition, intimidated, some thought, by the idea of going up against black players. When there are only 20 or so guys on a team, everyone is near the top of the pecking order. With 30 or even 40, a realistic goal for the season, there would be a third and, possibly, fourth string. While a typical suburban school might have 50 or more players, with strong programs registering 100-plus when freshmen and junior varsity squads are counted, the numbers at Shorewood, with 750 students, grew smaller every year. In part, it was a product of the losing, which led to an erosion of interest in football as other sports, notably soccer, flourished. There was a comfortable complacency surrounding the program. Losing was expected, even accepted.

With the new players from Messmer, some would lose
their guaranteed starting spot or have to change positions
completely. That included Drew O'Malley, a Shorewood
senior, who had played some receiver last year and now
wanted to play running back. He was sent to the line to
make way for the fleet-footed receivers from Messmer —
Ronell Halbert and Maurice Ragsdale. His buddy, Evan
Rivera, another Shorewood senior, had started at fullback
last year. He, too, was sent to the line, to make way for big
Nate Shorter.

There were other problems, too.

Pertrell Mallett, the prototypical Messmer stud, was
missing. The coaches had him penciled in as a starter on
both offense and defense. But with no real football experience, he was raw. A missed practice today would mean a
missed tackle tomorrow. The day before, Trost had cornered Nate Shorter, Pertrell's friend, in the locker room.
"We gotta find Pertrell," Trost said. "What do we do?"
Nate half-shrugged and said he had tried to reach Pertrell,
but his phone was out. "You gotta find him," Trost said.
"You gotta find him."

There was Nate's knee. Nate hadn't told the coaches,
but a few weeks earlier he had gone to the family doctor
who prescribed rest. Possible tendinitis. Perhaps fluid on
the knee. Nate ignored the doctor and the throbbing pain.
How long had he waited for this? In the week between
summer workouts and the first practice, Nate quit his three
jobs, but played basketball, lifted weights and dreamed
about the start of practice.

And there was Mark's shoulder. It wasn't the shoulder
itself, which had healed just fine after the spring surgery.
The worry for the coaches was Mark's head. His confidence. Mark was a talent, yes. A major talent. He had a
body built for the college game. Yet Mark was often hesi-
tant. The coaches were worried he might favor the shoulder, be afraid to hit. Indeed, he had yet to go to the doctor

to get clearance for full contact. If that wasn't enough, Mark was a captain, and though this team clearly would be his team, the coaches didn't see him leading by example, policing the ranks when players sat down on the field or didn't run hard. If anything, Mark often fell in with the rest of the squad.

Now the coaches lined the first string up for another run in the pursuit drill. They had run five straight, maybe six. There were grumbles and curses.

"How many more we have to do?"

It was Mark.

Trost frowned and blew his whistle. Maurice Ragsdale, in at running back, started to the right, pivoted and ran to the left, around the first cone and up the sideline. The defense bought the fake, though none were supposed to be allowed, and started one way, then doubled back.

"Shit," came a shout.

Then, the rest, one by one: "Hit. Hit. Hit. Hit."

Finally, after a few more runs, Trost called for the second group, and the first group wobbled and staggered toward the water trough, dizzily taking off their helmets and letting the water run over their heads, their necks, their tempers, cooling it all.

After a dinner break, as the second session of the day began, Trost carried a box of brand new practice jerseys outside. They were ordered before the merger and said "Shorewood Greyhounds" in red letters on white mesh. The real jerseys, new game jerseys, would say "Shorewood-Messmer." The team was already planning a weight-lifting fund-raiser for Saturday, and each player was supposed to line up pledges for every pound lifted, with a goal of $40 each. The game jerseys, at least in Trost's mind, would be purple. "You know, like the Northwestern University jerseys," he had told the team the day before. The players smirked and argued that with the red helmets, it would look ridiculous. Why purple?

"Red and blue make purple," Trost told them.

The partnership meant a lot to Trost, the off-the-field symbolism as much as the on-the-field promise. In the spring, he bought T-shirts for the team, white with the words "Shorewood," "Messmer" and "We will make it happen" printed in purple. And Trost vowed to have the players learn the school songs for both Messmer and Shorewood and sing them at the end of practices and at mid-field after each game, win or lose, just as his team at St. Pat's had. A sheet with the words to each song already was tacked to the bulletin board in his office and the players got copies the day before. Though the songs wouldn't start for a few days, there were already groans about the singing.

Now, as the players wandered outside, Trost laid the practice jerseys out on the grass, numbers up, so the players could choose, seniors first. It was early evening, but the sun was still uncomfortably hot. Everyone swatted at biting flies.

"I got No. 3," Drew O'Malley called out.

"You gotta work hard for this," said George Lasley, stepping in front of the underclassmen.

The jerseys were something tangible, something real, the first piece of the prize.

None of the Messmer players seemed to mind they only said "Shorewood." They were all so crisp and new. The players pulled the jerseys on over their T-shirts. Without pads they were loose and cool, and there everyone stood, looking the same, more so when they pulled the helmets on and lined up to begin stretching. The players clapped louder, more precisely. There was a renewed level of excitement. It was the jerseys. It had to be the jerseys.

Trost walked between them doing a silent count, crossing names off his list. There had been 33 players before. Now there were 31. One kid had been excused. The other, a Messmer sophomore, was AWOL. Trost went inside, called his house and a few minutes later reported back to the other coaches.

"He thought they had to get dinner themselves," Trost said.

Part of the idea behind the meal during the break was to keep kids at Shorewood. Another part was to be sure they had a decent meal. Two-a-days were both physically and mentally draining. Trost had asked everyone to pay $10 to help cover the cost of the meals, but said he'd take less if anyone couldn't afford it. "There was a time I didn't know where my next dollar was coming from either," he said, though no one seemed to believe it.

Trost had asked the player if he could come back, catch some of the evening session. But he couldn't.

"Why not?" Coach Trawitzki asked.

"No bus fare."

The evening session was dedicated to offense, a crash course like the afternoon one on defense. It was like learning a second new language. If defense was Latin, offense was Greek. The team broke into units again, each group starting with the basics. The groups would then be gradually brought together to form the full 11-man offense, which would run some plays against a phantom defense.

Trost, who served as offensive coordinator, had developed the team's system himself. The basic formation was a bit unusual. It called for the standard five linemen, two receivers and quarterback, with the three others in a triangular backfield — the fullback set behind the quarterback, a running back set a couple yards off to each side. The left running back was deemed the Liz back, the right running back the Roar, with the fullback labeled the Bull. The Ls and Rs, of course, corresponded to left and right. To Trost, the Liz spot was for the speedier back. That was Mark Moore. Roar was for the tough slasher, a player Trost had yet to settle on. And Bull was the most powerful of the three. That was Nate.

On each play, every position had a specific assignment and that assignment was built into the call made by the quarterback in the huddle. The quarterback would wear a wristband, with the plays written out next to a corresponding number. In theory, all Trost had to do was call out a number, or send it in with a new receiver or back, and everyone on the field would know exactly what to do.

The offensive groups were very similar to the afternoon, with the defensive backs turned around to be receivers, the defensive line becoming the offensive line, and the linebackers mixed in at a variety of spots. At each, the technique was raw and rough, but not nearly as clumsy and awkward as at the start of the summer camp, when the team would attempt the same footwork drills with the grace of a gorilla learning to waltz.

The receivers — Lee on the left, Rover on the right — were given different routes to run, each route with a designated number: One for an "in" pattern, two for an "out," three for a "fly." Some of the players, including Ronell Halbert from Messmer and Marty Wallner from Shorewood, grasped it quickly. They had played football before. Maurice Ragsdale, penciled in opposite Ronell at starting receiver, had to watch everything a few times. That was natural, of course. This wasn't basketball. Football was all new.

"Ragsdale," Coach Carroll called out at one point.

Maurice looked up. His stance was awkward and off balance. He cringed as the coach walked toward him.

"Are you left-handed?" Carroll asked.

"Yeah."

"Then you're left-footed."

Coach Carroll demonstrated the opposite foot placement.

"That feels very comfortable," Maurice said, in an overly formal voice.

"Well, I'm glad you're comfortable."

As the receivers ran their routes, the linemen worked on holding their stances, eyes on the ball, not flinching until it was snapped. The running backs and quarterbacks, meanwhile, ran through some handoff drills, then tried some basic plays. Trost explained the hole system. The Zero Hole is right where the center is. Straight up his butt. Odd holes are to the left — the One Hole between the center and the guard, the Three Hole between the guard and the tackle and so on. The evens were in the same fashion to the right.

While most players only had to master one specific assignment, the quarterbacks had to know everything. Dave O'Harrow, who had played at Marshall, nodded easily. George Lasley watched carefully, repeating the hole numbers to himself and pointing as he counted them out, imagining the players in position. Micah Moore, Mark's brother, was also on new ground. As a sophomore, he was trying quarterback for the first time.

Trost would demonstrate how to take a snap, how to get the ball up to the ear on a pass play, how to conceal it on a fake, how to slide it into the gut of the fullback, or get it out to a running back on a pitch. The standard count was "999-999-Set-Red-Hit."

Dave lined up first, yelled out the count, pitched the ball fluidly to Mark, who followed the other backs — his blockers — around the imaginary right end.

"Nice," Trost said.

"You go," George, the would-be starter, said to Micah, stepping back.

"Wait," Trost said. "I haven't seen what you've got."

George stepped in, waited a second or two, and shouted out the count.

"999-999-Red-Set-"

"Set-Red-Hit," Trost interrupted.

"-Hit," George finished.

Trost's offense was highly choreographed. Everyone had to execute the timing perfectly or it wouldn't work. On some plays, a running back was to go in motion on "Rrrr," the start of Red. On other plays, he'd go in motion on "dddd." Or even the "tttt" in Set.

They tried the plays over and over, Trost on his knees, snapping the ball to the quarterback and watching the backfield's moves. Each time they ran a play, they got a bit more precise. Eventually the receivers were brought over, and they were lined up, too. Then a center was sent over, then the rest of the linemen and finally, the full first string was together, though at this point the slots on offense and defense were mostly a guide. Players could be moved up and down the depth chart — or around on it — at a moment's notice.

Justin Owen, a Shorewood sophomore, was in at center.

He had transferred to Shorewood over the summer, after his family moved there from Indiana. He didn't know much of anyone on the team. He was nervous.

Micah took a turn at quarterback and the ball came up

Photo courtesy of Michael Tucker

Players gather around assistant coach Jim Carroll. With many Messmer players new to the sport, the team needed frequent encouragement.

late, causing Nate, at fullback, to plow into Micah who bumped into Justin, like a series of dominoes.

The quarterbacks were rotating on each play. Dave stepped in. He called out "Set-Red-Hit" and waited. No snap.

"On 'Hit,' you snap it up," Trost said. "Everybody re-lax."

Football, coaches will tell you, is the ultimate team sport.

There are eleven players on the field, and on every play, each has a specific responsibility. On a simple running play, the most basic in the play book, the responsibility may be to block a man, open a hole as the fullback, or distract a defender with a pass route. The quarterback may have to execute a fake, the running back hit a designated gap at a precise moment.

On every play, there are dozens of ways it can go wrong and sometimes only one in which it can go right. A team is always in search of that moment, that flash of perfection, because perfection can only be replicated once it is achieved.

Now George stepped in at quarterback. Sweat glistened on his face. His eyes were tired. His movements a step slow.

"Set-Red-Hit," Trost reminded him.

"Ready, Set," George called out and paused. "Hit."

"Don't move the ball twice," Trost said to Justin, who had shifted it during the muddled count.

The rest of the players stood watching in a loose half-circle. The other coaches watched, too. A few parents had arrived and stood leaning on the fence in the distance. Everybody watched. The team had practiced for more than six hours already. The sun was disappearing into the clouds. In the distance there was the squealing hum of cicadas.

Dave O'Harrow was back now at quarterback.

"Again," Trost said, arms crossed.

This time they got it.

"Good," Trost said.

Same group.

"Again."

They got it again.

"Excellent," Trost said. "Again."

The practice nearly over, some players sat dazed against the fence, damp towels on their foreheads or ice packs on the back of their necks as the rest lined up for sprints. The sky had gone fuzzy in the dusk — not quite daylight, not quite nightfall.

The linemen ran in one group, then the receivers and backs, each lining up first in the correct stance.

"This is conditioning," Coach Groser shouted. "This is getting you ready for the third and fourth quarter. The first quarter is easy. Three and four are about attitude."

Trost looked the players over as they ran, many pulling up before the end or jogging the whole way, wheezing and breathing heavily.

"C'mon, guys," Trost said. "We have lazy stances all up and down the line."

They ran harder. Then faded, like an echo. Then harder again.

Finally, Trost called them together.

Some of the players were still gasping for air. Others stood with slumped shoulders, eyes lost and vacant. This was football. Legs sore and screaming, necks weak from running with the helmets, arms tight and tired. This was not a pickup game in the gym. This was not summer workouts. This was not the movies. Some of the players had been embarrassed in the drills, tripping over their feet. Others felt awkward, out of place, not sure where to line up or what to do or even who to watch in order to try and fake it.

"There was some intuition out there today," Trost said. "Some of you are not confident of what is going on, what you should be doing. But don't be discouraged. Those things work themselves out over time."

He looked the team over.

It was so easy to quit. Too easy. Trost knew this. He had almost quit once himself, after his sophomore season when he was unsure about whether, at his size, he could make the jump to varsity. Then, one day outside of the St. Pat's gym, he ran into one of the coaches, John Gruber, and confessed that he might cash it in. Focus on wrestling or something else. Gruber told him not to. Said he had no reservations about Trost's size. Said he'd get a fair chance with varsity. He had to try. That conversation, Trost would say later, one that lasted two minutes, maybe three, had changed his life forever.

The players looked back at Trost, waiting for something more, some perspective, some words to put the day neatly in its place, some assurance that it would get easier and hurt less and that, one day, football would actually feel right and comfortable.

"We need you," Trost said. "All of you. You guys gave a pledge. You got a jersey today because you're gonna come back tomorrow. If somebody doesn't show up tomorrow, they're a quitter. And we can't have that."

The players nodded. Some slapped at their legs. The biting flies were fierce.

The 31 players around him, two less than started the day, were among more than 1 million boys across the country that would play football that fall, more participants than any other high school sport. In some places, the hopes of a town would rise and fall on the field every Friday night, the stands packed with hundreds — thousands — of fans, everything that was pure and simple coming together under the lights. Here in Shorewood, where football is an afterthought, where the glory is gone, lost in the yellowed pages of yearbooks and the dust on trophies in the back of the case, the coaches and players alone carried the dream. They alone thought it mattered.

"We're here together as one team," Trost told them. "Raise your hand now if you're not going to be here tomorrow."

No hands went up.

"Because then I want the jerseys back."

Still no hands.

"OK. Good."

The coaches turned and went inside. They were tired, too. Trawitzki put his hand to the base of his back and groaned. "That's it, tomorrow I'm getting the golf cart out," he joked. Mark Moore, the captain and star running back, stepped to the middle of the team.

"'Soldiers' on three," Mark said.

It was how they had ended every workout over the summer, after the camp sessions down on the big field. Everyone raised their helmet over Mark's head. The helmets clicked together.

"One-two-three," Mark said.

The shout came back loud and clear.

"Soldiers!"

Chapter 2
"You guys got a football team?"

Interstate 43, with its six lanes of traffic, cuts through the heart of the north side of Milwaukee, an asphalt gash through what were once blocks upon blocks of tidy, middle-class houses. Messmer High School, a hulking cream-colored building, sits hard on the edge of the freeway, long a landmark for the cars headed into the city during the morning rush hour or home to the northern suburbs at night.

If you get off the freeway at Capitol Drive, the city's busiest streets, and head east, you will pass Messmer on the left. On the right there is a dingy office building with a dirty maroon awning that reads, "Health Care For the Homeless." There is a bus stop on the corner, a bench but no shelter. There are weeds at the base of nearby buildings, litter on the ground and a stoplight that makes you wait — somewhat uncomfortably if you're not familiar with the area — for traffic on Seventh Street to cross.

You are in the heart of Milwaukee now, or at least the heart of the north side, which historically is quite different from the south side. Although the 2000 Census revealed Milwaukee had become a minority-majority city, with the white population accounting for 45% of the 596,974 residents, there is a stark split when it comes to where people live. The white population is concentrated on the south side, an area where less than a generation ago, black police officers weren't even allowed to patrol. And blacks, for the most part, live on the north side.

If you stay on Capitol Drive, you pass a bank and a car wash and a pizza place, its tall sign dull and faded. You pass a strip mall anchored by an auto parts store, a Popeye's Chicken, another car wash and another strip mall, this one with a Dollar Tree and a Fashion Bug and Club XXL, the city's largest hip-hop joint. The street could be picked up and plunked down in virtually any major city in the country, so familiar that it's all but anonymous. There is a U-Haul and a Wendy's and a Burger King and, on the site of what used to be an American Motors Corp. plant, a Wal-Mart, which replaced the defunct Builder's Square, all part of the manufacturing-to-retail shift that has characterized the city's job market.

You are still in the city, but not once you cross the Milwaukee River. On the other side of the bridge, you come upon a park and a bustling restaurant and a new custard stand and then, on your right, Shorewood High School. You pass the football stadium first, an old scoreboard off in the distance, framed by two sets of bleachers, one with a small red press box on top. Then you pass the school, its light brick buildings set back from the street, a perfect lawn unfolding in front. The school feels like a small college campus, minus the ivy. There are separate buildings for the auditorium and the swimming pool and, tucked in back, there is the gymnasium and the old Manual Arts building, which once housed shop classes, but has long since been turned into a community fitness center, filled with treadmills for the indoor runner.

If you kept going east, you would soon reach the vast blue of Lake Michigan and Lake Drive, the area's most exclusive address, where mansions at the top of the bluff overlook the white waves that crest and crash silently down below.

This is Shorewood.

Like all of Milwaukee's suburbs, The Village of Shorewood is white, overwhelmingly so. Of the 13,763 people counted in the 2000 Census, 91% were white, 2.4% black and the rest Asian, Hispanic or of other races. Indeed, after many years of ranking behind only Detroit, Milwaukee became the most segregated metropolitan area in the nation. While other ways of measuring racial housing patterns suggest the ranking is too high, the distinction — and the related label of "hyper-segregated" — seems impossible to shake, even as the city itself becomes more and more diverse. The ranking is due to the black and white split within the city, but more so to the split between the city and the suburbs — one that is only getting wider. Under one study that looked only at youth, nearly nine out of 10 black children in the four-county area would have to move to a less black neighborhood to achieve full racial balance.

The segregation ranking is only one of the regular headlines that make the city a frequent case study in race relations and racial disparity. For instance, when it comes to approval rates for mortgage loans, the city has long had the nation's greatest disparity between black and white borrowers, though both do better than the national average. The Milwaukee metropolitan area ranks sixth in the nation, tied with Chicago, when it comes to the disparity in the value of homes, with those owned by blacks worth 29% less than those owned by whites, even when adjusted for differences in income. And when it comes to household income in the Milwaukee area, black households earn $24,957 a year, or 49 cents on the dollar to the $50,754 earned by whites, a gap that puts Milwaukee behind only San Francisco among the nation's 50 largest metropolitan areas.

In Shorewood, the median family income registered $67,589 in the 2000 Census, nearly double that for Milwaukee. And nearly 30% of Shorewood households earned $100,000 or more a year, while in Milwaukee fully 17% lived below the poverty level.

In Milwaukee, though, such numbers and rankings are frequently greeted with a shrug, each latest result foretold in the previous report or study. Indeed, race is the community's silent conversation, one often conducted in whispers or in code. But it is there. It is there in the suggestion made to Shorewood newcomers that they don't really want to buy groceries on the other side of the river. And it is there in the understanding in Milwaukee's central city that blacks will get extra attention when driving through the suburbs at night.

An outsider, though, would know little of that. Shorewood, particularly in the summer months when the breeze comes gentle off the lake, is an intensely pleasant place, with bookstores and coffee shops, gardens filled with flowers and quiet streets canopied with trees. It is a nothing like the hot asphalt and rutted sidewalks and exhaust-filled streets that define the city, or at least the northern part that surrounds Messmer, which itself has a security buzzer at the front door and, in back, a barbed-wire fence.

To get to from Messmer to Shorewood, to get from one world to the next world over, you have driven just over a mile. It takes mere minutes.

It was back in September of 2000, a year earlier, the football season two games old, when Coach Jim Trost of the Shorewood Greyhounds, desperate for players, more desperate for victory, got off the freeway and headed east down Capitol Drive. He had been making the trip for weeks, just as he had the season before, to and from practice. And already, the blocks and businesses were beginning to blur, one into the next, into the next.

This time, though, he pulled over.

Trost was across the street from Messmer High School, a school he knew little about. He banged his car door shut and walked to the bus stop. There was a clutch of kids waiting. None of them wore letter jackets, which seemed odd. The kids were black, all of them. Trost knew that much about Messmer. Knew that it was Catholic. And black.

"Hey," Trost said. A few heads turned.

It was Trost's first year as head coach at Shorewood, a promotion from the top assistant job he held the year before, and already he knew something had to be done. The team had lost 33 consecutive games, a streak well on the way toward rivaling the school's infamous 63-game losing streak. But that was not the problem. There were 22 players on the team and 10 were seniors. That was the problem. Shorewood football, long rumored to be on its last legs, needed bodies to survive. Large, athletically gifted bodies preferred. A few years earlier, the school had weighed the idea of merging its football program with Riverside High School, a Milwaukee public school located about two miles to the south. But that talk quickly fizzled, and Riverside had turned its program around. Meanwhile, Shorewood remained one of the worst high school football programs in the Milwaukee area, the state and even the

Photo courtesy of Michael Tucker

The team works through a play against a phantom defense. While the players came from dramatically different backgrounds, once in uniform some of the differences disappeared.

nation.

Trost was running late, so he got right to the point. "You guys got a football team?"

The two schools, Shorewood and Messmer, were built around the same time. Indeed, they were designed by the same Milwaukee architectural firm, Herbst and Kuenzli, for two areas that in the 1920s were not so different from each other. If anything, the neighborhoods were separated by wealth, not race.

When the first building of the Shorewood High School campus was completed in 1925, Shorewood was barely Shorewood. The community, which began growing after railroad and trolley lines were completed in 1873, had long been part of the Town of Milwaukee, itself adjacent to the City of Milwaukee. But in 1900, residents dissatisfied with the allocation of tax dollars, including for police protection, decided to separate from the Town of Milwaukee and become East Milwaukee. In 1917, to distinguish itself further from the city, the village adopted the name Shorewood.

The same year Shorewood students moved into their new building, Milwaukee Archbishop Sebastian Messmer authorized the construction of a new high school — the first under the auspices of the diocese — on the north side of Milwaukee, where the Catholic population was growing rapidly, one booming parish spawning the next. Initially, a ninth grade was added to Holy Angels, then in 1926, the 166 students of Diocesan High School moved to the nearby St. Elizabeth's school building, with the first class graduating in the spring. A new building was begun in 1929, constructed at a cost of $750,000. It opened in February of 1930. By then, the school had already been renamed in honor of Archbishop Messmer, with the school's Blue Wave nickname giving way to the Bishops in 1939. The school, designed to hold 900 students, grew so rapidly that by 1944 — 15 years later — it boasted some 1,600 students attending classes in two shifts.

Of course, the area is different today.

As in all big cities, the changes in Milwaukee's central city were fueled by a mix of factors, large and small, some trends only clear in retrospect. There was the promise of industrial jobs that led to the great migration of blacks from the South, the rise of the suburbs with their wide streets and cookie-cutter houses, the disturbances of the 1960s that intensified white flight, the loss of wealth that resulted in urban ghettos and the army of bulldozers that cleared the way for the freeway, which now hums with so much traffic that plans call for extra lanes to be added.

Enrollment at Messmer began to decline, and in 1984 Milwaukee Archbishop Rembert Weakland moved to close the school, which at the time had a 48% minority population and was the only naturally integrated school — public or private — in the Milwaukee area. With little money and less hope, a group of parents and alumni rallied around the school and after countless marches, raffles, petitions and even a lawsuit to halt the removal of furniture and equipment from the building, the Save Messmer Committee bought the building from the Archdiocese and re-opened it as an independent, Catholic high school, mere weeks before the start of classes that fall. Most of the money came from the DeRance Foundation, a local entity that was one of the world's largest supporters of conservative religious causes. The price — $375,000 — was exactly half what it cost to build the school some 55 years earlier.

Messmer reopened with 28 freshmen, 45 seniors and some 150 students overall, less than half the number of the year before.

In effect, the school started over.

For years, Messmer struggled to survive, but today has more than 550 students, recently opened an elementary school, has a waiting list for lower grades and is one of the fastest-growing high schools in the state. Today, the school is more than 80% black. Most of the students are from families living in poverty, 70% are from single-parent households. About two-thirds attend through the state's school choice program, which provides a voucher for low-income families to attend a private or religious school, though the voucher does not cover the full cost of educating a student at Messmer. The rest is made up through contributions from alumni and grants from outside groups. The school carries a reputation, both in Milwaukee and across the nation, for strong academics, hard-nosed discipline and as a place where students with poor academic backgrounds can turn their lives around. About 90% of those who graduate go on to college.

A prime example is Sherelle Owens, who came to Messmer in 1986 after two years in public high schools, where she had accumulated 118 absences and a .450 grade point average. Her mother sent Sherelle to Messmer before the choice program, so Sherelle had to work extra hours to pay tuition. She went to summer school, taught herself how to type and graduated with her class in 1988 with a B- average, before going on to college. Her story generated local headlines and prompted creation of an award in her name.

Of course, there have been other headlines. Consider Jeremy Armstrong, who in 1997 was sent to prison for 20 years for killing a man during an armed robbery, an incident in which the 16-year-old fled, then later returned to the scene to take $500. He had been carrying a straight-A average at Messmer, where his record was free of any discipline problems and no one knew about a home life that newspaper reports of the case said included a schizophrenic mother and an alcoholic, cocaine-addicted father.

Among the Messmer staff and the school's supporters, such stories are reminders — like the battle to keep the school open — of how thin the line between success and failure can be.

The differences between the two schools — and the areas that surround them — were shaped in the 1960s, a period of upheaval for the nation and the city. Messmer had graduated its first black student in 1953 and the minority enrollment began rising in the early 1960s when a nearby neighborhood became an enclave for middle-class black professionals. But Shorewood didn't get a sharp dose of diversity until 1969 with the arrival of a program created by Dartmouth College called A Better Chance, or ABC.

Through the program, a handful of black students from around the country — places like Philadelphia, Washington, D.C., and Jersey City, N.J. — were moved to a house in Shorewood to attend high school. The idea, seen as innovative at the time, was to take the youth out of their rough environment, provide positive role models and give them a chance at college. Some Shorewood residents fought the program using local zoning laws that limit the number of unrelated people who can live under one roof. Nevertheless, the program arrived and soon offered eye-opening moments such as the one when a class was watching a movie about the problems of urban ghettos and one of the students from Philadelphia exclaimed, "That's where I live."

Of course, after 1967 and the summer of riots, there were similar examples much closer to home. In Milwaukee, the first riot broke out on July 30. The disturbances centered on Third Street — now Dr. Martin Luther King Jr. Blvd. — north of downtown, though some longtime residents recall National Guard troops being stationed miles away at the bridge between Milwaukee and Shorewood. By the end of the disturbances, four were dead, 100 injured, 1,740 arrested and Milwaukee received a spot on an unwelcome list: One of eight major disorders of the summer, as ranked by a U.S. commission. Later that summer, the upheaval continued, as Fr. James Groppi, a white

Milwaukee Journal Sentinel photo by Benny Sieu

**Messmer senior Revay Wright helps Shorewood sopho-
more Martin Wallner with his uniform before a home game.
It was this sort of bonding that administrators at the two
schools hoped for when they formed the partnership.**

Catholic priest, led open housing marches across the 16th
Street viaduct, from the increasingly-black north side to
the still-white south side, often meeting opposition in the
form of tossed bottles, rocks and eggs. A few Shorewood
students participated in the marches.

It was also the time of the Vietnam War, and while
student protests at some area high schools led to confrontations with the administration, at Shorewood, a teach-in
was organized on the front lawn. Black History was offered for the first time in 1970 as an elective, with white
students eagerly filling five sections to learn about ancient
Africa and Crispus Attucks and Marcus Garvey. Those years
marked a switch for the community, which had long been
considered conservative, once hosting the state's own Sen.
Joseph McCarthy in a packed auditorium. The conserva-
tive-to-liberal shift became official, perhaps, in 1984, when

the village backed Walter Mondale for president, while the nation went for Ronald Reagan in a landslide. The newspaper headline: "Shorewood turns left."

By then, the ABC House had been closed for five years, some 25 students having gone through the program. At the time, a few more black families had moved to Shorewood and a voluntary transfer program with the Milwaukee Public Schools, which faced a court order to desegregate, was bringing more black students to Shorewood. The system exists today as Chapter 220, which allows suburban districts to open a set number of slots for Milwaukee residents, with state funding following each student. The program has brought more minority students to the suburbs — and some additional white students to Milwaukee. Nevertheless, Milwaukee's public school system, which in 1976 was 57% white, was 17% white in 2001. In effect, it was more segregated than ever, thanks to white families leaving the school system or the city all together.

Today, Shorewood High School is considered one of the best in the Milwaukee area. It features a renowned drama department, a top-flight science program and every year a parade of National Merit Scholarship semifinalists. Of the 750 students, about 74% are white, 17% black, 5% Hispanic and the rest of other races. More than 90% of Shorewood graduates go on to college.

One of the few links that remain between the two schools can be found in the architecture, especially the colorful ceramic tiles chosen to brighten entrances and hallways near the gymnasiums. The tiles, in both buildings, are images of athletes — boys and girls playing tennis, basketball or running.

All are white.

It was a Friday, that day when Trost pulled over at the bus stop near Messmer while on his way to Shorewood. It was the third week of the season, and in two losses — to

Whitefish Bay and Riverside — Shorewood had been outscored 86-0. And, if anything, the first conference game of the season, set for Saturday, was a bigger mismatch. The opponent, Watertown Luther Prep, had never lost a game in its three seasons in the Parkland Conference.

When Trost arrived at Shorewood he went to find Cindy Wilburth, the athletic director. She was in her office, tucked inside the gymnasium building.

"We've got to do something," Trost told her.

Everybody knew that much. They had to do something. With so few players, the team was no longer just in danger of losing every Friday. Players were being put at risk. It was dangerous to put them out there in the fourth quarter, worn and weary, as the other side shuttled in fresh players. At most practices, the Shorewood team didn't even have enough players to go 11 on 11 unless some of the coaches stood in. So they would simulate plays, the right side of the offense vs. the left side of the defense. Or they would shadow block, a football version of the air guitar.

"What about Messmer?" Trost asked.

Shorewood already had cooperative agreements with nearby Whitefish Bay for gymnastics and with Whitefish Bay and Nicolet for boy's hockey. But a partnership with Messmer posed different problems, the first being that Messmer was a Catholic school. There was nothing that prevented public schools and private schools from forming sports co-operatives. But in the year since the Wisconsin Independent Schools Athletic Association, which represented private schools, disbanded and all the schools joined the Wisconsin Interscholastic Athletic Association, there had been very few public-private pairings. The ones that existed were mostly in individual-oriented sports such as swimming and tennis. Certainly none as high-profile as football.

Yet Trost's idea was an interesting one. It was at once simple and bold, so obvious that no one had seen or ex-

plored the possibility. Wilburth, in her fourth year at
Shorewood, said she'd look into it. Any noble intentions
would come later. For now, it was largely a question of
self-interest. One school needed players, the other needed
a team.

The next day, Shorewood lost 56-0.

A week later, before the game against St. Francis, Trost
again asked Wilburth if she had called Messmer. She hadn't.

That night they lost 41-6.

The next week it was Pewaukee: 43-8.

Then it was Greendale Martin Luther, 27-6.

The next Friday, Trost asked again. Wilburth returned
to her office, looked up the number for Messmer and called
Joy Bretsch, the athletic director there. The two had worked
together a few years earlier at Nicolet High School. No
answer. Wilburth left a message.

That night was the homecoming game for Shorewood,
a 63-6 loss to Slinger.

At Messmer, before Bretsch left for the day, she checked
her voice mail. Bretsch, in her second year, had been telling students they were trying to put together a football
team, but she knew the promises were all but empty. She
listened to the message and ran upstairs to find Principal
Jeff Monday.

"You better sit down," she said. "You're not going to
believe this."

In Milwaukee, Messmer has always been known as a
basketball school. It boasts seven state private-school championships, five of which came in the years since the school
reopened, including three straight from 1987 to 1989. At
any given time, several Messmer graduates are playing college ball. There is, of course, some football history as well,
though most of the names and games have been consigned
to memory, relived and retold mostly at class reunions,
where the drama and glory is amplified a bit with each

passing year.

One player, running back Greg Jones, a 1979 graduate, went on to play for Alcorn State University and then
the NFL's Washington Redskins. Another, quarterback Bob
Leszczynski, class of 1975, played for Navy, and until 1996
held the Holiday Bowl record for the longest touchdown
pass, a 65-yarder to Phil McConkey in 1978, when Navy
defeated Brigham Young University and its quarterback,
Jim McMahon. While McMahon and McConkey went
on to the NFL, Leszczynski signed up for a stint as a pilot.

During its years in the city's legendary Catholic Conference, which became the Metro Conference when Milwaukee Lutheran was added in 1974, Messmer was always competitive, but rarely dominant. One team, the
1948 squad, won a state private schools title. The tournament, though, was small — four or eight teams per division — and usually only conference champions could make
it. In the decades that followed, perhaps the closest the
team came to state was in 1969, the first year for Herm
Buechel as head coach. Buechel led the team to a 6-2 record
in the conference, the only losses coming against perennial power Pius XI High School and, the devastating one,
to Waukesha Catholic Memorial, an improving team in
the one of the region's fastest growing suburbs. That game,
an 8-6 loss, was labeled "a nightmare in mud" in the
Messmer yearbook.

In those days, there were usually 60 or more players
on the varsity squad, though Buechel insisted on dressing
only 44. It made for a neat four-deep lineup at each position and gave the other players something to shoot for.

Practices were held at nearby Lincoln Park, since
Messmer didn't have a field. With Buechel as the driver,
the school's rattling and wheezing bus made two trips out
each day, with freshmen and sophomores having to jog
the half-mile there and back. At Messmer, football was
the center of things in the fall, with hundreds of students

attending home games and a Bishop mascot with a giant paper mache head joining the cheerleaders on the side-line. Before each game, the football mothers group would serve a meal in the school cafeteria, the players dressed in sport coats and ties. Then it would be off to the locker room, then the chapel for words of wisdom from the coaches and athletic director, Fr. Robert Berghammer — "Bergie" to all involved. After every win, it was a longstanding tradition to stop at the convent in back of the school, ring the doorbell and then — as the nuns ap-peared in windows and doorways — kneel to count out the score, pounding helmets on the sidewalk for empha-sis.

In 1972, Messmer finally got its revenge against Catho-lic Memorial, by then an established power. Messmer came into the last game with a 3-4-1 record. Memorial, mean-while, was undefeated for the second year running. With a few minutes left in the game, Messmer trailing 14-13, one of the receivers, Mike Dorn, declared he could beat his man on the opposite side. With assurances from the linemen that they could hold Memorial off long enough, Buechel allowed Leszczynski to call the little-used play — "Popcorn Pass." The result: A 65-yard touchdown pass to Dorn. Back at Messmer, outside the convent, the players pounded their helmets on the ground 20 wonderful times.

Buechel was replaced in 1977 by Mike Ostopowicz, an assistant known to the players and students as "Mr. O." By then, the school had an agreement with the Koss Corp., a company located about two blocks to the north that manufactured stereo headphones. For $1 a year, the school could use a field north of the plant for gym class and football practice. The field was rutted and uneven and after heavy rains, rocks would often surface in the mud.

Football remained at the center of the school, or close to it, during those months of fall, with pep rallies in the gym before big games, each class trying to out-shout the others, and cheerleaders posting elaborate good-luck signs on player lockers each Friday, which students would sign yearbook-style. The school played most of its home games at either Custer or Rufus King, two public high schools. But as those neighborhoods grew rougher, officials looked for other options and in the early 1980s shifted some home games to Shorewood. Indeed, Shorewood and Messmer played twice — Messmer winning 36-8 in 1979 and 28-0 in 1981.

The program, though, was slipping. After the 1982 season, Messmer dropped out of the Metro in football, with officials blaming low numbers and saying the team could no longer be competitive. Coach Ostopowicz left, taking a job on the Catholic Memorial staff. And, though no one realized it at the time, the next season — 1983 — became the last for Messmer football. The team finished with a record of 1-7. In the yearbook, the varsity football picture showed only 20 players.

After the school closed and reopened, the numbers were too small for football, though officials tried to start a junior varsity squad a few years later. To the best of anyone's recollection, the team played a single game, scratching out a victory against University School, a well-to-do private school in the northern suburbs.

For a few years, Messmer scheduled its homecoming around a basketball game. Later, boys soccer was added as a fall sport, and that became the homecoming focus, until the team was dropped in 1999, after several years of allowing girls on the boys squad in order to have enough players. That left cross country as the only fall sports option for boys.

The school still had homecoming, but it was hardly the same. In high school, in the heart of the Midwest, in all of America really, homecoming means football.

Period.

Shorewood, if anything, is a soccer school, though in

the fall, boy's volleyball is a close second. Both programs are routinely near the top of the conference and ranked among the best in the Milwaukee area. In 1997, when the 25-0 soccer team made it to the semi-finals of the state tournament, even the football players boarded a bus to Madison to cheer them on. The team won a championship that year. Indeed, throughout the 1990s, Shorewood periodically considered focusing homecoming activities around soccer.

The decline of Shorewood football paralleled the rise of soccer, though one former football coach, Dennis Williamson, noticed a bigger impact when boy's volleyball was added and all of his tight ends and receivers were suddenly pounding down spikes in the gym instead of wearing them on the field. In any case, the fact remains, while dozens of boys play football at Shorewood Intermediate School, which fields 7th and 8th grade teams, when they reach high school, only a handful come out for football.

To be sure, Shorewood has its own football history, though to find it you have to look at the red banners that hang on the west wall of the gym. The football team won conference championships in 1927, 1936, then four consecutive seasons in the 1940s, then four out of five years from 1956 to 1960, then again in 1967 and 1981. That season, 1981, was marked by a victory over rival White-fish Bay, the win securing the traveling Glory Cup trophy for the first time in six years. The 6-3 record was good enough for first place in the small schools division of the Suburban Conference and the team made its first — and only — appearance in the state public school playoffs, losing 27-0 to New Berlin Eisenhower. The football team continued with respectable records through the 1988 season, when a Shorewood team that ended 3-6 upset rival Wauwatosa East in the final game, 25-14, to keep East out of the playoffs.

Coach Williamson lasted a single 0-9 season longer, stepping down just before the 1990 season to focus on coaching basketball, and for the first time in memory — perhaps ever — Shorewood turned to an outside coach for the football team.

First was Rick Bolanos. When he started, the losing streak was at nine games. When he left, voted out by the players three games into the 1993 season, the tally was 39 straight losses. And the streak had become The Streak. The replacement for Bolanos stepped down midway through the following season, after being charged with second-degree sexual assault of a minor. He was arrested right on the practice field and later acquitted. Next was Christopher Words. Then, in 1994, Lonnie Heller.

By then The Streak was at 45 games, its weight heavier all the time, persisting despite a move from the reconfigured and renamed North Shore Conference to the more manageable Parkland. By now, debating the reason for the decline of Shorewood football had become a veritable parlor game. Was it the success of soccer and the other fall sports? Or the fact few students needed a sports scholarship to make it to college? Was the brutality of the sport at odds with a life of privilege, inviting more sneering than respect? Were Shorewood boys simply smaller, less tough, than those from opposing schools?

Was it something in the water?

A year later, in 1995, The Streak was at 54, now the longest active stretch of futility for any high school in Wisconsin. With 34 varsity players, Heller's team opened the 1995 season against Riverside, another local doormat that had been scheduled simply because it would mean one of the two teams would end up happy. Shorewood officials even put a plan in place to protect the goal posts in the event of a victory. On the field, the team took a 7-6 lead, only to slip in the end and lose 18-7.

When Coach Carlton Hutcherson took over the next

season, The Streak was at 63.

And then, on Aug. 30, 1996, it was broken.

It was the season's first game, again against Riverside, and again at Shorewood. That night, the jubilant crowd could be heard throughout the village, first the roars from the stadium and then the honking of cars and shouts of students as everyone left, parading down the streets. The team made ESPN for breaking The Streak, believed to be the longest in the nation. Sophomore Aaron Hyche, who scored the first touchdown on a three-yard run with 1:26 left in the first half, would later tell the school newspaper: "It was amazing, like the whole thing was just a dream. Everything people said about us in the past just vanished once the clock ticked away."

The team won one more game that season, then one the next year. And then the new streak began, under Hutcherson until 1999, then under Dave Geis, a 1980 Shorewood graduate, who hired Trost to coach the defense, though Trost was soon installing the offense as well. After one season, Trost was promoted to the top job, the eighth coach for Shorewood football in 12 years.

Despite it all, football games have remained community events in Shorewood, with hundreds of students, parents, graduates and residents filling the stands on Friday nights. These days, fans are conditioned to cheer first downs as loudly as other schools cheer touchdowns and to measure success by the margin of defeat, not victory. And, even now, when the leaves turn yellow and drift to the sidewalk, there are still some groups of children who, after a game in the street or at the park, come home to declare to Mom and Dad they will be the ones, yes, the ones that turn Shorewood football around.

There are some, but not many.

At Messmer, officials were thrilled to receive the call from Shorewood. Although many students were clamoring for football and the administration felt it was losing potential students to other high schools because Messmer didn't have a team, it was too expensive to start a program from scratch.

The school didn't have any equipment, not so much as a knee-pad or chin strap. A few old football pads and other pieces of equipment had been found a few years earlier, when the school started construction on its gymnasium addition. But the rest — the silver helmets with the block blue M, the blue jerseys and the striped silver pants — had been shipped out or discarded years ago, when the school closed. It could cost as much as $50,000 for new equipment alone, perhaps $10,000 for a coaching staff, plus up to $8,000 a year for insurance. Then Messmer would have to find a place to practice, pay rent there, and find a field to play home games. More rent. Then there would be the travel costs in a far-flung conference.

At one point, Washington High School, a public school about three miles away, approached Messmer about joining forces, but just as Shorewood was leery of pairing with Riverside and having to play in the City Conference, Messmer wasn't much interested in joining Washington to do the same. Seeking a private school for a partnership, Br. Bob Smith, the school's president, had once broached the idea of Dominican High School, a Catholic school in Whitefish Bay, a well-to-do suburb. But members of the school's board who were Messmer alumni immediately shot it down. Dominican had been a bitter rival, back in the days of the old Metro Conference. Very bitter.

Shorewood?

Bretsch called Wilburth back first thing Monday morning.

"We're interested," she said.

Later that week, Shorewood won its first game of the year, a 51-19 pounding of Brown Deer under a full moon on Friday the 13th. The game ended the 38-game losing streak and the 51 points was the most by a Shorewood team in at least 30 years. There were tears on the sideline, pictures taken in front of the scoreboard and, once the bus made it back to Shorewood, fake champagne — brought in by joyous parents — in the locker room.

On the way home, the team bus stopped at a hotel, where Coach Carroll's wedding reception — planned long before he took the job as a Shorewood assistant — was in full swing. Carroll had told the team they could come crash the event, but only if they won. So it was in the middle of a dance that he looked up and saw the coaches, Trost in his trademark red shorts, standing in the doorway with wide, delirious grins. Carroll and his wife, Drea, went outside to accept the sweaty hugs and handshakes from the team.

A week later, the ball finally rolling on partnership talks with Messmer, Shorewood lost its final game of the year, collapsing after being tied at the half. The final score: 41-27.

The opponent: Dominican.

When it came to the partnership, officials at both schools knew there would be more to the arrangement than football. In a community where the racial divide is always present, but rarely confronted, there had to be more. By itself, of course, the partnership could not resolve all problems, or even put a dent in them. But officials at both schools decided it was worthy — and it was worth it — to try.

In Milwaukee, as in other big cities, it is said the most segregated hour of the week comes on Sunday mornings, when whites go to white churches and blacks go to black churches. But in area schools, that same dynamic is played out every day at lunch. Whites eating with whites. Blacks eating with blacks. Everyone separate.

At Messmer, the school used to participate in an exchange program with several Catholic high schools from the Green Bay area. A group of students from Oshkosh, Appleton and Menasha would spend a few nights in central city homes, the Messmer students up north. More recently, the school began running a daily bus from a Hispanic neighborhood on the city's south side, in order to add diversity to the student body. Nevertheless, white students are few and the main opportunity for racial mixing comes on the basketball court against opposing schools from places like Brookfield, Delavan and Burlington.

At Shorewood, meanwhile, officials had long wrestled with the question of whether its efforts in the desegregation program were truly working or simply creating new pockets of self-segregation. School board president Emily Koczela had begun conducting her own study on the matter. In one of her survey questions, all teachers, students and parents were asked to finish the sentence: "A well-integrated school environment ..."

The answers ranged from snide ones — "Doesn't give pointless surveys" — to thoughtful ones lamenting how people of other races shun attempts at friendship or noting little will change until Shorewood itself becomes more diverse. At the time, the school did not have a single black teacher. One senior wrote that during the lunch hour, when students can leave campus or eat wherever they want, the black students tend to congregate by a phone booth outside the gymnasium building.

"I sometimes feel uncomfortable walking through that area," the senior wrote. "It would feel strange for me, a white student, to walk up to one of them when they are congregated and start talking to them, even if I know the person, just because — I don't know, it would feel strange."

At both schools, administrators believed a key to bridging racial differences was to get kids from different backgrounds working together in non-racial projects, such as the band or drama club or the forensics team.

Or football.

In the fall of 2000, Shorewood High School had a new principal, Rick Monroe, who was quite familiar with the football situation. Monroe had lived in Shorewood for years and his son, Nick, had been a senior on the Shorewood team the year before. Monroe joined the staff from St. Francis High School, another school in the conference. St. Francis was one of the city's more blue-collar southern suburbs, a place where football was king, with more than 50 guys routinely landing on the varsity squad. Indeed, if a big and strong kid from St. Francis decided not to play, he'd run into neighbors demanding to know why at the grocery store, bank, drug store, even church.

Back when there were rumors about the potential partnership with Riverside, Nick Monroe wrote a scathing column in the student newspaper trashing the notion of a team destined to become the "Greytigers," instead of the Greyhounds.

"A Riverside-Shorewood combined football team spells doom for the future of athletics at Shorewood," Nick Monroe wrote. "The fact that it is even being discussed sends chills down my spine. Shorewood has a fine football tradition; before you laugh and say football is worthless, hear me out. Who packs the stands for EVERY home game? What brings in the most money for the athletic department? What made ESPN's SportsCenter? What has been one of the top five teams to watch this prep football season in the *Milwaukee Journal Sentinel*? Shorewood football."

Never mind that the team made SportsCenter only because it had finally broken the streak. Or that the newspaper named Shorewood a team to watch ... to see if it could break the newest one.

Now as principal, Rick Monroe remembered the fall Fridays when he arrived home from work, passing Nick and his friends in the driveway as they left for the game,

vowing every time that tonight would be different, tonight they would win. Monroe saw Friday night football
as a slice of Americana, nostalgia under the lights, a piece
of history that had to be preserved. He knew there were
troubles with Shorewood football. A year or two earlier, at
a Parkland Conference principals meeting, Monroe overheard the Shorewood principal at the time, Art Ellis, lamenting the cost and trouble of keeping the program going, almost wishing the team would disappear. "Is that
you talking, or the school talking?" someone asked. Ellis
did not respond. In any case, Monroe, a former high school
athlete and a father who had another son a few years away
from high school, wouldn't have that.

Across the nation, only 27 states allow athletic partnerships — co-ops — of any kind, and most of those do
not allow a public-private mix. Of the few dozen sports
co-ops in Wisconsin, only six paired public schools with
private ones, none in football. That alone would make the
Shorewood-Messmer partnership unique.

Around the country, there are perhaps two-dozen public-private partnerships in football. They generally fall into
two categories — two schools from the same place, such as
Austin High School and Austin Pacelli High School, located across the street from each other in Austin, Minnesota, or schools in neighboring small towns, such as the
partnership between Suttons Bay High School and Lake
Leelanau St. Mary High School in the Traverse City area
of Michigan. Of all the pairings in the country, the
Shorewood-Messmer partnership would be the only one
to combine a central city high school with a suburban
one.

The arrangement was quickly and unanimously approved by the boards of the two schools. Under the deal,
Messmer would pay Shorewood $300 for each student
that participated in football. The agreement would be for
two years. If all went well, it could be extended in two-

year increments.

Other schools in the conference, though, weren't so sure it was a good idea.

Shorewood had about 750 students, Messmer more than 500. The combination would create by far the largest pool of students in the Parkland Conference — even without Messmer, Shorewood ranked second in size, behind only Slinger High School. And Messmer, being private, could bring in students from anywhere, with those qualifying for the choice program attending free. Some believed Messmer could become the back door for Milwaukee players — black players — who otherwise couldn't get into Shorewood.

For perhaps the first time in years, Shorewood football was seen as a threat.

The first hurdle was a vote by conference athletic directors, where the plan passed 4-3. Monroe went to a meeting of the principals a few weeks later, assuring them the combination wouldn't be an instant powerhouse. Anything but. Indeed, the idea behind an athletic partnership is not to create one strong team but to give both schools a chance to build interest among their own students so, ultimately, they can be separate again

This time, only one school — Dominican — objected.

At Shorewood, the partnership in place, the administrators and coaches held an after-school meeting to talk with the returning players about how it would work. About 17 kids attended, some of whom were ineligible anyway. Monroe would later think that some came just for the free pizza.

Meanwhile, at Messmer the word quickly spread that something was happening with football, that by fall they might have a team.

Finally, in March, at the end of a prayer service, Athletic Director Joy Bretsch stepped to the podium and announced the partnership with Shorewood. Her words were lost in the screams, as students jumped up, pumping their fists, whooping and hollering, a reaction that quieted long enough for Bretsch to call Nathan Shorter up to the stage. He would be the school's honorary captain. Bretsch tossed him the ball.

Nate carried it with him the rest of the day.

The announcement was all the guys who were interested in football could talk about in classrooms, the hallways, the cafeteria. This was it. Football. Finally, football. It was touchdown passes and end zone dances, cheering crowds and marching bands. It would be like on television, like in the movies. It would be all that. It would be all of that and more.

If the Messmer kids had any impression of Shorewood, the high school or the community, it was a vague one — white, rich, big. In fact, some of the would-be players from Messmer had never set foot across the river.

Nate remembered driving past Shorewood High School a few times, seeing the football team out on the field, the uniforms so clean and bright, he figured they had to be good. Between classes that day, Nate stopped in the computer lab and looked up Shorewood's record from the last season.

1-8.

Oh, Nate thought.

Chapter 3
"They aren't your guys. They're my guys, too."

The day was hot again. And though the coaches pushed the first practice session back several hours to avoid the direct afternoon sun, the air was still heavy and humid. It was like a weight, extra pounds to be carried. The temperature again was more than 95 degrees, with the heat index making it feel somewhere on the wrong side of 100.

It was the second day of practice. Wednesday.

And, despite the end-of-practice admonition from Coach Trost and the promise that came with accepting the practice jerseys, not everyone came back. There were 26 players on the field, plus two in the locker room getting ready, down from 33 the day before. As the team stretched, Trost wandered between them with a roster in hand.

"Westmoreland?" he called out.

A hand went up.

"Acevedo."

Another hand.

"Kwiatkowski."

No hand.

It was so easy to quit. Too easy.

"Mallett," Trost called out. He looked around. "Pertrell?"

Still missing.

This team, with so little experience, didn't have much time. There were three days and six practice sessions before Saturday's Red and Blue intra-squad game, then another week before a scrimmage in nearby Random Lake, where four other teams would participate. A week later and it would be opening night, a game against Whitefish Bay, a traditional Shorewood rival and possibly the toughest team on the schedule. With so little time, everything carried a greater urgency and everything seemed to go faster, the week accelerating into a blur. The team mostly worked on the basics. There was the tackling dummy, which some quickly mastered and others danced around as if they had brought an elephant to the prom. There were passing drills, catching drills, blocking drills. There were sprints. More sprints. Still more.

Yet everything, each day, felt new.

So when the dinner break was over, turkey sandwiches and potato salad again, and Trost told the team to head down to the stadium, the players could hardly wait. They ran toward the field and down the steps, practically dancing across the track that circled the grass. Some tossed footballs ahead of them, then ran after the balls, which bounced crazily on the turf. Others took it all more slowly, walking, as if approaching a mirage, worried it would vanish if they went too fast.

Trost, running behind them, shouted a reminder of what was to come.

"Just remember guys, that's Friday night football right there."

The sun was nearly gone, with just streaks of pink and purple clouds on the horizon. The lights were on, casting competing shadows down below. No lines had been painted on the field and in the warm night, the grass seemed to stretch forever into the darkness. The moment stretched with it.

"This is what I like," George Lasley said, then shouted. "This is what we worked for boys. This is what it's all about."

The shouts came back.

"You know it."

"Here we go."

The season was only a day old, but Trost was already tinkering with the lineup.

Dave O'Harrow was definitely the quarterback. Even if he had flamed out at Marshall, Dave had played varsity football before and, if his father was to be believed, could throw the ball 50 yards. He seemed more confident than the other likely candidates and was an easier fit. With Nate Shorter and Mark Moore, two thirds of the backfield was set. But Trost still needed someone in the other running back slot, the Roar position, ideally a slasher to complement Mark's speed. He had tried Jonathan Williams, a sophomore who had transferred to Shorewood, but wasn't satisfied. Now, as the offensive unit walked through formations and plays, Trost told George Lasley — who had been slow to pick up the quarterback calls — to try the running back slot instead.

"You might like that better," Trost said.

"Yes, I would," said George, politely.

But George was still miffed about the locker room incident from Monday, in which Trost ignored his suggestion they pray. And he still wanted to be quarterback. Ever since he was a boy, whenever George and his cousin and the neighborhood kids played football in the street, he was the quarterback. Sometimes, if no one had a football, they'd use a deflated basketball, or treat a rock or piece of wood as the ball, whatever was handy, a light post or car bumper serving as the goal line.

Dave lined the team up. No defense. Just offense. George watched from his new spot, hands on knees, adjusting to the running back stance.

"When he says 'Set'," you're gone," Coach Smith told him.

George nodded.

"Flee like the police are on me," he said.

With anyone else, such a statement would have been a joke. With George, it was personal history. He had tried to run before, wanted to run the day he was arrested as a freshman at Bay View, the day when he felt something was wrong and slipped the bag of marijuana to one friend, the wad of cash to another and walked casually out of the classroom and into the long hallway, only to see a police officer coming toward him, only to turn and see another. As much as he wanted to run, George had been caught. And now, at the start of his senior year, he knew it was for the best. George may have grown up next to a church, but he hadn't found God and direction until he was sent to Messmer, located on his side of town. Now, if Trost told the team to "take a knee," George was liable to respond: "We praying?" He planned to go to college and had the idea of going somewhere outside Milwaukee. Somewhere distant, where there was no past to run from at all.

"9-9-9, 9-9-9," Dave began the count, "Set-Red-Hit."

At "Set," George started in motion. Dave turned easily, naturally, and pitched the ball to him and George, smooth and fluid, followed his blockers around the end, no defenders ahead, no barriers. Of course, George was supposed to be the one making the pitch. But that, too, was lost in the perfect glow of the lights.

The second day became the third day.

Before practice, Trost and Coach Groser handed out shoulder pads and the rest of the equipment to the team. The players picked up the pads from piles, as directed by Groser — thigh pads and knee pads and whatever-these-are pads. Some knew what to do with them all, but to others it was an utter mystery, as if they had just been handed a Barbie doll and a little pink dress. After collecting everything they needed, an armful, each player walked up to Trost who, like a stressed-out tailor, sized them up, grabbed a pair of shoulder pads and plopped them over the player's head. Hitting would begin tomorrow, and for the first time in years they might need to order extra equipment.

Nate Shorter, the biggest of all, walked back into the locker room, where the other players were changing or just listening to music from the boom box. Hip-hop, as usual. On Tuesday, despite the long first day of practice, Nate went home and played a game of pickup football in a vacant lot. Tackle of course. No pads. His knee still hurt.

"Damn, they're still too small," said Micah Moore, looking up. "They look like quarterback pads on you, man."

Nate shrugged. They were the biggest they had.

Now Maurice Ragsdale walked out, smiling through a red mouth guard.

"Makes me feel like a gladiator," Maurice announced, over and over, to anyone who would listen. It came out: "Mwakes me fweel wike a gwadiator."

Before they hit the field, Trost ducked into his office and ran through the phone list, trying to round up missing players.

"Tracey there?" he said into the phone. "Coach Trost from Messmer ... Well, he's supposed to be at practice right now."

Trost hung up, dialed another number.

"Coming today?" he asked, barely pausing. "How come? ... But you can come and watch. Why don't you do that?"

Trost looked irritated. It was easy to imagine the other side of the conversation.

"Is your heart in this Sam?" he continued. "Or not?"

Trost shook his head at the other coaches and frowned. One minute Trost was an equipment manager, the next a salesman. Indeed, Trost had once taught himself enough about the stock market to create Trost Investment Corp., developing a confident patter to disguise his inexperience.

Trost would be the team secretary when necessary, the travel agent when required, the disciplinarian, the task-master, the nanny and, on occasion, the friend, but mostly the father. In his mind, a football team was a family and the head coach was the father, who sometimes let his play-ers test their limits and other times guided them where they needed to be, whether they liked it or not.

Trost pressed on.

"Is it too hard for you, is that it?" he asked. "Do you want to play football?"

Another pause.

"All right. Then you've got to come out here and work."

When Trost finally made it outside, there were 28 play-ers, plus two nursing injuries — a twisted ankle and a sore back.

"You're hitting a wall," Trost told the team, everyone gathered in to listen. "We gotta fight through the wall."

In a few moments, Trost received an unlikely assist.

The day was hot again, but a touch cooler and windy, clouds sliding across the sky until they stacked up over the edge of Lake Michigan and seemed to double back. The clouds thickened and went gray and then, finally, raindrops pelted down.

"It's like *Any Given Sunday,*" declared Maurice Ragsdale. "Monsoon weather."

He was grinning when he said it. So were others, who remembered a scene in the movie about the NFL where the rain came down in sheets and the ground became mud and the mud sent everyone flying and crashing. The rain came harder.

"The monsoon is here, baby!" Maurice shouted.

Harder still.

"Oh yeah!"

As practice continued, shouts of glee mixed with the slapping hiss of the rain, Steve Wittemann, the trainer, stood in the doorway, scanning the horizon for lightning.

He was in his second year at Shorewood, after the previous trainer clashed with Trost and quit. Rain was OK. But lightning would put everything on hold. Practice would have to stop. In the distance, from within the gray, the lights on several TV towers blinked.

And then there was lightning.

But the shouts were growing louder. The players lost their footing, but got right back up, kept after the play. No one cared. This was fun.

"Hey, Jim," Wittemann shouted.

Trost looked over and Wittemann pointed to the sky.

Trost raised his arms as if to say "Where?" He lifted his glasses onto his forehead.

"I haven't seen anything," Trost shouted back.

The water was cascading off the roof of the nearby Shorewood Intermediate School building. There was a rumble of thunder. More lightning.

Finally Trost waved everyone in.

The shouts came back: "C'mon. One more."

After dinner in the cafeteria, before the promise of another night under the lights, Coach Carroll and Coach Trost walked down the hallway to the locker room, turned a corner and stopped cold.

"Oh," said Carroll.

"Wow," said Trost.

There was Pertrell Mallett, tall, strong, sturdy. He wore a pair of blue Nike shorts, a matching sleeveless shirt and a wide, embarrassed smile.

After Nate Shorter couldn't find Pertrell, Trost succeeded in tracking down Pertrell's father. Trost called Messmer, got his work number and, since Pertrell's father was on the factory floor, left a message with his own cell phone number.

"It's like seeing a ghost," Trost said.

They stepped into the locker room, where Pertrell was

greeted with slaps on the back and questions from the Messmer kids — "Where ya been at?" and "You gonna play?"

"I've been moving," Pertrell said simply.

Indeed, he had been moving, though the coaches only knew pieces of what was happening. Pertrell never allowed much more than a glance at the details of his home life. He was the oldest among seven children, naturally guarded and protective. Pertrell's father and step-mother were getting divorced and, in the temporary setup, he and two brothers had moved in with their father. Plus, Pertrell was finishing a driver's education class, which his father said must come before football, no matter how much Pertrell wanted to play.

There was a difference, Trost had already decided, between the Shorewood kids and the Messmer ones. The Shorewood kids, for the most part, came from stable, two-parent families. They were reliable. Dependable. They hardly ever missed practice, or complained about it when they were there. If anything, they might make a wise-ass remark, then follow orders. Those from Messmer, while good kids, were dealing with so much more. Absent fathers, working mothers, the allure of the street. While Maurice Ragsdale, the son of a single mother, picked up potato chips and pies for dinner at the gas station each night on the way home, Marty Wallner's mother baked cookies for the team, which she sent over on Fridays in old shoe boxes lined with aluminum foil.

Yet Trost needed the Messmer kids. In addition to Nate Shorter at fullback, Rob Wyatt was slated for starting duty on the line and Ronell Halbert was in at wide receiver. So was Maurice. George Lasley, out at quarterback, was still a starting linebacker and the heart of the defense. Others were pushing for starting spots.

And, of course, there was Pertrell, penciled in at linebacker and tight end.

"Now I got the schedule right," Pertrell assured Trost, who tossed him a practice jersey.

Nate knew what was going on with Pertrell, knew more of it than Trost knew, or ever could have guessed. But it was between them as friends. Nate walked over, hand out, and Pertrell took it, pulling Nate in until they bumped chests. The two had met at Messmer during their sophomore year in geometry class. They just started talking one day, about sports, girls, stuff, and made a connection.

"Sorry, man," Pertrell said.

Nate nodded.

"I hope you'll apologize to your teammates," Trost said, more of a demand than a suggestion. "Is that what you want to do?"

"Uh," Pertell said and paused. He shook his head. "No."

But he was there. That was something.

That was a relief.

Pertrell followed the team outside, down to the big field, where some of the players were already tossing footballs around. The lights were on again. And the grass, still damp from the rain, felt extra fresh, as if the world had just stepped from a shower.

There were no goalposts in place and one of the six light standards was out. A power line had been cut while work crews were digging a hole for new goalposts, so a corner of the field was left deep in shadow. None of the players had noticed the shortcomings the night before — it was so perfect under the lights. But the coaches grumbled that it was typical Shorewood and predicted they'd have to move the opening night game to Whitefish Bay. Or else, the joked, they'd bring flashlights and, for field goals, stand in the end zone and hold hands to create a human goal post.

The drills began.

Pertrell, who hadn't turned in his physical card, tried

to watch from the back of the group, but as the team lined up for the pursuit drill, chasing out to the designated cones, Trost tossed Pertrell the ball. He caught it. Surprised.

"Let's see that speed of yours," Trost said.

Pertrell half-smiled and shrugged.

Then he ripped off a run in which he nearly beat every defender to the designated spot — "Hit. Hit. Hit." Pertrell jogged back, flipped the ball to Trost and again tried to escape the attention. Pertrell liked the background, not the spotlight.

In that regard, he fit in with the team just fine. There were some players who were flashy, who possessed that tinge of cockiness that was needed to line up across from an opponent and know, know way deep down, that you cannot be stopped. But, by and large, from the captains on down, the team's voice was a mumble, not a shout. When each captain spoke briefly at the team meeting on Monday, the other players strained to hear them over the hum of the air conditioner.

There were four captains, two from each school.

Nate Shorter, of course, was one of the captains from Messmer. That was a given. The other Messmer captain was Rob Wyatt, who had transferred from Marshall and with some commitment over the summer in the weight room had gone from bench pressing 215 pounds to lifting 315 pounds into the air on the final day, arms wobbling all the way. The captains had to sign a form, along with their parents, stating they understood the expectations of leadership. "People who want to get things done find a way, others find an excuse," it read. And: "The speed of the leader determines the rate of the pack." From Shorewood, there was Mark Moore. Again, no doubt.

And, finally, Timmy Lathrop.

Timmy, who was white, was a Shorewood senior. He had hair that seemed to perpetually be out of place, even though it was cut short. A splotch of hair was lighter than

the rest, which was your basic brown. After three years on
the wrestling team, Timmy's nose looked like it had a dent
in it. He played soccer when he was young, but gave it up
because it was too soft. It didn't demand the anger and
release that football did. Timmy came off as the classic
square peg. During dinner breaks, he often sat by himself,
or at a table with another Shorewood player, Brandon
Blanke, who would listen to a CD on a headset rather
than talk with him. Timmy didn't fit in easily with the
Messmer players either, admitting he had little contact
with blacks before the season. But the Messmer players
respected Timmy, if only because he always worked hard.

Seeing holes in the lineup for fall, Timmy worked over
the summer on the footwork needed to play quarterback,
practicing regularly with friends at a park near his house.
Timmy asked the coaches for a shot, but they never really
considered him. Instead, he was sent with the linemen,
though on defense he could also be used as a linebacker or,
in a pinch, safety. Wherever he was needed. Timmy was
strong, but not quick. Determined but not overpowering.
Attitude compensated for any lack of athleticism.

Back in the spring, Trost also had named Shorewood
seniors Evan Rivera and Drew O'Malley captains. The two
lived down the street from each other, just a few blocks
from the high school. And though Drew went to St. Robert Elementary School while Evan was in the Shorewood
system, they didn't really remember a time when they
hadn't known each other. Evan had played football all four
years, six if you counted the two at Shorewood Intermediate School. Drew joined last season, as a junior, after playing soccer for two years — one of the few players at
Shorewood to make such a switch. Over the summer,
though, Drew was a counselor at a YMCA camp and Evan
worked a lot, so they both were sporadic weight-room
participants and had been stripped of the titles.

Due to the influx of Messmer talent, they also lost their

positions from last year, Evan fullback and Drew wide receiver, and, though disappointed, they moved to other spots. Like Timmy, they loved to play football. They'd have played it anywhere.

That's what the Shorewood players brought to the table. They wanted to play, all of them. You had to want to play football to play at Shorewood. It certainly wasn't because of any hallway glory that came from wearing a uniform.

It was that way with Marty Wallner, the undersized sophomore who was aiming for a spot at wide receiver. Or running back. Or kick returns. Somewhere. Anywhere.

In seventh grade, in the first game of the season, Marty, in at running back, went more than 50 yards for a touchdown the first time he touched the ball. The moment is immortalized in a family photo, Marty in Shorewood red splitting a bunch of Nicolet players in blue. He scored against Nicolet again in the first game of his eighth-grade season, but in the second matchup was injured. It happened as Marty tried to cut back, feet moving even as he was being wrested to the ground. There was a quiet in the stands, the quiet that only comes when a player is down. After a few minutes, unsure whether he should intervene, Mark Wallner — Marty's father — stood up, picked up his cane and slowly went down to the field. Mr. Wallner had suffered from polio as a baby and walked with a twisting limp, both legs partially paralyzed. The only reason he and Marty could do their "football walks" years ago — the ones in which Marty would race ahead for the passes — was pushing Jack, Marty's brother, in the stroller allowed Mr. Wallner to make it up and down the long Shorewood streets. As he walked across the field toward Marty, a Nicolet coach remarked, "He's so little." Mr. Wallner turned and snapped: "Yeah, well, he scored a touchdown against you this year."

Later, Marty stood on the sideline, grimacing at the pain. His ankle was broken. Coach Trost and Coach

Trawitzki, who had come to the game, were standing nearby and motioned him over. You'll be all right, they said. Stay tough. Take some Advil. They, too, thought Marty was small, impossibly slight. But back when Trost was in high school, in that hallway conversation, his varsity coach told him he had no reservations about his size, he just saw a football player.

Trost tried to see the same with Marty.

After the pursuit drill, when the team broke into units, the running backs did a cut drill, zig-zagging between a series of orange cones. When it was his turn, Marty was fast, faster than Mark Moore. He was sharp, sharper than Mark. Coaches stopped and watched, called to others to do the same. The players had recognized Marty's skills even before the coaches did, sometimes picking him first when choosing sides for the pick-up games at the end of the summer camp sessions. Some joked that catching Marty was like trying to catch a mouse. Now Marty's feet seemed to slice along the damp ground, but the noise was his sharp breaths. He shifted the ball in his hands, back and forth, always to the outside.

This is how a position is won.

A few minutes later, when Trost lined up the first-team offense to run through some plays against a phantom de-fense, he put Marty in as the second receiver. Maurice Ragsdale, head hanging, was sent to work with the second team. The two units lined up back to back and ran the same plays at the same time. It was like looking into a mirror.

Marty snagged a pass. Maurice dropped one.

Marty dove. Maurice pulled up.

This is how a position is lost.

"I love that kid over there," Trost said out loud, to no one in particular. He meant Marty. But Trost finished the thought in his head, as he had so many times before: *If only he weighed another 20 pounds.*

Later, Maurice stood on the sideline, arms crossed, muttering and frustrated.

"I know Marty's got the experience, but dog," he said, to a group of Messmer players.

"Maurice, you gotta give it to Marty," one replied.

Maurice was competitive, of course. And, in truth, he had nothing against Marty. The two, despite their battle for the same spot and their near-opposite backgrounds, had begun sharing a locker and a tentative friendship. Like any friendship, it was hard to say just when it started, but there was a day over the summer, a Tuesday or a Thursday after a weight lifting session at Messmer, when the two went straight to Shorewood, even though the camp session wouldn't start for hours. Maurice, who sometimes bummed rides home from the coaches, said he'd rather not take the bus. Marty didn't ask why, which would be impolite. Didn't offer to pay, which would be condescending. They just walked. And when they got to Shorewood, they spent hours playing catch in the sun, Marty tucking the ball under his arm after each catch, ever the perfect example.

Maurice liked Marty fine. But that was his spot.

You gotta give it to Marty."

The words, especially coming from a classmate, cut deep.

The fourth day blended into the rest, until it was hard to separate all the days. Players came and went, new plays were installed, new drills added, new terminology introduced, everyone's head jammed with numbers and names and assignments. Sometimes the team was smooth, other times sluggish, always, it seemed, teetering between the two.

On Friday night, after the first day of hitting, the coaches had arranged a sleepover in the Shorewood gym, with the Red and Blue intra-squad game for parents and others to follow Saturday morning. The coaches had talked about doing the session at Messmer, but the gym floor was being refinished that weekend.

After the end of the second practice session of the day, sometime close to midnight, the team was herded up to the gym, lights flicked on. A series of red banners hung along one wall listing all of Shorewood's conference and state championships by sport. There was a boy's cross country state title from last year, 2000. Boys soccer from 1997. This year's boys volleyball team was ranked among the top teams in the state. It was quite a contrast at Shorewood. Over the last five years, while the other boys fall sports were the best in the state, helping fill the trophy case, the football team had won exactly one game — and that was considered an improvement. The most recent championship listed on the football banner was 1981, before any of the players had been born.

In the gym, the wooden bleachers were pushed back against the wall. The players lugged in their sleeping bags and blankets and pillows, setting them down along the edges, near a giant fan that struggled to push the stale air around the room. Some walked around, looking up at the banners. Others grumbled about having to be there at all, especially on one of the last good Friday nights of the summer.

All things considered, the first week of practice — the first week of the great experiment — had gone well. Nevertheless, there was still a tentativeness between the players from the two schools that was tied into all the differences. During dinner breaks, they sat separately in the cafeteria, though some were beginning to mix together, the starters mostly, which was a different division in itself. The coaches were still worried about how the team would function once the season began. Would they blend their talents together and become one? Or split and splinter, one school here, the other there?

The night's agenda involved a series of team-building exercises, the stuff of retreats and seminars. In the first, a tennis ball was set on the floor and the players had to pick it up and pass it around without using their hands. A snap. In the second, the team was bunched together and wrapped in a volleyball net, then had to get to three designated spots in the gym, lights out, everyone laughing as they inched along. The message: If one guy falls, everyone falls. It was basic stuff, kinda hokey, really, but it didn't seem quite so embarrassing when it was only the team and the coaches.

When Trost was in high school, back in Chicago, the coaches once took his team to Plano, Illinois, for three days of practice and two nights of bonding. Another time, it was to a nearby park. The park was only a few miles away, but to the St. Pat's players it felt far, far away from their world.

In the gym, the Shorewood players were home.

The Messmer ones were not.

Though few would ever admit it, it was a test for the Messmer players to arrive in Shorewood for practice every day. Most Messmer players took the bus, while several from Shorewood had their own cars. When they went home at night, the Messmer players faced stares for something as simple as waiting as a group at the bus stop. For one Messmer player, a plastic grocery bag doubled as his gym bag. He'd quickly stow it under the locker room benches when he arrived. In contrast, one Shorewood player who quit after a week or two complained that when coaches cleaned out his locker a Rolex watch was thrown away.

For the last exercise, the coaches put everyone in a wide circle. The tennis ball would be tossed from one person to the next. Whoever caught it had to say why they were on the team, what their goals were for the season and what person influenced them the most — who they were playing for. The circle was large, so when it came time to talk, time to dig down and share secrets, the words seemed to be spoken louder than they were, with greater emphasis. It was late, pushing 1 a.m.

The tennis ball was tossed.

One person. The next.

The words came slowly, at first, basic stuff. There was talk of winning games and winning championships. Mark Moore said he wanted to break the Shorewood rushing record, which, so far as anyone could tell, stood at 1,203 yards, maybe even notch 2,000. There was talk of former coaches as role models, talk of mothers and fathers. And, from those who were missing one parent or both, there was talk of friends, teammates, grandparents and teachers, someone who had filled the void.

That group included Dominique Ross, a Messmer sophomore, who always had a smile on his face. He lost his mother years before and never really had his father around, living instead with a grandmother. He, more than the others, seemed to enjoy the camaraderie of the team, just hanging around, being with the guys, being part of something. Sometimes he would lean an arm on a teammate's shoulder, or just listen at the edge of a ribbing session. Dominique wanted to stick with the varsity, though the coaches wanted him to go down to the freshman-sophomore team where he would get more playing time.

"You guys," he said, tears welling in his eyes. "You guys are about the only thing I've got."

There was no laughter, no snickering. Instead, several players stood to hug him.

That seemed to open up everyone.

Mark Williams, a Messmer senior, was with his grandmother, too. He had transferred to Messmer, located just across the freeway from his house, after two years in a public high school, where he was struggling with motivation in the classroom. He had grown up in Philadelphia, living for a time with his "god family," until his grandmother

Photo courtesy of Michael Tucker

Revay Wright and Blake Comer, two players from Messmer, listen to instructions from the coaches. Many of the Messmer players came from central-city neighborhoods. Some had never been to Shorewood before.

figured they had to get away and, when Mark was 10, moved them to Milwaukee. His mother later followed them, but Mark rarely saw her. She drifted in and out of his life, Mark figuring she didn't care much about him. Mark said he was playing for his grandmother.

"She told me to never quit," he said.

Montreal Miller, another Messmer senior, lived in perhaps the roughest neighborhood of all the players, one filled with litter-choked lots and houses with chipped paint and rutted porches. He often heard gunshots at night, followed by the inevitable wail of sirens. Montreal's father died when he was 10. Heart attack. But his mother, a drug and alcohol counselor, kept the four kids on track. Growing up, Montreal was sent every summer to a youth leadership program for boys. At Messmer, he did well in the classroom. And though he had a "Superman" logo tattooed on his arm, he was soft-spoken with an almost gentle demeanor. During practice, he wore pads on his forearms to provide some cushion against the blows he got going

up against the likes of Nate and Rob on the line. Sometimes, on his way home, seeing women wandering the
streets in skimpy dresses and men drinking in cars and on
porches, Montreal would look around and repeat to himself his self-created motto — *"I will never surrender. I refuse
to die."* Over and over. *"I will never surrender. I refuse to
die."*

When the ball was tossed to George Lasley, he started
talking about his past, matter-of-factly, as if there was nothing shocking about it at all. Some Shorewood players sat
amazed — at the story and the ease with which it was
told. At one point, George stood up, as if a witness at a
revival meeting, walking among the group. It was all easy
to talk about, he would often say, because it was all past.
Long past.

George talked about how his father was gone and his
mother may as well have been. He and an older sister were
put in a foster home for a while, when their mother was
strung out. But the wealthy white foster family only
wanted George, who had lighter skin. After a few days, an
aunt came and took them both home. As a boy, George
had trouble reading and writing and was held back a grade,
considered stupid by his classmates. Even in high school,
when he came to Messmer as a sophomore, the guidance
counselors tested him to see if he was suffering from a
learning disability.

George talked about the drugs and the drug dealing.
At the start, it was just about smoking a little dope, though
George soon turned to selling it. Sometimes he'd give buyers
$15 worth of marijuana for the $25 they paid, using the
extra cash to build the business. He sometimes took in
$300 a week, rolling the blunts in the back of the class-
room, all the while pulling down decent grades. George
had robbed people. He had been beaten up. He lived for
the thrill. That day when George was caught, he wound
up handcuffed to a table at the police station, waiting for

his aunt to come and get him, putting his head down and trying to sleep, trying to dream it all away.

"I wanted to quit," George told the team. "But now I'm staying."

As the ball went around the circle, some players cited George and other teammates as their new role models. Trost, who at the start gave his own goal for the season — bringing the team together — listened to it all, struck by the candor and the contrast, a team being built before his eyes.

"I want to win," one player said. "I never won anything before in my life."

"I saw him out there," said another, "and I knew if he could do it, I could do it."

They kept at it for more than an hour, when the coaches finally went downstairs to sleep. In the gym, no one really settled down until about 4 a.m. The players tossed a lopsided old volleyball around for hours. George ran around shouting out the quarterback cadence, the one he kept forgetting the day before, his bare feet slapping across the floor. Someone started doing impressions of Coach Trost: "Let's go, let's go, let's go." And soon everyone was into it. Flex had the team in stitches, joking about how one player was so skinny he looked like a stick figure with an Afro. Somewhere amid it all, the ice was broken. And come morning, after breakfast in the cafeteria, two players sat outside, bleary-eyed, a slight chill in the August air.

One was from Shorewood. One from Messmer.

One was white. The other black.

Both were seniors, neither a big star. They had that in common. And now, they had a little bit more. They laughed about the antics in the gym and compared bruises from the first week of practice.

The two, if only for that moment, both felt at home.

On Monday, at the start of the second week of prac-

tice, there were only 17 guys out on the field stretching. Trost glowered and stalked through the locker room, telling players to hurry up, dammit, and get moving. He went to the office and started calling missing guys. By now, he knew some of the numbers by heart.

Outside, the other coaches tried to coax some enthusiasm from the players, who looked around and saw how much their numbers had fallen from a week earlier. To be sure, the first practice of the second week always is among the worst, if not the absolute worst, of the season. Players have had a day off, so their muscles have tightened. There is no game at the end of the week, so there is little to look forward to but more practices. There is a lot of hitting, but only hitting each other.

"Can't give them a day off, I see," said Coach Carroll, standing with Trawitzki and the other coaches.

Trost walked out.

"Couldn't get a hold of Pertrell," he announced. "George is missing in action."

All around them, there was activity. The other fall sports at Shorewood had begun practice, so the boy's soccer team was down on the big field, kicking balls into the net. The two cross country teams jogged past. The girl's tennis team was on the courts behind the middle school. The girls volleyball team was in the gym. The boys team would practice later. After a week in which the football team had everything to itself, the team — small and weary — was back in its proper place, at the bottom of the pecking order.

There had been a decent showing of parents and fans on Saturday, at the Red and Blue game and the cookout that followed. But it was hard to judge the team's talent or progress. The star of the day was Marty Wallner, who had a long touchdown reception and an interception in the end zone. Several key players, including Nate Shorter, sat out with injuries and others limped off field, bruised but mostly queasy and tired. The pads and equipment added 15 pounds, which left many wobbly on their feet. The team still had trouble getting organized in the huddle, so Trost and Trawitzki made adjustments while standing in the middle of the action on the field, choreographers as much as coaches.

Two more football players walked outside, lugging shoulder pads with them. Nineteen now. Last year, it was the same two dozen guys every night. This year, the numbers hovered between 25 and 30, though the mix was always changing.

The coaches broke the team into groups and they went station to station, doing the same drills from a week before, from the first day. The cuts and shuffles, the high-steps, the dives and weaves. This time, the echoes were angry: "No. Let's go. Do it again. C'mon, you're walking on a football field. Again. Let's go, let's go, let's go. Hustle, hustle."

After the dinner break, the team returned to the field even more lethargic than before. As players stretched, Trost dragged some large cushioned pads to the center of the field, laying them out in two sets of chutes. The players knew what was coming.

Oklahomas.

That was Trost's name for the two-on-two drills, in which an offensive lineman and a running back squared off against a defensive lineman and linebacker. In the drill, the pads serve as an out of bounds line for the four players, who line up as if in a game. The offensive lineman tries to create a hole, the running back tries to skirt through and the defensive players try to tackle him. The drill is meant to approximate game situations. It's all about pride. Aggression. No tentative, tippy-toe stuff. The running back must plunge ahead and the defense, the linebacker especially, must hit him, tackle him, somehow stop him. As a

player, you either embrace it or shirk from it. You relish in
the chance to make a big hit or try to disappear into the
back of the line. It is football at its rawest and most emo-
tional.

Trost had introduced the drill Friday, in the first practice where full contact was allowed. Before they were done,
an ambulance had to be called to remove Carlo Albano, a
Shorewood junior, from the field after he injured his knee.
The injury was a bit of a fluke — Carlo was locked up
with Nate when his knee gave out — but it left the players nervous and afraid. Now it was as if a cloud hung over
the drill.

The team was split into two groups, with the most
skilled facing off against each other. They had already done
the drill in the morning session, when Trost felt he had to
spice things up a bit. This second session would be longer,
more intense. It was a challenge to the players, but one
they were ill-equipped to face.

The first players lined up, waited for the whistle.

There was a thrust forward and a push back. Then a
casual banging of pads, all delicate and dainty. Over in
the second group, Maurice Ragsdale swung a guy around
but couldn't bring him down. Jason Davis, a Messmer
sophomore, ran through, untouched, over and over. He
tried to give the ball to another runner, but no one took it.
In the top group, Nate pushed guys around, clearing wide
holes as the offensive lineman.

"Guys, hit somebody," Coach Carroll said. "It sounds
like a ballet."

The coaches paced. Trost twirled his whistle, angry.
No pride, he thought. *None.*

"I should have guys fighting to get in there," he said,
teeth gritted.

The intensity picked up again, at least a touch, as players
were goaded and yelled at: "C'mon. Hit him. Harder. You're
getting pushed around. Get up. Stand up and fight."

Then, a crunch of helmets, and two players slumped to the ground.

One was Timmy Lathrop, in at linebacker. The other, Ronell Halbert, in at running back. They had met, helmet to helmet. The two stood up woozy and were led to the sideline. Steve Wittemann, the trainer, sat with them, looking into their vacant eyes, and the hitting continued.

"Don't dance him around. Hit him. Stay with it, stay with it. C'mon. C'mon. Let's go, let's go, let's go."

Finally, the whistle.

"Go get a drink," Trost said.

The team ran past Timmy and Ronell, who sat against the fence, dazed.

One hit, two concussions.

After practice, Trost returned to his office and slumped into the chair. It squeaked loudly as he sat down. He took off his glasses, tossed them onto a mess of papers on the desk, leaned back and stared hard at the ceiling. The day had been a disaster, all of the progress lost, collapsed back to where they had been at the beginning.

Trost knew the road ahead was brutal. After Whitefish Bay, the team caught a slight break with Lakeside Lutheran, but then it was the four toughest teams in the conference, before the three easier ones. Trost still believed in the play-offs and, though he earned only $3,500 a season as coach, had promised to pay for a weekend trip to Las Vegas for all six coaches if they made it. But he had begun to look at the season as a mountain to be climbed. It wasn't enough, he decided, to give the players the proper equipment, or even a map of the mountain. Somehow, the coaches had to get the team to the top and explain to them only later how they got there.

As Trost fretted, Coach Trawitzki called some of the missing players. He tried George Lasley, getting his aunt, who reported she hadn't seen George all day.

One by one, the other coaches wandered in. They sat
on the desk, on the bench or leaned in the doorway. Some
absently picked up footballs, tossed them from hand to
hand.

"For some reason, we don't want to hit," Trost said.

He was right. Everyone could see it, plain as day.

The conversation took off from there. The coaches questioned who was tough, who wasn't. Who was scared, who
was lazy. They were disappointed in the captains especially. Rob Wyatt, they thought, was dogging it. Nate
Shorter took some plays off. Timmy Lathrop tried, he always tried. But Timmy didn't have any great physical gifts.
Even Evan Rivera and Drew O'Malley, who in battle-field
promotions had been reappointed captains during the afternoon session, were too loose and casual in the evening
one. The coaches had the most questions about Mark. Was
his heart in it? Was he ready to carry the team? Was he
even able to? Last year, on the first day of hitting, Mark
hit Drew so hard in one drill that Drew flew through the
air. The kids talked about that hit all season. But this year,
no one was hitting like that. Hell, Mark had yet to have
the doctor check out his surgically-repaired shoulder and
clear him for contact. Some of the coaches thought he was
delaying it so he wouldn't have to play in the scrimmage
Saturday.

"We have to tell Mark it's his team to carry," said Coach
Smith, shrugging.

"No, we don't," Trost said quickly.

"Leadership has to be earned," said Coach Trawitzki.

The locker room had cleared out and a janitor walked
through the hallway pushing a mop. The season, merely a
week old, already felt long, impossibly long. A week earlier, on the eve of the first team meeting, Trost had called
up Coach Smith, put the receiver by a stereo speaker and
cranked up "Ain't No Mountain High Enough" — the
theme from the movie *Remember the Titans*. The movie

recounted the story of a football team in 1970's Virginia, created when two high schools, one black and one white, merged. The team split along racial lines, but the hostilities eventually gave way to a championship. This team, on the surface, had echoes of the movie. Indeed, last year the Shorewood team had gone to see the movie as a group the night before their victory over Brown Deer. And the Messmer players watched it together one day in the spring.

Talk turned to the Oklahomas.

"They're a meat grinder," said Coach Larsen. "The kids aren't ready."

"They have to be ready," Trost said. "We have a scrimmage in five days. If we aren't ready, we're in a world of trouble."

Although Coach Smith had been hired at Messmer, where he ran the Saturday morning detention hall and subbed in some classes, Larsen was the only true coach from Messmer. The rest, including Smith, had been on the Shorewood staff last year. Larsen was a Messmer science teacher, popular for hands-on experiments. But he had not coached before and at times appeared out of his element. There was still a distance between the coaches, just like with the players. The night of the sleepover, Larsen went to sleep outside while the other coaches crowded into the air-conditioned "S" Room, Trost talking strategy all night with whomever was awake at the moment.

Now, feeling outnumbered, Larsen looked for support.

"You agree, don't you?" he said, turning to Steve Wittemann, the trainer, who stood behind him in the doorway.

Sides were being chosen. Lines drawn.

Wittemann spoke carefully. He said he was concerned about how long the afternoon Oklahomas session went. Concerned there were two sessions of the drill in one day.

"Five minutes for one," Trost said dismissively. "Ten in the other."

Milwaukee Journal Sentinel photo by Benny Sieu

Shorewood senior Tim Lathrop listens to music on his headset before a game. The coaches often cited Timmy's never-quit attitude as a model for the rest of the team.

"And they went on while I was tending to injured players," Wittemann continued, words even more careful now. "I needed to see what was happening."

"They're a Level One drill," Larsen argued. He meant the most sophisticated, too sophisticated for this team.

Trost looked perplexed.

"They're a microcosm of the game," he said.

And they were. The drill replicated a matchup that happened on the field every play, up and down the line. Football was all about beating the guy lined up across from you. It could be done with greater skill, yes, greater heart, certainly. But it often came down to strength and the desire to physically punish an opponent.

That was all true. But so was this: The kids were scared. Nervous. It was something new and intimidating to be knocked to the ground. Saturday's scrimmage would include live hitting. None of the teams would care that Shorewood-Messmer had guys who had only been playing for 10 days. Indeed, some would have guys who had played organized football for 10 years. The team simply had to improve its technique, and the players had to get past their fear. If not, they wouldn't be embarrassed Saturday. They'd get hurt.

"I've always done Oklahomas," said Trost. "They're part of football."

"I have to be concerned about the safety of my guys," Larsen said, looking evenly at Trost.

"Wait a minute," Trost shot back. He snapped forward in the chair. "They aren't your guys. They're my guys, too. This is the Shorewood-Messmer team."

The room seemed even smaller. Tighter. As if being tied into a knot.

Larsen tried again, voice steady.

"If Messmer is concerned about the safety —"

"No," Trost said, agitated. "You're not the one who's gonna pull the trigger on this. I care about these kids, too.

This was my idea."

The words hung there. Finally, they dissolved.

There was a sudden, almost apologetic, knock on the door frame. The coaches turned. It was Marty Wallner. He had missed the evening practice session to attend the last meeting of a speed-reading class, and told the coaches he'd stop in to be sure Tuesday's schedule hadn't changed. The coaches couldn't read his face, since he was in the shadow of the hallway. Had he heard the argument? If so, how much?

"Thanks for coming in, Marty," said Trost.

"No problem," Marty said.

Marty seemed unsure of what he had walked into, whether he should say anything more or not. He shuffled his feet. Trost told Marty they'd be on the normal schedule.

"See ya tomorrow," Trost said after a moment.

Marty left.

"If only we had 20 guys like Marty," Trost said.

At the end, once Larsen and Wittemann left as well and it was just the coaches from last year, Trost had a final message for everyone. A warning, really.

"If this thing goes to hell," he said, "they'll be coming after all of us."

On Tuesday, the coaches were determined to work on attitudes. From the very beginning, Trost told the team the second practice session was cancelled, so long as they worked hard in the first. The harder they worked, the sooner they all went home.

"I think we need a break," he told the team. "Is that a deal?"

They went through everything quickly. Punts. Kick-offs. Offense. Defense.

Montreal Miller arrived late and got the news from Revay Wright, another Messmer senior. Neither was on the first team, but they came every day. Both were already losing weight, due to the heat and the intense workouts. In the locker room, Montreal didn't want to even take his shirt off in front of the guys.

"He said he's giving us the second one off," said Revay. "Why?"

"Don't ask why," Revay said, shaking his head.

The shortened practice was really meant to let the dust settle. Coach Larsen had gone home Monday night and called Joy Bretsch, the Messmer athletic director, who in turn, called Jeff Monday, the principal, who in turn called Rick Monroe, the Shorewood principal, who called Trost, who would have to meet with that group, plus the Shorewood athletic director, Cindy Wilburth, and Br. Bob Smith, the president of Messmer, before practice Wednesday. Everyone.

In the meantime, Oklahomas would have to go on the shelf. But the coaches knew they also had to build in some intensity. So at the end of practice they tried a new approach on sprints. Five teams of five, competing against each other. Each runner ran five yards, came back, then 10 yards and back, then five yards and back. The idea was to hustle, make sharp turns. And to encourage the next guy.

"Do them right and we go home," Coach Smith shouted.

Mark Moore, suddenly a leader, repeated the admonition.

"Run 'em hard."

On Wednesday, the team returned to the tackling drills. Back to the basics. Whistle. Thrust up. Whistle. Thrust up. Whistle. Thrust up.

George Lasley made his return, stepping into the locker room to sarcastic applause.

"Where ya been?" Nate asked. "You're out of sick days."

George shook his head. Not in a dismissive way, but as if to say you don't want to know. He barely spoke to anyone. He was nothing like the George of the week before, the one who at Friday's overnight session vowed never to quit.

It was mostly meaningless now, football. And George wondered why it had seemed so important before. His great-great-aunt, his "auntie," who lived a few blocks away from him, the one he looked in on every day, the one who at age 92 had long been frail, now was seriously ill, maybe dying. It started with a few minor seizures, but was clearly getting worse. And fast. George wanted to be able to do something, to be in control, but was left helpless. If that wasn't enough, over the weekend, his father, the father he didn't remember, came to Milwaukee unannounced from Missouri, along with the twins from the new marriage: Another George and Georgeanna. His father had gotten his life together and said he wanted to reconnect. After much thought, George went to meet him, standing on the porch wondering until the last moment if he should knock.

It was too much to process, way too much. But George had said he wouldn't quit, made a promise to the team. He wrestled with the two commitments.

Now he stepped outside, where the team already was doing its stretching.

"I expect a lot out of you today, after your hiatus," Coach Smith said.

Smith had no idea what was wrong.

George nodded. He carried his helmet with him, but now there was so much more to carry. Last week, when he tried on the shoulder pads for the first time, they made him seem stronger, more powerful. Now the pads made him look weary and tired.

"Don't end up like us in Oklahomas, man," said Ronell Halbert, in street clothes, leaning against the wall near the doorway. He and Timmy Lathrop were out for a week, due to the concussions.

"I ain't doing any," George said flatly.

"You'll do what the coaches tell you," Coach Smith said.

Just then, Coach Trawitzki called for George to hustle up and get going on the stretching. Instead, George stopped, dropped his helmet and went inside.

Coach Smith caught him in the hallway and, talking on the steps, the story spilled out. Trost, who was headed out to the field after his meeting with all the administrators, stopped to talk to him, too. They told George to think about it. "Doubles are almost over," Trost said. "Then there's a game every Friday." It gets better, he stressed. It gets fun.

Oh, how this team needed a game.

It needed a lift.

A spark

Anything.

George said he'd think about it, hung up his pads and went home.

Trost walked out onto the field, eager to get away from all the questions and the scrutiny from above. He hated dealing with it all, jumping through hoop after hoop. For Trost, the concept was simple: The players play, the coaches coach and the administrators, well, administrate. Coach Carroll looked over at him and raised his shoulders in an inquiring shrug. Could they go back to hitting? Or did they have to kid-glove it some more?

"Everything's copacetic," Trost said. "At this point."

Hitting was fine. But Oklahoma would still have to wait.

Trost wore a pair of gray pants and a button-down shirt, looking more the part of a middle-school teacher, which he was, than a football coach. While working on his master's degree, Trost taught middle school students with cognitive and learning disabilities. Later, with a cock-eyed grin, Trost walked up to the other coaches. He loved to tell off-color jokes, but this was better. Trost swallowed a wide grin, hiked up a pant leg, and revealed white tube socks with his black loafers. He let out a cackle of a laugh. The wardrobe change had been a wink all along.

The day was better in a lot of ways, as if a cloud had passed overhead without spitting rain. Pertrell Mallett had made it to practice, a victory in itself. The only injury to speak of was Tracey Cunningham, a Messmer sophomore, who held an ice pack to his mouth. "Take a hit son?" Trost had asked. No. Just hot sauce in the mouth guard.

After practice, the coaches sat outside and talked. The season, less than two weeks old, already had been a roller coaster. No one had ever seen anything like it, the team up one minute and down the next, players coming and going, attitudes changing with the flick of a switch. As they talked, Nate, Pertrell and Jerrel Jackson, a Messmer sophomore, walked out the door and headed across the field toward the bus stop, gymbags in tow.

"Last day of doubles tomorrow, guys," Trost shouted. "When we get done, there will be a party. Nice cake."

They laughed and kept walking.

"Hats and horns," Coach Carroll called out.

"I jump out of the cake," Trost said, then added: "In a thong."

"Oooooh," Pertrell said, over his shoulder. "Now I've got to sleep with that in my head."

But of all the developments that day, the most encouraging was this: Mark Moore had been cleared for full contact. He went to see the doctor that morning, and appeared on the practice field in his pads, sleeves rolled up and tucked under the shoulder pads to show off his arms — his "guns," as the players called them. Mark was looser. Almost cocky, though at one point Flex wiped him out on a play, winding up more surprised than Mark was himself.

When coaches lined up the team for the dreaded pursuit drill, the one in which the defense ran to assigned cones in an attempt to beat a runner there, Mark volunteered to carry the ball. He took it and raced up the right sideline, the weight of the pads not slowing him at all.

"Hit."

"Hit."

"Hit."

The shouts started coming back, but Mark was nearly beating the defenders.

As he ran, players on the sideline did a quick calculation of who would wind up at the last cone. Mark had told them to watch.

"Hit. Hit. Hit."

"That's Jay White," announced Dominique Ross.

Indeed, it was White, a Shorewood senior, the biggest guy on the field. He had just reached the last cone when Mark got there. Mark ran through him, delivering a massive hit that sent both tumbling to the ground. There were "Ooohs," from the players. Last year, Mark had wiped out Drew. This year, Jay. The two got up in the distance and Mark patted Jay on the shoulder pads.

Yes. Mark was back.

Chapter 4
"All you need is this much faith."

It was late evening, still a few days before the start of classes, but there was activity everywhere at Shorewood — a boy's volleyball game in the main gym, cheers echoing out through the open doorway; a dance for freshmen in the old gym, the first arrivals nervously waiting outside for reinforcements. Some of the freshmen were dropped off by parents, who were quickly sent away. Others came on their bikes, which were set aside as they sought out familiar faces and fell into small groups, boys here, girls there. No one wanted to stand alone. The football players hung around on the sidewalk, casually taking in the scene.

It was the night before the Whitefish Bay game. The night before opening night.

One of the players had brought a copy of the *Shorewood Herald*, the weekly newspaper, which had its high school football preview section inside. There were two pages about the team, with a headline that spoke of "better things to come" and a list, as identified by Trost, of three players to watch — Mark Moore, Nate Shorter and Rob Wyatt. Mark, the article said, had come back "bigger, faster and stronger." Nate had "drawn interest from a number of colleges, including some Division 1 programs." And Rob was "expected to be an anchor along the line." Heady stuff.

The players crowded around to read it.

The section included other area teams and when someone finally flipped to the Whitefish Bay preview, all eyes focused on one of their players to watch.

"Booker ain't no 5'10"," declared Coach Smith, after a moment. "I've seen him and he's up to here."

Smith held out his hand at a height just above his shoulder.

"They got all of them wrong," said Mark, shaking his head. "I'm listed at 6'1", and I'm not even 5'11" yet."

Trost brushed past the knot of players.

"I always boost my guys up a little bit," he said.

Indeed, even Marty Wallner had gotten bigger, going from 5'5" and 115 pounds, to 5'6" and 135 — adding, on paper at least, the 20 pounds Trost figured he needed in real life.

As always, Trost was eager to get started. He headed downstairs, arms full of equipment and folders, leaving son Bryce napping in the car. He came back out a few minutes later and drove the car around to the practice field, out along the edge of the grass, near the stadium fence. The players, in shorts and T-shirts, were already doing their stretches. There would be no pads the night before a game, just a brisk walk through.

Over the past week, the team was like a series of light bulbs being turned on. Indeed, the team had its best showing in years at the scrimmage in nearby Random Lake, winning two of its three matchups. And every day since, someone else would emerge, pick up the right blocking technique, take the right angle on a tackle or make the right adjustment on defense. In some cases, the light bulb would flicker, even burn out, but in others it stayed on. Now, on the field, the team clapped in unison. They counted out each stretch. There was a precise rhythm about everything, a new and focused energy. A confidence, almost.

They would need it.

All of it.

Because Bay was good. Very good.

The series between Shorewood and Whitefish Bay, two

neighboring suburbs on Milwaukee's north shore, dated to 1934, one of the oldest high-school football rivalries in the area. In the first game, some 4,500 people crowded into the Shorewood stadium to watch their beloved Greyhounds fall 7-6 to the dreaded Blue Dukes, time expiring with Shorewood lined up at the Bay 1-yard-line, trying to get off a final play. Seven of the first 10 games were decided by a touchdown or less. The football series was full of venom, with students from both schools known to egg the opposing building on the eve of the game. One year, a group of Shorewood students drove over to Bay at night and poured a chemical concoction on the lawn to spell out "Go Shorewood, Beat Bay."

All told, Bay had won 41 games, Shorewood 23. But Bay had won the last 15, most by lopsided margins, including a 76-0 victory in 1991. That helped prompt a break in the series in 1995, when Shorewood's losing streak was at a mere 54 games. In a newspaper article at the time, Shorewood officials said it was a mutual decision to put the series on hold while the school changed conferences. But Bay officials said it was Shorewood that wanted to stop playing. In other words, they were chicken. When the game was revived four years later, Shorewood administrators cited the tradition involved, though everyone knew it remained a bad matchup. It wasn't a rivalry any more, so much as a proximity. After so many losses in a row, none of the Shorewood players had even seen the Glory Cup, the trophy that went to the victor.

The coaches acknowledged the tradition, but didn't see history when they looked at Bay. They saw a bulldozer. Bay was ranked 7th in the state in its class and returned senior running back Booker Stanley, who was being recruited by the University of Wisconsin and the University of Nebraska, among others. Word on the street was he just had to decide what shade of red he liked best. Bay also had experienced players at other key spots. Quarterback. Receiver. Line. The year before, Bay beat Shorewood 38-0.

While the game was a rivalry for Shorewood, the Messmer players didn't see much difference between Whitefish Bay and Shorewood, both white and wealthy. In the Milwaukee area, many referred to Whitefish Bay as "Whitefolks Bay." It was Shorewood to the next degree. Bigger houses. Bigger lawns. More money. "They're both the same," Messmer senior Sebastian Negron declared one day in the locker room. "Uh uh," said Marty Wallner, a Shorewood sophomore, his voice earnest and intent. "No, we're not." At Shorewood, where the yearbook would sometimes salvage bad seasons with headlines such as "JV beats Bay," and a spoof story in the student newspaper told of Shorewood seizing its neighbor to the north, Whitefish Bay was a constant comparison.

As the team stretched, Trost went inside and reappeared

Milwaukee Journal Sentinel photo by Benny Sieu

The Shorewood-Messmer captains, right, listen to referees during the coin toss before the opening game against Whitefish Bay High School. The historic game was covered by the *Milwaukee Journal Sentinel* and several local TV stations.

with a box of bright red jerseys, which he began spreading
out on the grass so everyone could find their number. They'd
wear the game jerseys tonight, then set them out on the
benches in front of their lockers so the jerseys would be
waiting on Friday. It was a ritual, meant to show there was
something significant about the jerseys, a pride involved.
It may only be a Shorewood jersey, but if you wore one, it
meant you were a football player and that counted for
something.

The plan all along had been to buy new uniforms, or
at least new jerseys that would say "Shorewood-Messmer"
on the front — the purple jerseys Trost had envisioned.
Each player was supposed to get $40 in pledges for a
weight-lifting fund-raiser held the morning before the Red
and Blue game. But only a handful of players participated.
One Shorewood player simply brought in $40 and handed
it to Trost. Without the money, the team would stick with
the Shorewood uniforms — red jerseys, white letters, gray
pants — with a blue "M" decal added to both sides of the
red helmets to signify Messmer.

Trost checked the jersey numbers against his roster and
his roster against who was on the field. Several players
were late. Trost couldn't believe it.

"Hey, I need to get padded up."

Trost looked up. It was an unfamiliar face, someone
who had been at one, maybe two, practices.

"Where ya been?" Trost asked. "Are you even on this
list?"

It had been a problem from the beginning, this revolving door. There were guys who signed up in the spring
but never showed for fall practice. Guys who came on the
first day and disappeared, mumbling about how hard it
was. Weeks later, the locks would be cut from their lockers, the pads and helmets retrieved and assigned to that
day's new guy. Some showed up after the grueling two-a-
days were over, or turned the two-a-days into personal

one-a-days by coming for just the second session. Several missed one day because it was raining and decided practice must be cancelled. Others, such as Pertrell Mallett, had reasonable excuses, though the coaches fretted they were missing too much of the basics, especially Pertrell, who no longer was penciled in as a starter.

Most games are won, the coaching adage goes, in the off-season. If not, then certainly during the weeks of practice leading up to the first game, when the offense and defense are installed. In an ordinary situation, anyone who missed the first weeks would be out all together, but as the coaches worked their way into the season, it was clear they had to be patient. Most of the Messmer kids had never played organized football before. They didn't understand the commitment expected. They didn't know the fundamentals, the rules or, in some cases, even where the backfield was. For weeks, the team spent 10 minutes each day on form tackling — the basketball equivalent of learning to dribble.

Nevertheless, Trost had managed to cobble together a respectable opening-night lineup. About two-thirds of the 36 players listed on the roster were from Messmer, but the starters on offense and defense were split nearly evenly between the two schools. And when the transfers were figured in, nearly all had played some varsity football before.

The team, done stretching, drifted over to the jerseys.

"Hey, we got more people here tonight," said Rob Wyatt, a lineman from Messmer, looking over the scene.

"Yeah, that's what happens the night before the game," said Trost.

His voice had an edge of irritation.

"Holy Thursday," said Coach Trawitzki, to confused looks from the players.

That's what the coaches called the night before a game. Holy Thursday. When every sprained ankle and wrenched back, every sore shoulder and jammed finger miraculously heals. Hallelujah. Praise be. I can walk again. This time, the healing was going so well entirely new players were showing up in the doorway, like Lazarus from the tomb.

"OK, seniors first," said Trost.

The players snatched up their jerseys and pulled them on. Smiles slid across their faces, though some tried not to let on how cool it was. The jerseys. Finally, the jerseys. If there was time, some would have made an excuse to go down to the locker room and check the mirror to see if they looked as tall and strong as they suddenly felt.

Last year, before the Bay game, the coaches ran the whole practice on the main field, only to discover later that a few of the Bay coaches had slipped into the stands and watched the first 10 plays of the game, all scripted, unfold before them. As if they needed the help. This year, some Bay coaches and players watched the team's Red and Blue game, undoubtedly leaving unimpressed. Bay's own scrimmage was run by NFL officials as part of a clinic for high school referees. Trost looked down at the stadium, the bleachers empty.

The lights were on. They glowed in the distance like a dream about to come true.

What the hell, Trost thought and blew his whistle.

"Everybody down to the main field," he shouted.

The team chased after him, feet moving faster than they had in days.

On the field, all the light standards were working now, but even without them everything would have seemed brighter. And the goal posts, installed a few days earlier, had been painted — though in typical Shorewood fashion, instead of painting the goal posts while they were still on the ground, the crew waited until they were installed, then stood in the bed of a pickup, a roller attached to a long extender, and painted them white in the fog that

morning. There always seemed to be some technical mal-
function at Shorewood, from the lights on the field, done
in by the errant digging for the goal posts, to the perpetu-
ally-stopped clock in the locker room. Coach Larsen, who
taught physics at Messmer, helped work out a bug in the
scoreboard, which was working now, too.

"Can we tear these goal posts down tomorrow?" asked
Trost.

Coach Smith shook one and looked up.

"Yeah, you can tear 'em down," he said. "Don't know
if Shorewood will get that happy, though. Maybe
Messmer."

In truth, it wasn't clear just how anyone would react
tomorrow. Not the crowd, which would be somewhat
sparse since neither school was in session. Not the coaches,
who for once felt pressure in a Shorewood season opener.
And surely not the team, with most of the players in their
first-ever high school game. Even tonight's practice was
different. There were lines on the field now, numbers
painted to count out the yard lines. This wasn't a park or
a playground or an alley. On Friday night, there would be
no crazy made-up plays, no joking with the opponent.
When you missed a catch, it mattered. When your opponent scored, it went up on the board. When they hit, it
would hurt.

This was real.

First team offense, scout defense. They broke the huddle
and Marty Wallner, the Shorewood sophomore who had
dreamed of wearing the red jersey, reliable, dependable,
disciplined Marty, went to the wrong side of the formation. They were all called back.

"Hey, don't get flustered," said Coach Carroll, a hand
on Marty's shoulder. "Single slot left, you're on the right,
got it?"

Marty nodded.

How many times had Marty imagined all of this? His

grandparents had lived a few doors down from the practice field and when Marty would visit them as a boy, he'd
watch practice from the other side of the fence. When
Marty was in grade school, he'd play makeshift football
games with other kids in the shadows on the practice field,
while the varsity game went on down below. He was at
the game in 1996 when Shorewood broke The Streak
against Riverside — indeed, the trophy the team got for
being named Channel 12's Team of the Week was in
Marty's basement, bought a few years back at an athletic
department rummage sale. When Marty was in junior high,
he'd sit in the stands, about the only one in his group who
actually watched the game instead of flirting and gossip-
ing. Last year, as a freshman, Marty rode the team bus to
all of the road games, keeping stats, filling water bottles,
doing anything and everything, soaking it all in, ever closer
to the dream. Now, the red jersey was his.

And, as a sophomore, Marty was starting varsity. In
less than 24 hours, he'd be on the sideline, standing proud
as the band played the National Anthem, holding his helmet aloft for the long last words — "and the home of the
brave" — and then, when the announcer called out his
name, "At one receiver, Number 9, sophomore Martin
Wallner," he'd run through a line of teammates, slapping
hands and bumping chests, out onto the soft and beautiful grass.

The team huddled again and Dave O'Harrow, the quarterback, called out the new play. They broke with a unified clap and — again — Marty went to the wrong side.

He suddenly seemed too small for the jersey.

Meanwhile, other players messed around, high-step-
ping down the sideline with an imaginary ball, offering
their own play-by-play in a fake announcer's voice — "It's
Big Rob, Number 75, for a touchdown." There were more
than 30 players in all, enough that with an offense and
scout defense, there was a full third squad standing on the

sideline with little more to do than clap, as they were instructed, and, later, as the easily-irritated coaches demanded, shut up and pay attention. By now, Bryce was awake and running across the field, his legs trying to keep up with his father's quick stride. Bryce had poked his head up from the back seat of the car, watching his dad through the window, until Trost went to get him.

"He's about the same height as his dad," George Lasley joked, eliciting a few chuckles on the sideline.

Yes. George had come back.

As Coach Trost urged, he took a few days to think about his decision to quit. Football offered a bit of a break from home, time away from the pain of watching a loved one slowly slip away. A few nights earlier, George's "auntie" had awakened in the middle of the night, called out to George and said it was time for breakfast. No, George said, it's night out. She insisted: Breakfast. George opened the curtains. See. It's dark. What time is it when it's dark? Nighttime. OK, go back to bed. No, George, I'm hungry.

Finally: OK, I'll make you some breakfast.

Even George realized he needed a break, if only for a few hours a day. The time off had cost him whatever chance he had left to start at quarterback, but George was still starting at linebacker, where he brought a much-needed fire to the defense.

"Dave, where are you?" Trost called out and tossed him a brand new football. "Take this home tonight."

"Do you want me to sleep with it?" Dave O'Harrow asked.

It was a typical Dave response, understated and low-key. From the start, the coaches felt Dave was under too much pressure and figured they knew why. His father, Mike O'Harrow, who had coached Dave and several of the other players in grade school, would sometimes drop off old plays from the St. Bernadette's playbook scribbled out on a yellow legal pad. Many nights, Mr. O'Harrow would show up at practice, taking it all in from a bench in the distance. Or he'd be spotted walking around the track, a slight limp in his step. Tonight, he sat on a bench near the concession stand, watching silently, ankle over knee. The coaches knew there was more to the story, health problems of some kind, but they didn't know much more. Instead, they summed the situation up in four words no coach wants to hear: "Father playing through son."

Slowly, though, Dave, seemed to be getting more comfortable around the coaches and the players. He wasn't the confident, follow-me-to-victory kind of quarterback the coaches wanted, but he grasped the offense and was dependable. Dave, who was still leery of what classes at Messmer would be like, had a dry sense of humor. One time, when the coaches were on the team about tackling better, he deadpanned: "Coach, I've got a problem. I got a little dirty." Another time, after a blown Trost gasket, Dave looked at Trost and, in an entirely serious voice, said: "So, you want me to *complete* the passes?"

Should he sleep with the game ball? *Hell yeah*, Trost thought.

"Whatever you've got to do to get the feel of it," he said.

Trost smiled.

Yeah, Dave was all right. When he relaxed.

The team ran through the offense, the defense, kick-offs, kick returns, punts, punt returns and in a fit of optimism — at least based on last year's shutout — extra points. Finally, at the end, they worked on how they would run onto the field for warm ups, counting off into six lines, then running out row by row, stopping at five-yard intervals until half the field was evenly spaced in red. The captains, waiting at the back, would then run through the lines to the front. Trost wanted the team to appear disciplined, as if they had done this all before. They tried it a few times, but it was like a Keystone Kops routine, everyone bumping into the guy in front of him, eliciting giggles in the ranks.

"Can't we do like in *Remember the Titans?*" asked Maurice Ragsdale. He broke into the military-style rhyme and stutter-step from the movie. "Every where we go-ooo. People want to kno-ooow." He shouted out the next lines, a few players joining in the call-back response: "Who we are. So we tell them. We are the —"

The Greyhounds? The Bishops?

Nobody knew the answer to that one.

Finally, the sky gone black and a hint of dew on the grass, Trost blew the whistle and called the team over.

"Take a knee," he said.

One by one, the coaches ran through their speeches. Standard motivational stuff: We have nothing to lose. A team with nothing to lose is a dangerous team to play. Whitefish Bay? They have everything to lose. We can win. But you must give it your all. Give it everything — every single thing — you've got. When you walk off this field, you should have a hard time walking.

Across the way, a few kids stood talking, some sitting on their bikes. The freshman dance had let out. Several cars had pulled in behind the bleachers, lights on, and a few parents leaned against the fence. On the field, the shadows, which had raced across the grass with the team's newfound energy and adrenaline, were silent and still.

Now it was Coach Smith's turn.

Stanley Smith, 22, was the son of a Baptist minister from Mississippi, though it had always been mostly just him, his mother and two brothers, until his older brother died in a car accident. He had a picture of himself and his brother tattooed on his arm. Smith, the team's only black coach, had a special rapport with the black players, especially Mark and Micah Moore, who had lost their own mother and now lived with an aunt. Smith played some football at a community college, then a year at Jackson State University, linebacker, before he followed a girl north and stayed, working three jobs to buy an engagement ring. For a time, he talked about trying to catch on at the University of Wisconsin, but that never came about and he fell into coaching instead, literally walking onto the field one day last fall to volunteer. Deep down, he wanted another chance at the game.

Smith told the team he called his father before every game he had ever played or coached, even when times were bad and their relationship was frayed. He didn't tell them that when they talked the night before, about the impending game and all it meant for the team, for the first time in memory, Smith's father told him he was proud of what he was doing, proud of him. It was a statement Smith had always wanted to hear, from the days he would go down to Veterans Park in Jackson and watch his father quarterback a flag football team. His father was one of the best players in the state, eventually inducted into the American Flag and Touch Football League's national hall of fame. Smith always gave his father, who had remarried, a report on his own most recent performance: I had two tackles in the game. I recovered a fumble. I had five tackles. Six tackles. More.

But until now, the approval never came.

"I asked him how to inspire you guys," Smith said. "George, you may know this story."

The story was the mustard seed, a parable from the Bible, a story told and retold in black churches and in poor communities. The story seems to ring truer there, with people near the bottom. The seed is tiny, but when it grows it becomes a tree.

"If you have the faith of a mustard seed, you can move a mountain," Smith said. The team was silent, entranced, as Smith's voice carried across the field, drifting in the sudden, easy breeze. "Do you know how big a mustard seed is?"

There was no answer, but none was expected.

"This big," Smith said, thumb and finger almost touching. "A man once said that's all the faith you need in one another. All you need is this much faith and you can move a mountain. There's 35 guys here. That's 35 mountains we can move."

"I like that," Maurice Ragsdale said, nodding.

"It's true," said George.

George knew about small, about being called "pretty boy" and getting beat up on the playground. About being in school and having trouble with reading and spelling, being held back a grade. About being in church as a boy, impatient and distracted, and how a single look from his auntie would demand that he pay attention.

Yes, George knew this story.

"The mustard seed is not magical," Smith said.

He reached into his shirt pocket and pulled out a stack of sandwich bags, each carefully taped shut.

"If you believe we can beat Whitefish Bay tomorrow," Smith said, "you come up here and grab one of these mustard seeds right now."

Everyone stepped forward at once.

First he handed them to the coaches, Trost, Trawitzki, Carroll, the rest. Then the players: George, Maurice, Mark, Marty, Nate, Dave. Everyone reaching for one, holding the bag to the light to see the pinprick of a seed inside.

Only that much faith was required.

Friday night. Shorewood-Messmer got the ball first, but punted after three plays, Mark Moore never touching the ball on the opening series. The idea was to surprise Whitefish Bay and get the ball to Ronell Halbert, the wide receiver who was put in at one of the running back slots to take advantage of his speed. It didn't work. After the punt, it took two plays before Whitefish Bay scored, a 32-yard run up the sideline, untouched into the end zone, and just like that it all felt like last year again, hope circling the drain.

The stands were mostly full, the mood already restless. The players could sense it on the sideline, a few looking over their shoulders now and again, scanning the crowd. A small group of Messmer backers was on one end, a clutch of blue and white. The rest was Shorewood red. As Bay kicked the extra point, generating a roar from across the field, Trost found Mark and turned him by the shoulder. Along with Maurice Ragsdale, Mark lined up deep for the kickoffs.

Mark Moore had a mixed history against Whitefish Bay. As a freshman, he had been on varsity and made his debut against Bay, but ripped up a shoulder on the first play, trying to tackle Booker Stanley, also a freshman, and was lost for the season. As a sophomore, Mark scored his first touchdown against Bay, on the trick hook-and-ladder play, late, when it didn't matter much to the outcome. The following spring, after his mother's death, Mark thought about moving away, maybe to Texas, where an uncle lived and real football was played. But he had promised his mother he would stay, he would stay at Shorewood and play football and, more importantly, he would graduate. As a junior, Mark was ineligible when the team played Bay. Now it was senior year. His year.

"We need you buddy," Trost told him. "Now is your time."

Mark nodded. But he, too, seemed small in the moment.

Mark turned and ran onto the field. He had barely heard Trost, the words came off muffled and garbled, lost in all that was running through his mind. He took his position and waited, like the gladiator before the lions enter the ring.

The whistle blew and a referee dropped his arm.

"Let's go Shorewood," came a shout from the stands.

The kickoff came and Mark took the ball on the left sideline, right in front of the bench, coaches and players yelling encouragement — "Go, go." He caught the ball on the run, the field opening in front of him, as if the Bay players didn't expect the ball to go there, certainly not to Number 22. Mark tucked the ball, but as he started upfield — one step, another — his foot hit the white line and the whistle blew again. The coaches swore and cursed, telling the referees it was a horrible call. But Mark was out of bounds.

"Let's go Messmer," came another shout.

This time, the plays went to Mark. First, a pitch to the right. Caught in the backfield. Next play: A fumbled snap, recovered. Then a toss to Mark, a five-yard gain.

"Let's go Messwood."

The shout was lonely now.

Another punt and another Bay score.

And another.

And still more.

Halftime: 51-0

In the locker room, the team slumped on benches and leaned against lockers. The uniforms were muddied and bloodied. Clumps of dirt were on the floor, stomped free of the cleats. It had rained all day, a steady, misty drizzle that stopped an hour before game time. In the outer room, Evan Rivera sat on a table, feet dangling above the floor, face inside his jersey, hand to his forehead. Evan was in at fullback, the job he wanted all along, the position he played last year. Nate Shorter, the Messmer junior who held the spot for the first two weeks, had been shifted to the offensive line because the coaches wanted more bulk up front against the bigger Bay squad. Evan was dazed. At one point, he wobbled back to the huddle and blew the blood from his nose. It splattered on the shoes of his teammates. Dave was unsure if he should even hand Evan the ball. Now the trainer looked Evan over, caught Trost's eye, shook his head. Concussion. Out for the second half.

The coaches brushed into the locker room, Trost stepping to the middle, surrounded by misery.

"Guys, we can't get down on ourselves," he said.

But, of course, it was too late.

Two hours earlier, the room had pulsated with hip-hop music, Maurice bopping in the center of it all, while Mark sat quietly, getting focused. That morning, the team and the great public-private experiment had made the front page of the *Milwaukee Journal Sentinel* and TV trucks were parked behind the bleachers, reporters ready to interview the coaches and the captains. Dave O'Harrow, who had, in fact, slept with the football next to his bed, registered at Messmer that morning. He felt sick as the game approached, but shook it off and confidently slipped on the quarterback wristband with all the plays.

The locker-room mood had been light. Easy. Guys flirted with volleyball players outside the gym, kissed girlfriends for luck, vowed victory. They checked jerseys in the mirror and slipped the mustard seeds into shoes and helmets. The clock ticking toward game time, they dropped to their knees and, a hand on the next guy's shoulder, listened while George Lasley led them in prayer — "Heavenly Father, let us believe in each other. God, in the name of Jesus, don't let anybody feel like they're not loved." Then they rose in a burst, shouting and screaming, pounding lockers until the lockers shook and banged against the walls, the room roiling with emotion and energy.

Now, all the promise was gone, like air from a balloon.

"It's easy to quit," Trost said, looking around at them. They were angry, sullen, quiet. "But that's not life."

This time, the team rose slowly, filing out the door and up the stairs for the second half. This time, instead of running down to the main field, they walked, finally mustering enough pride to turn their steps into a stiff, uneasy jog. This time, their feet were heavy, hearts nervous and scared.

The second half went mercifully fast. Since the score was so out of hand — Bay ahead by more than 35 points — the officials used a running clock. No stoppages for missed passes, penalties, anything, unless Shorewood-Messmer could close the gap. After the opening series, another quick Bay touchdown, George Lasley returned to the sideline fuming. On the field, he had tried to do his job — line up the defense and call out the adjustments. But no one listened. George tossed his helmet to the ground. It bounced and skittered away. A teammate offered encouragement, but George just looked at him, sized him up in a withering instant. The player's jersey was still bright red.

Shit, you ain't even played, George thought.

"You don't know how hard this is," he screamed.

At times, the team didn't have enough guys on the field. The receivers kept lining up off sides. Flags rained down. Nate Shorter, replacing Evan at fullback, kept bulling into the line. Again. And Again. Now Mark to the outside, and finally a first down. There was a cheer in the stands, genuine, to be sure, but on the field it echoed down in sarcasm.

Some players stalked the sideline. Put me in, they said. Give me the ball. I'll score. Coaches grimaced. At one point, Mark was knocked to the ground and stayed there, rolled onto his side. That would be a disaster, an absolute disaster.

"Get up," Coach Smith said, not as a shout, but a mumble to himself, as if saying it would will Mark to his feet. "C'mon, get up."

Finally, Mark was helped to the sideline, where the bench was filled with the walking wounded, ice bags everywhere. Shades of last year, when the coaches felt the team had Purple Heart Syndrome — players, more bruised than injured, content to sit on the sideline with the nobility that comes from having taken a hit for the team. Mark returned to the game, but a few minutes later someone, a teenager, stood at the fence at the edge of the track and mocked his performance.

"Mark Moore, where you at?" he shouted and then laughed, a taunting laugh. "Turn around, you know you hear me."

The cheers in the stands grew slowly weaker and, eventually, the only sound was the chatter of students socializing, making post-game plans. Even that had nearly disappeared by the time the band stepped to the track and prepared to march away. Band members, informal in white polo shirts and dark pants, tested their instruments, a quiet rattle-tap of drums, a low groan of tubas. There were more than 110 band members in all, 15% of the student body at Shorewood. Sometimes the coaches thought the school kept a football team just so the band had somewhere to perform. Indeed, three former football players, all unhappy with Trost as coach, were in the band — two at saxophone, one at tuba. Now, as the team gathered at midfield and, helmets raised, sang the two school songs, the band followed the track behind the scoreboard to the exit.

Final score: 64-0.

The next morning, the team sat on the steps outside the gymnasium building. The steps had already become a Saturday morning gathering spot, as the players waited for the coaches to arrive. The building, like the others at Shorewood, was a light, cream-colored brick. It was long and low, the old gym on one end, the "new" gym, from a 1950 addition, on the other. There had once been ivy over the doorway, but all that was left was its brittle, brown skeleton, twisting across the bricks. In the parking lot, the

girls volleyball team was holding a car wash fund-raiser, so
the football players couldn't even suffer in private.

The sports section from the morning newspaper was
passed around and some read the statistics aloud. The
numbers were even more painful in black and white.
Booker Stanley, Whitefish Bay's star running back, carried
the ball just seven times, but had 80 yards, four touchdowns and a pristine jersey at the end of the night.
Shorewood-Messmer managed a mere 35 yards of offense,
24 on the ground.

"Shorewood shares misery with Messmer," said one,
reading the headline.

"Man, why'd they have to write that?" said another.

Finally, Trost arrived with a key and they all dragged
into the locker room. The room was clean again, the vague
lemon scent of detergent in the air. They sat and waited
for the coaches to get started. The only sound was the
shifting of ice packs — Nate's knee, Timmy's shoulder,
Dave's neck. Dave had been hit hard on the last play of
the game, after throwing an interception, and wound up
sprawled on the grass.

George Lasley was missing again. The day before, he
was late getting to Shorewood for the game. He had been
at home playing video games with his cousin, a Tupac CD
playing loud and angry in the background. The two played
video football, George as the Tampa Bay Buccaneers, a
team he considered much like his own — a good defense,
but not much offense. It was easy on the screen, so easy.
George in control. Everything working. After the loss, as
George drove home, he knew he wouldn't be back. His
auntie was now in the hospital, often asking where George
was. And he was off doing this? The coaches were weak,
George thought. The team was weak. Maybe he was weak,
too. But at least he wouldn't lose again. Not like that.
Screw that.

Trost stepped to the center of the locker room. Time

for some damage control. He apologized for having to play
Whitefish Bay, but said there was a contract. And
Shorewood still considered it a rivalry. He didn't mention
that he had gone to the administration before the season,
begged and pleaded with them to drop the game, to find
a more reasonable opponent. He looked at his players,
their heads hanging.

"Hey," Trost said, and a few looked up. "This was a
good team."

The rest stared at the tile, cracked and worn in places.

"This was a fast team," Trost said. "Fastest you'll see all
year."

No response.

Like the other coaches, Trost wanted to transplant his
love of football to the team, but it never seemed to take
root. Fifteen years after high school, Trost still kept a clasp
from his shoulder pads on his key chain. And he still had
his high school jerseys, home and away, No. 31. His 4-
year-old son, Bryce, wore them as pajamas.

In Trost's last game, the first ever playoff game for St.
Pat's, he walked out of Hansen Stadium a first-round loser.
For Coach Smith, his team lost in the state championship
game, a last-second field goal sailing through the Mississippi sky. Coach Trawitzki's team made the playoffs, but
lost 20-19, when the quarterback, desperately rolling toward the sideline, was tackled and the clock ran out. Coach
Carroll's team had a half-time lead in the playoffs and
collapsed. He still had dreams in which he was back in the
game and this time made it right.

All of the coaches, every one of them, felt a twinge
when they stepped on the field before a game. They all
longed for one more night between the lines. One more
chance to be a captain walking slowly out to midfield for
the coin toss, teammates on each side. One more chance
to wear the jerseys, to accept victory hugs on the sideline
and command respect in the hallways. If Mr. O'Harrow

was playing through his son, Dave the quarterback, in a way the coaches were, too. Playing through all of them.

It was early in the season, eight games left, a winnable one coming up. But the coaches knew the personality of a team was fixed at the start of the season. So when they went outside, the sun beating down, they didn't ask much of the players, only 20 today, lined up under the goal post, hands on hips.

Only this: Run without complaint.

Hit without fear.

And believe without question.

All three were important, but the last was the most critical. They had to believe, to believe the way a child believes a father will get him safely across the street, or catch him when he jumps into a swimming pool. A deep belief. Not a mustard-seed-in-my-pocket belief. They had to believe they could win, would win.

But the coaches worried this team would have to win before it believed. And to win, the coaches felt the players had to be tougher — against Bay, some were asking for a break after the first series. So now the players were told to run. And run. They griped and grumbled, most starting slowly, muscles tight, muscles screaming.

"This ain't no punishment," Coach Smith shouted as they ran. "You have to want it yourself."

Maurice Ragsdale won the first sprint.

Marty Wallner won the next one, Maurice second.

On the final play of the Bay game, Marty had chased down a Bay player who intercepted a pass and was headed for a certain touchdown. It was just like in the much-despised pursuit drill. Marty, who that week had declared Shorewood was not the same as sneering and uppity White-fish Bay, cut the player off on the sideline, knocked him down and gave an extra little shove and an extra little shout. Maurice, who was competing with Marty for playing time, could respect that. He wanted to be that.

More sprints. Ten, 15, 20.

"No pain, you don't feel nothing," said Smith.

"Don't feel it," Maurice repeated under his breath.

More: 25, 26, 27.

"How many times I gotta come in first?" Maurice gasped.

"Every time," Trawitzki said.

"Ask your teammates," said Trost.

Still more: 31, 32, 33.

Earlier that week, at the end of one of the practices, the team had run sprints, shouting "Beat Bay" at the start of each. Now they sniped at each other.

"You're cheating."

"Run to the end."

"C'mon," Maurice shouted, looking over at Mark Moore and Drew O'Malley.

The two, both captains and seniors, had played virtually every down the night before. Maurice had mostly made his mark by lining up off-sides.

"Fuck off," came the response, in unison.

As the players ran — 39, 40, 41 — the coaches replayed the game, searching for bright spots amid the wreckage. The team did have two sacks, one from Rob and one from Nate, as many as they had all last season. They had actually made Bay punt a few times, though it was mostly Bay's second and third string that was stopped. And, unlike recent years, Bay hadn't scored on its first play of the game. Never mind it was the second.

Actually, Maurice was a bit of a bright spot. He showed some shiftiness when returning kicks, though he had trouble fielding the ball cleanly. On one play, the ball bounced past him, Maurice averting disaster by scooping it up and picking his way back upfield to the 35-yard line. A week earlier, the coaches had to call and wake up Maurice so he could catch the bus to the Random Lake scrimmage, where he scored two touchdowns. Yes, Maurice was a bit of a clown, always talking in funny voices, or cracking jokes at the wrong time. But now, it was clear Maurice was striving to be more. He had asked Trost if he could be the Messmer player to address the team before the game, an honor that went to Dave instead. And in the locker room that morning, when Trost asked if anyone had anything to say, Maurice was the only one to pipe up. "The loss, as bad as it is, I think we can still come together," he said. "It's like, for me, a wake-up call. It's like all of us know now we gotta bring it up a notch. We can't dogwalk nothing." Trost nodded: "Well said."

Now, another sprint done, Maurice fell to the ground in front of the coaches. He wore a dark blue T-shirt, the words "School of Hard Knocks" in white across the front, sweat sticking the shirt to his stomach.

"Maurice get up," said Trost. "You're a captain this week."

"Captain?" Maurice exclaimed.

He bounced up and raced down the field, Wile Coyote after the Road Runner. The coaches laughed. If nothing else, Maurice was resilient.

"Maurice and Mark this week," Trost said to the team later. "The rest of you have to earn it back."

Chapter 5
"Good things will happen."

On Monday, the new week marking a fresh start, the last players hustled out to the practice field, Trost's shouts of "let's go, let's go, let's go" echoing behind them. Outside, a few players punted the ball back and forth, awkwardly, the ball veering off to the side. Others stood near the water trough, a plastic tube-like contraption that spit water from six holes. The rectangle of grass underneath was the greenest on the field.

"Man, we don't even need Messmer," said Mark Moore, the star running back from Shorewood.

His voice was disgusted.

"We're still doing what we did last year," he said. "Out there both ways."

He meant offense and defense. Although Mark was the team's best athlete, he saw himself as a running back, not a cornerback or a return man. Certainly not all three in one. He thought doing it all left him too tired on offense, where his college future was at running back. Mark was talking to some of the other players, starters mostly. Those standing nearby could hear the conversation but pretended they didn't. They leaned against the fence, looked away. The Messmer kids were athletes, supposed to be anyway. But nothing had changed. The loss to Whitefish Bay was worse than last year.

Losses, particularly bad ones, can bring a team together as much as drive it apart. This team, though, had barely been together. And, if it wasn't about to come apart, it was fracturing a bit. Cracks forming here and there, each crack becoming a line, each line dividing the team, by skill, by school, sometimes, even, by race.

"I didn't get any rest," added Drew O'Malley, a fellow Shorewood senior.

He was the kicker, the punter, a guard on offense, linebacker on defense.

Drew and Mark, along with four others, were captains. Or, at least they had been until Saturday, when Trost moved Maurice Ragsdale into a captain's slot, alongside Mark, and told everyone else they'd have to earn it back. But Maurice, a Messmer senior, was late for practice, a fact that wasn't lost on any of the others.

Trost walked outside.

"Where's Ragsdale," he asked, scanning the field. "That didn't last long, did it?"

The coaches gathered the players together and talked about commitment. As if to underscore the point, Maurice Ragsdale and Sebastian Negron, another Messmer senior, walked across the field on their way from the bus stop. A coach shouted at them and they jogged to the locker room.

Trost lined up the team. More sprints.

The coaches knew they should have done more conditioning early on, but the heat during the first week of practice was so brutal they were limited in how much they could do. Indeed, the week before practice started, Minnesota Vikings player Korey Stringer died of heatstroke while at training camp. In any case, with this team, it was always a delicate test to determine how hard to push the players: Too hard and they might walk away, they had so little invested. Too soft and they wouldn't be ready, which would mean more lopsided losses, which would also drive them away. It was an awkward balance.

The opponent this week, Lakeside Lutheran, was a new addition to the Shorewood schedule, replacing Riverside, which last year won 48-0. Lakeside Lutheran, a smaller school, was a better matchup and, in fact, a true chance at victory for the team. But, after the Whitefish Bay debacle, they desperately needed to get focused.

Before each sprint, the players lined up in their stances and waited for Trost's whistle. The stances were bad Friday night. And they had been offsides constantly, so the deal now was if someone left before the whistle, they all dropped for 10 updowns.

Updowns.

They are a hell only a football player can truly understand. You stand there, legs spread, and awkwardly start running in place. This is called chopping. Short, quick steps. The whistle blows, you drop to the ground. The whistle blows again, you pop up and return to chopping. This is one updown. You do this over and over, until the back of your thighs are straining and your breath comes hard and heavy and your chest hurts from banging the ground and your arms are sore from forcing yourself back to your feet and you chop some more, each step, up and down, getting harder, heavier, as if your cleats are made of concrete.

It was inevitable. The second sprint, maybe the third. The whistle from Trost, then a quick second whistle, sharp and accusatory. Offsides.

"Everybody chopping," Trost said.

"C'mon, man," said Drew to the offending teammate.

"Be a leader, Drew," said Coach Carroll. "If one person goes offsides, we all go offsides."

Drew was a leader, of course. Like Mark and Nate, Rob, Ronell, Dave, all of those with the most experience on a football field. They were leaders whether they wanted to be or not. The other players instinctively looked to them. They set the tone through attitude and example. So when Drew and Mark complained about the Messmer players, it was as if all of Shorewood was talking.

At 5'11" and 180 pounds, Drew still had the build of a soccer player, but in his second year on the squad was developing the mentality and swagger of a football player. Drills and techniques that were confusing last year now made sense. Everything clicked. A couple weeks earlier, Trost joked with Drew about how many dates he had lined up for that evening. "Chicks dig linemen," Drew said. Indeed, at a more sports-oriented high school, Drew would have been at the top of the jocks heap. But Drew didn't really want to be a lineman, all grunt work and no glory. He had seen the constant shuffle to fill the slot opposite Mark Moore in the backfield and wanted to try his feet there. So when the sprints were done and the team broke up for position drills, Drew casually followed Mark.

"I'm with backs," Drew announced.

"What did we say about complaining?" asked Trawitzki.

"I'm not complaining," Drew said. "I'm just giving you a helpful suggestion."

Instead, Trost sent Maurice, who was still tying his pants, over with the running backs and gave him a crash course in what to do, when to go in motion and who to watch. He would rotate at the Roar position with Jonathan Williams, a Shorewood sophomore, whose slumped shoulders and crossed arms underlined his disgust. Jonathan was once the starter, but every week there was a new guy auditioning for his job. First George Lasley, the one-time quarterback. Then Ronell Halbert, the wide receiver. Now Maurice.

Somehow, Trost had to find an answer at the position. Without another threat in the backfield, teams could key on Mark, often anticipating the team's favorite play — a pitch to Mark as he swept to the right side — and assigning a linebacker to crush him at the line. One of Trost's plays, Roar Back, was designed to exploit the defense by using Mark as a decoy. In it, Mark would cut behind the line of scrimmage. Dave O'Harrow, the quarterback, would fake a hand off to him, pivot, and give the ball instead to the Roar coming from the opposite direction. To make it work, the Roar had wait and let the defense over-commit. To get the timing right, Trost ordered the Roar to say "Mississippi" in his head before moving.

They had worked on this play many times before. It was more complicated than most, though its potential was much greater, too. Trost told them it should pick up first downs, it should gain big yards. It had touchdown written all over it. But everything had to be perfect. Not close to perfect or nearly so. Absolutely perfect.

"You say 'Mississippi' and then go," Trost said to Maurice.

"In my head, right?" Maurice asked.

"Yeah."

The ball was snapped and Maurice went too soon, bumping into Dave at quarterback. Dave mumbled. He was looking for some stability in the Roar position, too. And wise-cracking Maurice, a walking cartoon, didn't offer much in the way of stability.

Maurice checked his feet. His elbows. Hands. The stance right, he looked straight ahead, still as a statue. Dave gave the count again: "999-999-Set-Red-Hit."

Another bump and stumble.

Again.

This time Maurice shouted "Mississippi" out loud as he ran. He rushed it and it came out: "Missppi."

Again.

This time he shouted the full word, then turned and ran. It was better, but he was too wide behind the line, forcing Dave to stretch to get the ball to him. Mark Moore looked at Trost and shook his head.

"Just let him keep saying it," Trost said. "That's Ragsdale. Good job, Maurice."

The offensive work done, the team gathered around Coach Trawitzki, who talked about defense, about the need for everyone to toughen up. As he did, the padded bags were dragged out and lined up. Two chutes. And his words became a drone, static, the players looking past him. They knew what was coming. They dreaded it.

The return of Oklahomas.

The two-on-two drills had been all but abandoned after their second appearance, that bad Monday when Ronell Halbert and Timmy Lathrop were left with concussions, the others spooked and scared. After that day and the post-practice blowup between the coaches, Trost decided they had to tone everything down. So, for awhile, instead of Oklahomas, they went back to the tackling drills. It was necessary but remedial. Most teams wouldn't have had to spend any time on tackling technique, or if they did, only a quick refresher. With this team, it was like tracing the letters of the alphabet over and over.

Ordinarily, Trost wouldn't even do Oklahoma once the season started. The risk of injury was too great. But the Bay game made it clear the team needed more game-like experience. Some players were still making arm tackles, clinging to a runner like a cowboy to a bronco. Others would grab on to someone and go limp, their weight finally pulling the opponent down. Most would wait and catch blocks, instead of attacking the opponent. The team needed technique and toughness. Oklahomas could offer both.

They broke into the two groups.

"Does anyone not want to hit?" Trawitzki asked. "Is anyone scared? You get hurt if you don't want to hit. You get hurt if you're intimidated."

The players nodded. Trawitzki gestured toward the pads.

"This is the most important hour of the season," he said.

That, too, was the truth.

On Saturday, after the never-ending sprints, the team collapsed on couches and chairs in the "S" Room to watch a tape of Lakeside Lutheran's first game. Trost said they were mostly "tall, skinny white guys," and that had become the mantra for the week. Trost worked the room, player to player. "Mark, you ought to have a big day," he said. "Nate and Rob, on defense, you ought to be dominating." Bryce, his son, walked behind him. "Dominating," Bryce said. The players had started referring to 4-year-old Bryce, who had his own burr-cut, as Mini-Trost. On the tape, Lakeside Lutheran was playing Fond du Lac North. The score was tied 14-14. The players watched, trying to believe. "Hell, we've got four athletes on this team that can beat them by themselves," said Trost. "We're going to have a hard week, but at the end of Friday, you're going to be happy campers."

But, deep down, Trost and the other coaches knew Lakeside was dangerous. They were tough. Disciplined. You could see it on the game film, their stances uniform and perfect. Typical small town Wisconsin, a bunch of sturdy kids who knew each other and played together for years. Last year, Lakeside finished 7-2 and made the playoffs, though Trost — figuring his team didn't know better — told the players Lakeside was 2-7.

They lined up now for Oklahomas. The first players went. It was all slow and soft. There was no crash of pads. No burst from the running back. No pop, no excitement.

"Guys, you need to make contact," said Coach Carroll, working with the second group. "Do not stand up and shove the guy. That's not football. Hit."

"C'mon, somebody get in there," shouted Trawitzki at the first group. "Who wants to hit this week?"

Maurice jumped in at offensive line, across from Nate Shorter, the biggest and strongest player on the team. Maurice scratched a foot across the ground. He looked up, practically growled at Nate, who didn't crack a smile. Behind Maurice, Evan Rivera cradled the ball, waiting for Maurice's movement, which would start the drill. Maurice rose up and so did Nate and, in a burst, Nate drove Maurice back, into Evan and they both went down. Maurice shook his head and jumped up.

"Ragsdale's my man," Trost shouted.

Maurice adjusted his helmet, shifting it back into place with a tug of the facemask. He lined up again and jolted into Nate, bracing his legs against the oncoming crush. Slid back and finally knocked to the ground, Maurice stood again, slapped Nate on the helmet.

"God damn, yeah, baby," Maurice said. "That's what I'm talking about. That's some hard hitting."

"Ragsdale wants to hit," Trost said, loudly, to goad the others along.

"Yeah, I want to hit," Maurice repeated.

In truth, Maurice was always more about basketball than football. He came out for football mostly for fun, so maybe that was why he could forget about a bad play in a blink. Indeed, back on the first day of hitting, the day after Trost warned the players to "bring something for your package," Maurice had been spotted in the locker room — everyone else out on the field — slipping balled-up socks into his pants. Maurice was a piece of work. But from his summers playing basketball on the playground, enduring fouls that slammed you to the asphalt and left blood on your elbows, he got the concept: You may feel pain, but you don't show it. The street code.

"You'll be a guard pretty soon," Trost declared.

Drew slipped into the running back slot but Trawitzki stopped him.

"I want to run the ball," Drew said.

"Put me at center," Maurice said, in one of his funny voices. He was still responding to Trost.

"Put *him* at guard," Drew said, pointing to Maurice.

Trawitzki shrugged, motioned the two to go ahead.

Maurice stepped in as Drew's blocker against Rob, the second biggest guy on the team. Rob slipped past Maurice, shed him like a rag doll, and drove Drew to the ground, hard, bodies sliding across the grass. It was a loud smack of the pads that left those watching calling out "Damn!" — some with excitement, others with a shudder. Lest there be any doubt, Maurice was not a guard.

"I heard that one," shouted Coach Carroll, gleeful.

"Best hit all year," said Trost.

On Tuesday, there was toilet paper draped from the trees in front of Shorewood, from all of the bushes and even from the lone tree back by the practice field. The Messmer players got off the bus and shook their heads in bemusement. If they had cruised up and down the tony streets of Shorewood, past all the pretty houses and manicured lawns, from the smaller houses near the high school, down to the giant ones along the lake, they would have spotted similar scenes at the homes of all the teachers, administrators and freshmen, especially the freshmen.

Yes, at Shorewood, classes were in session.

There had been a picnic for the seniors the night before. The picnic was a Shorewood tradition and so was the overnight toilet-papering of the trees, a controlled rowdiness that had been pre-approved by the police department. The night before, Timmy Lathrop had gone home after practice and tried to take a nap, but was so excited he kept waking up every 10 or 15 minutes until it was time to go out. Drew and Evan, of course, were out in the same car, along with Jay White, another senior on the team. The three, along with another friend, stayed up all night, driving the quiet streets in Jay's black Chevy Blazer, part of a caravan of eight cars, stopping only to get out and launch toilet paper into the sky. Once finished, around 5 a.m., they hit a 24-hour diner for breakfast, then home, then school.

Not Mark Moore.

Mark and Micah, his brother, lived with their aunt in

a modest duplex on Milwaukee's northwest side, the house they once shared with their mother. The house, one of the nicer ones on the block, was located in a neighborhood that a politician, to put it politely, would have described as "changing." That is, becoming more black. While the area was more integrated than most in Milwaukee, it was following a demographic shift that started years earlier in the central city, now pocked with vacant lots and boarded houses.

The shift, as in other major cities, is marked by a complex and combustible mix of factors — poverty, income, education, unemployment — that in the end, announces itself in the form of crime and violence. In Milwaukee, during a five-year period, half of all the city's gun killings happened in four central-city zip codes, home to eight players on the team. Over the summer, the city's hot spot for violence had been in and around the Metcalfe Park neighborhood, where 13 people were shot and killed in the course of a few weeks, most of the incidents tied to gangs. In Milwaukee, violence has a way of creeping around and then exploding into the headlines. Stray bullets had killed children, grandmothers, people riding in their cars, people sitting on porches. There were stories of people sleeping in their bathtubs, stories that — even if they were only urban legends — carried a ring of truth.

In contrast, the crime blotter in the weekly newspaper in Shorewood, just over five miles away from Mark's house, was more likely to list people stopped for speeding or teenagers caught with beer or drugs, than robberies or assaults. The year before, in 2000, there was a single homicide in Shorewood. Some 461 crimes had been reported in all, an average of barely one a day. Indeed, one blotter listing said two unknown people, on May 7, had cut the lock on a delivery truck outside Sendik's Food Market, an upscale grocery, and stole 40 pounds of snow crab legs worth $168.40.

For Mark Moore, part of the football dream, at least a small piece, was to really hit it big. More than college. The pros. It was a common dream, to be sure. However unrealistic, others on the team held it, too. Once, a few weeks back, Mark and Coach Smith talked about whether college basketball players should finish school or make the jump to the NBA. Mark sided with the jump, pointing out the guy could get hurt in college and never get the chance at the big signing bonus. "I'd rather be hurt and living in the suburbs, than hurt and living in Parklawn," Mark said, mentioning a well-known Milwaukee housing project. "I'd rather be hurt and rich than hurt and poor."

Mark may have gone to school in Shorewood, but he wasn't truly part of the suburbs yet. So, as the other seniors celebrated the start of their final year, he called Leslie, away at college on a track scholarship, as he did most every night, and went to sleep. Why go all the way back to Shorewood and drive around with a bag of toilet paper rolls?

He didn't see the point.

In addition to the toilet paper dangling from the trees, Shorewood students were greeted on the first day by Principal Rick Monroe and a small group of students handing out flowers to welcome the freshmen at the front door.

They were also greeted by a wide variety of news from over the summer. There was the preliminary approval for a $1.9 million addition to the Science Building, where some labs dated to the 1950s. There was talk from the student council of creating student evaluations of teachers, like those many colleges have. And talk from administrators of instituting an honor code for students to curb cheating on papers and tests. A program planned for September to honor 1942 graduate William Rehnquist, chief justice of the U.S. Supreme Court, was prompting talk of protests by liberal student and community groups.

And there was this: A well-liked junior-to-be, 15-year-old Amanda Rockett, was killed in a July 21 car accident, when she and three others were driving home after attending a rave in Kenosha, about 35 miles south of Milwaukee. The driver, a 2000 Shorewood graduate, reportedly was under the influence of the drug Ecstasy and may have fallen asleep before the crash.

The use of drugs by Shorewood students is a poorly kept secret. Long ago, the school had picked up the nickname "Shoreweed." In 1990, a study at the school determined the use of hallucinogens among seniors was triple the national average. Three years later, nearly one-fourth of the seniors at the school reported smoking up to five cigarettes a day; one third of those said they had used marijuana in the past 30 days; and 36% said they had been drunk or high at least six times over the past six months. Indeed, the previous spring, when the student newspaper asked "What will Shorewood be like in 50 years?" then-junior Drew O'Malley joked: "A drug rehabilitation center."

At Shorewood, some students were Tommy Hilfiger prep, others goth or punk, their hair in wild spikes or bright colors, eager to test the suburban limits. Student groups included the usual — band, theater and yearbook — and the unusual: Amnesty International and Students for Homosexual Awareness, Respect and Equality (SHARE), which sponsored a school version of National Coming Out Day. There were student rock bands with names like Code Orange and Angry Daisies. And while some high school newspapers feature editorials about cafeteria food and detention hall, the pages of *Shorewood Ripples* were more likely to quote Gandhi, or carry headlines such as "Mugabe's tyranny must end peacefully," about the president of Zimbabwe.

Yes, Shorewood was different.

The day, Tuesday, brought another raggedy practice.
A good play here and there, but they were mixed in between so many bad ones they were all but lost. The coaches
were trying to instill some competitiveness into the players and told the scout defense if it stopped the first-team
offense for a loss, the starters would have to do 10 updowns.
It didn't work. At one point, Trost put all 13 available
guys out on the field for defense.

They still couldn't stop them.

Fed up with it all, Trost shouted the next play aloud
— Liz Motion Keep. Then, lest there be any doubt among
those on defense, he pointed to the line.

"He's running right there," Trost said. "I want 11 guys
right there to hit him."

Dave O'Harrow called the snap.

This time the offense was offsides. Ten updowns.

How could it be? The coaches wondered it constantly.
How could it be that if someone confronted one of the
players on the street or stepped on a shoe in the hallway,
they'd be ready to fight in an instant. Yet on the field, a
place where anger is required, there was no emotion. How
could it be that given the chance to set aside all of the
problems of home, all of the adult stuff, the players carried the problems with them instead.

They switched to Oklahomas.

This time, it was three on two, a fullback added to
take on the linebacker, making it even closer to game conditions. But it was like trying to start a balky lawnmower.
Tug, tug. Nothing. If a tackle was missed, the defender
would watch the runner. If the ball popped loose, no one
fell on it. All dainty and disinterested.

Finally, Trost ripped off his whistle and threw it to the
dirt.

"I'm not seeing this," he shouted, face red with frustration. "He gets past you, you run after him. You're standing and watching. That's not football."

The players were stunned.

Louder now: "That's not football."

At the end of the day, the team gathered around the coaches. Some players glowered with anger. It wasn't what it was supposed to be, football. It was supposed to come easy, it was supposed to be natural, it was supposed to be fun. There were moments like that, of course. But it was mostly confusion, long practices, sore muscles and — so far — nothing to show for it but the humiliation of the Whitefish Bay game.

"We had flashes today," said Coach Trawitzki, when it was his turn to talk. "But you can't get by on flashes."

As the team's defensive coordinator, Trawitzki could have come straight from central casting. He had a bald head, hunched shoulders, giant hands and a forehead that seemed to be in a constant, frustrated furrow. He didn't walk around the field so much as he lumbered, great heavy steps. But he had a loud, easy laugh.

Joe Trawitzki, 25, was never a great athlete in high school or college, joking sometimes that the position he played was "left out." He could laugh now at the football game during his freshman year, when his team, Thomas More, was beating rival Marquette and he was sent onto the field. He was so surprised to get the call, he grabbed the wrong helmet, yanked it down over his ears and lined up to kick off, knocking the ball maybe six yards along the ground. After graduating from college with a communications degree, Trawitzki went to Florida to train for six weeks in hopes of becoming a minor league umpire. That didn't stick, but he still coached his sisters' softball teams. Trawitzki was a salesman of supplemental health insurance packages, but the job didn't seem to fit him. He was more at home on the athletic field, around students.

"Look at Timmy," Trawitzki said.

He gestured toward Timmy Lathrop, a Shorewood senior. Trawitzki was also the Shorewood wrestling coach and Timmy was something of a star pupil. As a freshman, Timmy didn't score a point in any match. But he kept at it, dedicated himself, improved. It was the same with football. Timmy might miss a play. But if he did, face red and teeth gritted, he'd go at it again. Timmy sat there now, staring hard at the ground.

"Mark Moore," Trawitzki said, turning to find the team's star. "He's got a quarter of the talent as you. But all the heart in the world. My challenge is to get that heart in you."

That was the challenge for the whole team, really. To put it all together. If the Messmer students represented raw talent, some of the Shorewood students were pure heart. To see it that way, of course, was to buy into all the racial stereotypes. It was to see the black kid and just see the body, to see the white kid and only see the brain. It was to say one was a *great athlete* and the other *played smart*. To see it that way, was to think Nate Shorter got by on brute strength, not reading the quarterback and diagnosing the plays. And to ignore Marty Wallner, who was a strong athlete no matter his size. But the fact was, not enough of the players were the whole package. They were bits and pieces, minutes and moments. They were flashes.

Trawitzki continued.

"I quit my job three weeks ago," he said.

A few players looked up.

"Every day I go to the hospital for radiation treatments," he said. "Half hour every day. Then I go home and sleep for five hours and come to practice."

His voice was even, matter-of-fact. He swung a whistle in his hand. It wound around his finger. Then he twirled it the other way, unwinding.

A few more players had raised their heads.

"I was in a great mood today," Trawitzki said. "I thought we were over the hump."

By we, he really meant himself. Over the hump.

Trawitzki was battling a condition commonly known as gigantism. It was caused by a tumor on his pituitary gland, which controls growth. In effect, the tumor put the gland into overdrive, which meant a growth spurt when he was in college at the University of Wisconsin-Stevens Point. At the time, Trawitzki was on the wrestling team, struggling to put on weight in order to get to the heavyweight division, so as he got bigger, he figured it was due to the change in diet and the extra time in the weight room. It wasn't until January of 2000, when Trawitzki was at a wrestling meet that a doctor — a woman whose nephew wrestled for a different school — told him he had to be tested for acromegaly. Trawitzki had never heard the word before. It may as well have been gibberish.

When he was finally tested, the diagnosis was as predicted. Doctors tried medication to shrink the growth, but it didn't work. So in March, after another football season and another wrestling season had passed, he had surgery to remove the tumor and now was midway through six weeks of daily radiation treatments. The treatments left him tired and depleted. Trawitzki wasn't one to complain, although once in awhile he could be seen stretching and bending, as if he somehow had to loosen his bones.

"I was at the doctor today," Trawitzki said. "The doctor said, 'I see you lost by 64 points, saw you on the news.' He asked me, 'Why are you putting yourself through this?'"

The question lingered.

It could be asked of the coaches, or the players. Why? Last year, the coaches marveled that the team, despite all the losses, clung to the promise that the next game could be the one, would be the one, victory. They believed. And when they beat Brown Deer, in the eighth week of the season, they cried with joy, at last heroes for the night. The coaches could all have other jobs, jobs with better programs, programs where the victories came easy and often. But success would not be as sweet.

"I looked at him," Trawitzki said, "and told him, 'I don't know. There's something there. There's something about this team.' "

On Thursday, the first day of classes at Messmer, students were greeted by flyers posted in the hallways that stated "It's not too late" and exhorting them to "Make Messmer history" by joining the team. And they were greeted by Coach Smith, who rounded up anyone who looked big enough to knock somebody down or fast enough to run past someone and steered them to Shorewood for football practice.

In the locker room, there were grumbles about the new Messmer dress code, which required shirts with collars and pants to be worn with belts, not drooping below the waist, the latest urban style. At Messmer, there could be no bare mid-sections, no hooded sweatshirts, no visible tattoos and no caps, scarves or bandanas. If a shirt had a large logo on it, it had to be a Messmer shirt or from a college. The code of conduct already called for no music with vulgar lyrics. No pagers. No cell phones. No bad language. No chewing candy or gum. Anyone involved in a fight — on or off school grounds — could be expelled. Some students chafe at the discipline, which includes detention hall on Saturday mornings. But most students, in the end, come to appreciate the structure.

In a city where 20% of students in the public high schools are absent on any given day and the four-year graduation rate is 55%, lower still for black students, some 97% of Messmer students graduate, nearly all going on to college. Indeed, the school is a regular stopping point for dignitaries and officials who come to Milwaukee to learn about the state's private-school choice program, particularly as it relates to central city schools. In the spring, New York Mayor Rudolph Giuliani visited, bringing the entire New York school board and a contingent of newspaper reporters with him. The school's president, Br. Bob Smith, has been a guest at the White House.

At Messmer, extracurricular activities include the Art Club, Spanish Club, French Club, Movie Club and the Praise Team, which helps organize the twice-weekly prayer services. The buzz in the hallways, though, was all about football. The main questions — "You gonna play?" and "We gonna be any good?"

As Trost fumbled through the pile of message slips, medical cards and stat sheets on his desk, a new guy walked in. His name was Abdul. He was short, but had a sturdy, compact build. His hair was in dred locks. He wanted to play running back.

"You know Maurice Ragsdale?" Trost asked.

"Yes."

"You faster than Maurice?"

Well, Abdul said, he beat Maurice once in a race while they were on the track team. He told Trost he had played football in 6th, 7th and 8th grade, in the Athletes For Youth league. Nate Shorter had been in the same program.

"Anything happen to you around noon today?" Trost asked, playing it straight, though there was now a twinkle of mischief in his eye.

Abdul gave an uncertain look.

"Well," he said. "I decided at lunch to try football."

"Because I got on my knees and asked for a football player," Trost said. "Right around noon today. I got on my knees and asked for a running back."

He sent Abdul out to watch the practice. Trawitzki walked in and Trost relayed the story, racing through it to get to the end.

"Yep," Trost said. "We may have found our running back."

"Is he a cornerback, too?" asked Trawitzki, always thinking defense.

As the players stretched in the evening sun, Trost counted them out. "Thirty-seven," Trost said, including a few injured and in street clothes and the new prayed-for running back. Holy Thursday indeed.

"That's a record," Trawitzki said.

"What's the over-under for Monday?" asked Coach Larsen.

The tone was bright and casual, loose. But, in a minute, the cloud was back.

The team ran through its offensive plays, including the much-practiced Roar Back. The play required more than perfect timing in the backfield. On the line, the left guard had to hold the block. If a defender got through, it would absolutely blow up the play. Drew O'Malley was the guard. He had to hold the block for four, maybe five seconds — what seemed like a lifetime. Drew declared he couldn't do it. No way. He didn't have the body, the leverage. Why couldn't the coaches see it? He wasn't a guard.

Trost looked at Drew, waited a beat, then pointed him toward the second team.

"You're out," Trost said, then looked for a new body to plug in. "I need a guard."

Timmy Lathrop reached for his helmet, pulled it on.

"I didn't want line no way," Drew said, defiantly.

Drew stood off by himself. Now Trost said Drew was also out as starting linebacker. No offense, then no defense either. There had been moments of tension on the field before, but nothing like this. Coach Smith stepped toward him and offered some encouragement. But Drew turned and headed for the locker room.

"I didn't do nothing," Drew said, his voice sad and plaintive.

"You walk through that door young man, you're done," said Trost.

"Drew!" a player shouted.

"I didn't do nothing," Drew repeated.

"Drew!"

"Everybody thinks they should be something else," said Trost, turning to the rest. "You're a team. Not individual players."

But no one was paying attention, all eyes on Drew. He disappeared into the building, down the stairs to the locker room.

"Awww, Drew," said Nate Shorter and followed him inside.

Dominique Ross, a Messmer sophomore, went after Drew next. It was two Messmer kids, going after a Shorewood kid. Trost noticed it right away. He sensed a turning point and put everything on pause.

"Get a drink," Trost told the team.

Helmets came off and they trudged to the water trough, some questioning what happened, others questioning the coaches. Why pick on Drew? He came every day. The other coaches gathered around Trost, who softened his position. If Drew came back, everything was OK. He said it loud enough so some of the players could hear him.

Mark Moore ran inside.

Nate was already in the locker room. We need you, he told Drew, whose face was red, intense, sweat on his forehead. You worked too hard to quit now, said Dominique. Mark came in next. Come back, Mark said. For me. For Evan. For yourself.

For Drew, it was a moment of decision. An adult moment thrust into the rush, the emotion, of youth. Drew was a senior. There were eight games left. You never get those back. He could not, would not, quit. Wasn't brought up that way.

Outside, the team anxiously watched the doorway.

First, Nate and Dominique came out. Nate shrugged. A few minutes later, Mark Moore came out and nodded to Trost. Practice began again.

Finally, Drew came back outside, helmet on.

On Friday, game day again, the team wore ties to school.

The players wanted to wear their jerseys, but the coaches demanded ties. The ties made them stand out, as if they had something more important on their minds than hallway flirting or classroom clowning. Some ties featured giant knots. Others hung to the middle of stomachs. One tie had a bright Hawaiian theme, complete with palm trees, that clashed with a gray patterned shirt. Maurice Ragsdale wore a white polo shirt, a striped tie he borrowed from Mr. Wyatt clipped awkwardly to the neck. Mark Moore, meanwhile, was sharp in khakis, a yellow buttondown and a patterned blue tie, knotted tight. The night before, after practice, Mark had slipped into the office and asked Coach Trawitzki to tie it for him. He would keep it tied all year, loosening it just enough to slip back over his head. Drew looked out of place in shorts and a North Shore Fire Department T-shirt. He had plans to be a firefighter and during the last two periods of class he interned at the fire station, located a few blocks from the school and up the street from his house.

Marty and Maurice pulled their equipment out of their joint locker, tugging the white road jerseys over shoulder pads, inserting pads into the gray pants, and sliding it all into waiting gym bags.

"What would you do if you were a senior and there was this freshman girl who liked you?" Maurice asked.

"I don't know," Marty said. "I'm not a senior."

"She said she was coming to the next home game," Maurice said. "You'll see her. She looks like Jennifer Lopez."

Marty shrugged.

From the other side of the room, Rob Wyatt announced there was a new breakdown — the road breakdown — much more elaborate than before, involving a "Let's take it to the house," to be followed by a "Woo-ooo-oooh."

There were 35 guys in all, though some, such as Abdul, had not practiced yet and would not suit up. When the bus arrived, late, they had to double and triple up in the seats. On the highway, several players fell asleep. Pertrell Mallett, who had begun to make more practices, sat in the aisle. Eventually, he dozed off, his head on Nate Shorter's shoulder.

In many ways, Nate was the anchor for the Messmer kids, something solid they could count on. Nate was part of a group that rode the Capitol Drive bus home together each night. The group usually lingered in the locker room long after the others had gone, before heading to the bus stop where they would sometimes wait even longer, letting buses pass so they could horse around for a while. At times, Nate's face would seem strong and angular, but then he would laugh and it would be loose and soft. At the bus stop, Nate would sometimes demonstrate the swim move, or the best way to shed a block. The guys would all talk about the team, the coaches, the next opponent, always giving Nate the last word. If someone was short on cash, the group pooled its money so all could ride the bus. Nate would often get off with Montreal Miller, who lived in one of the roughest neighborhoods, and wait until Montreal caught his second bus, then walk the last few blocks home by himself.

The trip to Lake Mills, where Lakeside Lutheran was located, took about an hour and when the bus rolled off the highway, there was only 45 minutes until game time. The coaches clapped everyone awake and started going through the pre-game meetings. In the back, Dave O'Harrow, the quarterback, was feeling sick and queasy. Nearly all the starters were in the back, a hierarchy that was subtle but understood by all. The coaches practically shouted, so everyone could hear.

"We're scoring a lot of points tonight," Trost assured

Milwaukee Journal Sentinel photo by Benny Sieu

An exhausted Evan Rivera, a senior running back and linebacker, tries to forget the results on the scoreboard, after the team's loss to Lakeside Lutheran High School. The coaches and players felt they should have won the game.

them.

The bus rumbled into town and stopped for a traffic light in front of an American Legion hamburger stand. Everyone standing in line turned to look. The community of Lake Mills, population 4,843, is 97.5% white. The 2000 Census recorded eight black residents. If the bus broke down and the team had to stay overnight, the black population would have quadrupled.

The bus continued past a gas station and a taxidermy store and a bed and breakfast, set back from the road beyond a large front lawn. The town, small as it was, still had a crossing guard on Main Street. The bus turned onto a side street and the high school came into view. The players all looked out the dusty windows. It was a low brick building, off on a slight hill. The football field was on the edge of some houses and a few residents watched from their backyards, lawn chairs set up near the fence. The band was already playing, surrounded by a circle of students and cheerleaders carrying silver pompons. The team filed off the bus, feet crunching on the gravel, gym bags slung over shoulders. A few Lakeside players watched from a nearby doorway. They were, in fact, tall, skinny white guys. They had won their game last week on a late field goal.

The team was led to the girls locker room and three girls were shooed out. The room had a vague smell of perfume. There were powder blue lockers with navy blue trim. A hair curler was left on a shelf by a mirror. The team was quiet, businesslike, some players unsure if they even had time to go to the bathroom. Nate took a folded sheet of paper, on which he had written IHW — for "In His Will" — and slipped it into a shoe. Nate, who was a junior deacon at his church, wrote the same letters on tape wrapped around his wrist against Bay. A few others still had their mustard seeds, hoping they were magic after all.

"Reminds me of Brown Deer," Drew said, confidently.

He meant last year's victory. "Exactly how I felt before we whooped 'em."

There was little time to get loose. The team rushed through its pre-game routine. They couldn't return to the locker room, so they gathered around Trost and the other coaches in the end zone. No time for a prayer. A few words and off to the sideline.

"You ready, boy?" Nate shouted to Rob. "We're gonna win."

They butted helmets and ran out onto the field.

From the start, the game felt better. Lakeside Lutheran got the ball first, but the defense held and after three plays Lakeside had to punt. Trost, headset on, was already pacing, trying to calm his own excitement. There were two small sets of aluminum bleachers on the Shorewood-Messmer sideline, half-filled with fans, mostly Shorewood red. Leslie, Mark's girlfriend, was there. She stood in the first row with Mark's aunt, wearing a red Number 22 jersey, one from two seasons back, when the players bought their own jerseys. The team faced the setting sun, so the coaches and players squinted to see the action.

Maurice Ragsdale went back to take the punt, but he couldn't field it and, coaches shouting "get away, get away," the ball bounced to the 36 yard line. Two plays later, Mark got the ball. He ran to the right, shifted left, smooth and fluid, past one defender, then another. On the sideline, the team jumped and shouted and then Mark was free and clear and then he was in the end zone and it all seemed too easy and it was. There was a flag back where the play began. Yellow. Limp on the grass.

Clipping on Dave.

"That's horrible," Trost shouted to a referee. "Just horrible."

"Do it again Shorewood," came a shout from the stands.

The referee came to the sideline and bent down slightly,

hands on knees, ready for the next play.

"It's the quarterback," shouted Trost, his voice agitated and bewildered.

"What's your point?" the referee said over his shoulder, still chewing on his whistle.

"That was 20 yards away from the play."

"Doesn't matter where it is," the referee said. "Can't block him in the back."

The next play didn't go anywhere, it was 3rd and 21 anyway, and they had to punt. Trost continued to fume. "That's enough, coach," the referee said. "I don't want to hear about it." Now Dave came back to the sideline, muttering as he pulled his helmet off.

"Did you clip him?" Trost shouted, loud enough for the referee to hear.

"Naw," Dave said. "He came and hit me."

It was forgotten a few minutes later when Evan Rivera, the fullback who was so beaten up in the Bay game, burst up the middle, cradling the ball with both hands, and reached the end zone. He casually dropped the ball behind him, as if he did this sort of thing every day. The players were ecstatic, slapping hands and pounding shoulder pads.

The team went for two and got it, 8-0.

"We need more, we need more," Trost shouted, then congratulated Evan when he hit the sideline. "That was a big-time play, young man."

The flag was forgotten even more on the kickoff, when Martin Wallner — yes, Marty, the smallest on the field — stuffed the receiver and, legs churning, held him up long enough for some teammates to wipe him out.

"We got this," said Maurice, on the sideline.

A few possessions later, Shorewood-Messmer worked its way down the field, slowly, methodically, to the 48, then the 21, then the 15, then the seven, then the five. Mark was working the edges, Evan plowing up the middle.

For a change of pace, Trost called Roar Back. It was the play of the week, the one Maurice had been working on when he kept saying "Mississippi" out loud, the one Drew was supposed to be blocking on when he had the argument with Trost the day before. This time, Jonathan Williams, the Shorewood sophomore, was back in the Roar position.

The sun had set and both sidelines, which had crackled with energy, were nearly quiet.

"If you guys can't get excited about this, get off the field, this is football," said Coach Carroll, and the players began shouting encouragement.

"Let's go."

"C'mon."

"Yeah."

"C'mon Jonathan," Trost yelled, pacing again. He shouted the reminder: "Mississippi."

Jonathan nodded.

Dave took the snap, faked to Mark, who went right. Now Dave pivoted and slipped the ball into Jonathan's gut. Following a guard who had pulled out to block, Jonathan ran left, ducked toward the end zone and ... and ... everyone on the sideline craned their necks ... and .... and ... there was a clamor of bodies on the field. The blue jerseys popped up first, players running to their sideline, the football held aloft.

Fumble.

Jonathan would tell the coaches he heard a whistle and was trying to toss the ball to the referee. Some of the players who were on the field would say it looked like Jonathan was trying to reach the ball out and over the goal line, just like the pros do it, when the ball slipped out. It hurt. Definitely. But the team still led 8-0.

At half-time, they gathered behind a goal post, sitting on a slight hill. Some players leaned back, gasping for breath. Most were playing offense, defense and special teams. At one point, when Lakeside Lutheran missed on fourth down and Shorewood-Messmer got the ball, the coaches yelled "Offense" and only Maurice, in at receiver, ran onto the field. Nate Shorter sat on the ground, his left leg stretched out, rubbing his knee. He had made tackle after tackle, but the announcer kept saying, "Tackle by Albano," since the wrong number was listed on the roster. Nate didn't care. Hardly even noticed.

"You guys want to win a game?" Trost asked.

Mr. Wyatt, Rob's dad, passed out bottles of Gatorade. He had become a sideline fixture, even running water out to the team during timeouts. The players cracked the bottles open, chugged them down.

"Mark, you've got nine carries," Trost said. "You're going to get 35 by the end of the night. Dig down."

That was one way to protect the lead — to hold on to the ball. And the best way to do that was to keep feeding Mark Moore. Trost looked at all of them, faces streaked with sweat, hands twitching with anticipation. This game was theirs.

If only they grabbed it.

"I'm not walking off this football field without a win," Trost said finally. "The coaches have been hard on you all week. I've been an asshole all week and I want to win."

He asked a captain to step up and talk, but it wasn't Mark Moore or Maurice Ragsdale, it was Rob Wyatt. He had played at Marshall High School, and with his teammates there — Ronell and Dave — had more wins than anyone under his ample belt.

"The score is zero to zero," Rob said, voice raspy, urging them to take nothing for granted. "We need to go out there and set the tone. We gotta stay together to win."

In the second half, Lakeside Lutheran scored first tying the game, 8-8. That wasn't the plan, of course, the plan was to hold them and win on defense. But it was early. No worries. Shorewood-Messmer took over, but soon punted.

"They know our plays," Dave said to Trost on the sideline.

"They don't know the plays."

In truth, in high school football — particularly low-level high school football — there aren't many secrets. The plays are all pretty basic and familiar. And Trost had developed the offense with Mark Moore in mind, so it was no secret Mark would get the ball, most often on the pitch that took him to the opposite side. Evan, still at fullback due to Nate's problem knee, would work the middle to keep the defense honest. And, once in a while, Dave would drop back to pass, with Ronell Halbert almost always the designated target. The routes were short. No one trusted the line to provide protection for very long.

Dave's family was in the second row, one of the few from the Messmer side to make the trip. After the season of frustration at Marshall, the dispute with the coach, the punch to the locker, the lost season, this was Dave's time, back with Mark Moore and the rest of the guys. Dave's father followed the action with a video camera. Mr. O'Harrow had never been an athlete himself. He was born with club feet, which made it impossible to do more than play football in the park or whiffle ball in the backyard or one-on-one basketball in the driveway, usually with a friend who was the star athlete at the local high school and went on to play football at the University of Akron. Over the summer, when the family was vacationing in Pennsylvania, Mr. O'Harrow made a side trip to Ohio to see his old friend. They talked about Dave and his prospects with the new team. Mr. O'Harrow, never having played, couldn't see himself in Dave. He saw his friend.

So, yes, Mike O'Harrow wanted to see his son do well, to see him fit in at a new school, to see him comfortable and confident. Any father would. But, as the coaches suspected, there was more to the story. Back in January, one of Mr. O'Harrow's lungs had collapsed, then he had a heart attack, then heart surgery. The complications lingered. This might be his last season, too. He smiled as he trained the video camera on the action, on his son.

There was no more scoring in the third quarter, each side having trouble moving the ball for more than a few plays at a time. Early in the fourth, Lakeside Lutheran got it going and crept closer and closer to the end zone, tension on the Shorewood-Messmer sideline rising with each play. They finally reached the two-yard line. Trawitzki paced. This was his defense. They needed a stop. But in his third season with the program, he had never seen a Shorewood team make a goal-line stand. Not enough skill, not enough character. Trawitzki shouted out adjustments, the rest of the team clumped together behind him, quiet again, nervous and uncertain, all eyes on the field.

C'mon, Trawitzki thought. *Just this once.*

"Hold 'em Hounds!" came a shout from the stands.

Now, Ronell made a tackle on a run to the outside. And then Nate grabbed a runner's ankles at the line, dropping him to the grass. Another shout. If this was a movie, the dramatic music would have already begun. Third down. A Lakeside Lutheran receiver was wide open to the left side, but the pass was dropped. Deep breath.

And then it was fourth down.

The Shorewood-Messmer players stood in the huddle, their feet in their own end zone. They looked around at each other, eyes meeting. No time to be tired. One more, they said. We got this. The week had been a rough one, but now they were united: We gotta hold 'em. They clapped in unison and stepped to the line, cornerbacks running out to match the receivers. The Lakeside Lutheran stands were nearly full. The lights glinted off the band instruments and the silver pompons of the cheerleaders, who shouted and stepped through a routine on the track. But their voices were lost in the wind. It was as if everything operated in silence, the game already on film and in slow motion.

The Lakeside quarterback eased behind the center, shouted out the play.

One more, Trawitzki thought. *One more stop.*

Snap.

Now everything happened fast. The quarterback rolled right and Nate Shorter and the rest of the line plunged forward. A receiver spilled out into the open, into the end zone and Mark rotated over to cover him and Evan Rivera burst around the end of the line, untouched, and lunged toward the quarterback, reaching out, pulling at his jersey. The quarterback lofted the ball and as it sailed through the air, Mark saw it, jumped and tipped it away. On the sideline, there was the slightest pause as the ball harmlessly fell to the ground, and then they went absolutely nuts.

"Yeah, yeah, yeah."

Thank God, Trawitzki thought.

Maybe he was right. Maybe there was something about this team.

But there was a whistle and another flag. Back of the end zone. Pass interference on Dave O'Harrow, in at cornerback. The call sent the coaches into another fury. They cursed the referees, drawing a warning for poor sportsmanship. With another chance, Lakeside Lutheran scored. It was 14-8.

Dave walked back to the sideline, dejected.

The best athletes possess the ability to forget about a bad play, to instantly wipe the slate clean and move on. With Dave, it was as if he couldn't forget, as if he was standing at a chalkboard, writing the same words over and over: It is my fault. It is my fault. It is *my* fault.

There still was time to regroup, 9:56 left in the game.

A touchdown would tie it. An extra point would mean a victory. But on the next drive, Dave threw an interception. The defense held. On the next possession, another interception. Again the defense held. This time the team got the ball on their own 14 with 1:57 left. A pass went behind Marty who was open up the left sideline. They tried the halfback pass, Mark to Ronell, but Mark was tackled before Ronell could find an opening. The clock ticking away, Maurice lined up on the left side and Ronell on the right. At the snap, Maurice cut across the middle. Dave dropped back and launched the ball behind him. Another interception, this one returned for a touchdown.

On the sideline, a teammate told Maurice he should have looked for the ball sooner, but Maurice shook his head: "Look, look, look, it's a one route." He meant the ball was in the wrong spot. Dave walked past them, past everyone. Trost stepped through the players, heads hanging, and sought out Dave.

"Don't worry about it," Trost said to him. "We come back tomorrow and get to work."

"Fuck it," Dave said, turning away. "I quit."

Final score: 21-8.

By the time, the team reached midfield, several players were already crying, the tears mixing with sweat. Pertrell Mallett had hardly played, but his eyes were wide and sad. Others stood, hands on hips, staring at the scoreboard or at the Lakeside Lutheran players, who after soberly shaking hands with the Shorewood-Messmer squad were slapping backs and shouting and laughing, reveling in this terrible, horrible moment.

"The score doesn't mean anything to me," Trost told them. "You guys showed character."

Dave took off his shoulder pads and dropped them to the ground.

"You know what?" Trost said. "This is what we're up

against. Nobody wants us to win."

True or not, this team always seemed to be starting first and long. On the field and off. It always had to go farther and run faster, try harder and dig deeper, do better and do more, just to get back to even.

Dave's father put his camera away. The lights on the scoreboard went out, section by section: Period, down, distance, finally, the score. Oh, what a victory would have meant. Vindication. Validation. Momentum. The team needed it all.

"Good things will happen," Trost said, emotion creeping into his voice. "We did enough tonight to win a game. It didn't happen, but we will win. We will win."

Trost stepped away, lifted his glasses to his forehead and rubbed his eyes.

The season is going to be one wild ride, he thought. *A wild ride.*

"Daddy, daddy, daddy."

It was Alexis, age 5. She ran up and hugged his legs.

Chapter 6
"I'm not a quitter."

The next morning, the players gathered again on the steps outside the gym, waiting for the coaches. Dave O'Harrow was the main topic of conversation. All the wild passes. The penalties. The interceptions. After the White-fish Bay debacle, there was no single person to blame. This time there was Dave. In truth, it wasn't all Dave's fault, but he made for a convenient target, especially since he was nowhere to be found.

The coaches pulled up one by one. It was Labor Day weekend and some families were squeezing in a last trip, so the group of players was smaller than usual. They filed into the basement, 20 guys in all, footsteps echoing in the long hallway. Most were already in shorts. They waited for the others to change before everyone went outside.

The loss had exacerbated some of the problems on the team, particularly the split between those who weren't playing and those who were playing all the time. In the locker room after the game, several reserves confronted Coach Smith about the lack of playing time. One of the Messmer players, senior Justin Moore, was nearly in tears. "I'm sick of this shit," he shouted. "I've been practicing since March." Mr. Wyatt, with a son and grandson on the team, comforted other players, telling Nate Shorter, "Now you know what it was like back in the day." He meant racism. Maurice Ragsdale, stuffing clothes into a gym bag, said he was through, but Mr. Wyatt told him to hush that nonsense. No quitting.

Robert Wyatt Sr. grew up in Birmingham, Alabama, where he went to a segregated high school, drank from segregated water fountains, went off to the Army, served in Germany, then came home to the still-segregated South, where he marched a few times with Dr. Martin Luther King Jr. On election day, he would drive residents to the polls, which often were in rural areas, set far from bus lines to discourage black participation. Mr. Wyatt soon moved north to Milwaukee, the hometown of his first wife. He knew things were different when he ordered a Cherry Coke at the Gimbel's Department Store lunch counter downtown and didn't have to go out back to drink it. He could drink it right there, which made it taste that much better.

Mr. Wyatt had retired from the Milwaukee airport, where he worked for almost 30 years as a baggage handler. He was divorced, a single father. Yet he came to all the games and every day picked up Rob and Ronell and some of the other guys to drive them home from practice, figuring it was safer that way. His battered brown van, with a "You Have A Friend in Jesus" plate on the spare tire, had more than 200,000 miles on it. Mr. Wyatt played high school football himself, way back when, running back. Hooper City High, class of 1956. Mr. Wyatt had a knack for catching kids before they quit, turning them back. He felt if he didn't check in on the team every day things had a way of going wrong.

"Ya'll just get 'em next time," Mr. Wyatt said after the game, gray hair poking from under a black Shorewood-Messmer cap. "That's what ya gotta do."

Outside the locker room, where Coach Trost and Coach Trawitzki sat on the hallway steps, the dissension came off as a murmur, muffled by the closed door, which would occasionally swing open, another sad or angry player walking out to the bus. Maurice emerged apologizing to the coaches, teammates, anyone who would listen, apologiz-

ing for not catching a pass he could never have caught. At
one point, the referees walked past from the other direction. "Excellent job tonight, you are excellent," Trost said
and then, once they were out the door, shouted: "You
guys are pathetic." Finally, he and Trawitzki followed the
last players to the bus. "Ain't nobody talking on this bus,"
Rob Wyatt said once the door was pulled shut. And on
the way back there was no sound but the coaches talking
up front, hushed and huddled. At one point, Coach Carroll
turned to the seat behind him. "Marty," he said, "better
tell your Mom to start baking cookies."

Nevertheless, there was something different about the
team.

A week earlier, after the Whitefish Bay disaster, the feeling was one of defeat but also, in a sense, one of relief, like
a small town that survived a tornado. The night before, it
was all anger and disgust. The team didn't feel as if it had
lost something, but as if something had been taken from
them. Stolen. Whether it was the result of racism or not,
it stung the same. Of course, if anyone had stepped back
as the team cried its tears onto the field, they would have
realized this: If the team was hurting, it was because the
players felt something. The game meant something.

Trost could see it now, on the morning after.

There was, finally, emotion.

And he could work with that.

Trost wanted the team to play with attitude. An edge.
As if the players had something to prove, to all the doubters, to themselves. He'd always played that way. On the
defensive line in high school, it was Trost, at 5'3" and 135
pounds, who demanded double-teams, not the all-conference tackle next to him. In a newspaper interview at the
start of his senior year, in the fall of 1985, Trost described
his approach: "If you think about someone who is bigger
and stronger than you and it gets in your mind, then you're
beaten. I used to think about it, but not anymore. When

you go against a bigger guy and you don't have the inner desire, you won't beat him. You'll beat yourself."

He felt the same as a coach. So he woke up that morning, still sour and surly from the Lakeside loss. He banged around the house so loudly, his wife, Sheila, took their three children — Alexis, 5, Bryce, 4 and Cierra, 1 — out to get doughnuts, so they wouldn't have to see Daddy so mad. Trost needed a target for his anger, for the team's frustration, and a perfect one was coming Friday.

Slinger.

By now, all the Messmer players had heard the stories about Shorewood's last trip to Slinger, a town of about 3,900 located 35 miles northwest of Milwaukee, where some of the players reported hearing racial slurs on the field. And after the game, as the coaches tried to conduct a meeting, the team was ordered out of the way so the homecoming fireworks could begin. Even quiet Nate Shorter had vowed "we're gonna bust some Slinger heads." If that wasn't enough, Trost accepted a position on the Slinger staff three years ago, but backed out just before the season began when the top assistant position opened at Shorewood, along with the potential of becoming head coach a year later.

So Trost, who lived in nearby Hartford, had something to prove and this could be the season to do it. Indeed, despite all the talk about Lakeside Lutheran, this game was more important. It was the start of the conference season. The team was once again, in the old sports cliche, 0-0. To make the playoffs, they needed four wins in seven conference games. The way Trost figured it, the last three were certain victories: Whitefish Bay Dominican, Brown Deer and Greendale Martin Luther. That meant they had to win one of the first four. And Slinger, in the midst of an off-year, was as good an opportunity as any.

The theme of the week: No excuses.

"We can't go around saying the referees cheated us,"

Trost said, as the team gathered outside. "It's no secret what happened, but let's keep it on the field. We just have to be that much better. We have to beat a team by that much more."

Everyone nodded.

Drew O'Malley, who on Thursday nearly was kicked out of practice, said they should do 21 sprints — one for each point they let Lakeside Lutheran score. There already was a change in Drew.

"I'm not even going to tell O'Malley to pull up his pants," said Coach Carroll, as the team ran. "Being kicked out of practice was the best thing that ever happened to him."

After the sprints, which went fast and easy, they gathered in the "S" Room to watch video. Martin Wallner's father had taped the Lakeside game and the camera zoomed in several times on Marty, even if the play went somewhere else. Marty blushed a bit and tried to deflect the jibes. At away games, when the Shorewood backers were sparse, Mr. Wallner could often be heard shouting "Hold 'em Hounds" to the team, or "All right, here we go buddy," to Marty, who would acknowledge it with a slight raise of his fist. Here it was all caught on tape.

As they watched it now, the game seemed even closer. A few plays. Two, maybe three, made the difference — and all had gone against Shorewood-Messmer. There was the clipping call against Dave, which brought back a touchdown. The fumble at the five-yard line. The second-chance touchdown for Lakeside after the pass interference penalty. The frustration came back as the play flickered on the screen: The quarterback rolling right. Evan Rivera, coming untouched through the line, pulling on the quarterback's jersey. The ball in the air.

Trost rewound the tape.

And there was Evan again, tugging on the quarterback's jersey, the ball fluttering out, and there was Mark flashing across the background, jumping and the ball changing directions. It was tipped. *Hell yes*, it was tipped. That was the argument the coaches had made on the sideline to the deaf ears of the officials. If Mark tipped the ball, there was no issue with Dave bumping anyone. It was all fair game.

Trost rewound the tape again, pointing as the play unfolded a third time.

"Mark tipped the ball," Trost said. "See."

If Dave O'Harrow had been there, it might have made a difference. He could have seen for himself it was a bad call, not a bad play. Maybe it would have built back some of the confidence that had crumbled away. But Dave was gone. The tape with "O'Harrow" written on it was already ripped from above his locker, the locker empty. "Well, I guess I'm QB now," Micah Moore had said when they arrived in the locker room an hour or so earlier. His voice was one of resignation, not excitement.

Now they turned to the Slinger tape. Slinger had lost the night before to Cedarburg, 31-0. That left them 0-2, with the other loss, 16-6, coming against Random Lake, a team Shorewood-Messmer handled in the scrimmage a few weeks back. If Lakeside Lutheran was "tall, skinny white kids," Slinger was "short, stocky white kids." As the coaches discussed the Slinger defensive scheme, how to attack it and the strategy for the week, everyone seemed more intent. From the back of the room, Ronell Halbert, the lanky wide receiver, offered up his own game plan.

"We should open up with a three-route," he said, confidently. He meant a pass. To him, of course. Down the sideline. "I can see it."

"You'll be throwing it," Trost said, matter-of-factly.

He paused as two heads swiveled toward him in surprise.

"You or Micah."

One thought he already had the job. The other didn't much want it. But they both would have to compete for it.

The Monday practice, Labor Day, was scheduled late, 7:30 p.m., so those who went out of town could make it back. Still, most players were missing, so there was little that could be done but get a head start on resolving the quarterback question.

On one hand, there was Micah Moore. The year before, as a freshman, Micah played wide receiver and cornerback. He had been working out at quarterback from the start this season, but began in the third spot, behind Dave O'Harrow and George Lasley, who quit the week before. Like his older brother, Micah came off as reserved, but where Mark Moore was confident, Micah seemed timid. Sometimes the coaches wondered if he really wanted to play football, or just came to practice because his older brother did. On defense, the coaches had initially put Micah at first-string linebacker, but he lacked the needed fire, and soon was drifting between different backfield spots and the sideline, depending on the mix of players there on a given day. In the locker room, Micah was the one who manned the CD player, content to let others bop and groove and carry on.

On the other hand, there was Ronell Halbert, a junior. He was always at the center of locker room attention. He had the bearing and attitude of a wide receiver — the frizzed out hair, the shrugged shoulders after a catch, a walk that was more of a strut. On the last day of summer camp, Ronell had hung with Mark Moore in the timed sprints, running them with his shirt off to demonstrate how much the weight room work had paid off. As a sophomore at Marshall, Ronell had played on the junior varsity, yet still talked about playing college ball, certain he'd go, in his words, "D-One" — Division One. He used money from a summer job to buy receiver gloves. Being quarterback, he felt, would hold him back.

The two watched as Trost, back in his role as tutor,

stepped through the plays in slow motion, exaggerating the movements to emphasize the turns and the footwork.

The offense was meant to be simple. On every play, the call in the huddle would tell each player his responsibility. It would list the routes for the receivers, the blocking assignments for the line, the hole the fullback would run through, the spot where the running back would go. In most cases, a receiver would run in the play, giving a number called by Trost to the quarterback, who would look down at his wristband and read off the full call, such as "D-Slot, Liz Motion Toss, Bull 1 (PT, BT, C)." Simple.

But while the other players only had to execute one assignment, the quarterback had to know where everyone would be and see each play as it was meant to be run. He had to understand a hard fake to the fullback was needed to get the linebackers to bite, or that hiding the ball at his hip on a pass play could buy critical time for the receiver. It was instinct as much as practice. Running a play over and over could make it second nature, but in a good quarterback, there was something else, something more.

Micah and Ronell each did the same play a few times until they had it down, then on to the next. Quickly, no thinking allowed, just go.

"It's only Monday," Trost said at one point. "Thank God."

Once, back in Chicago, Trost had to go with a quarterback he described as "box of rocks dumb." So, risking penalty, he rigged an ear piece for the player's helmet and set it to pick up the discussion between the sideline and the booth.

This wasn't that bad. Yet.

"We're keeping it simple," Trost said a few minutes later, as much to himself as the team. "Not putting a lot in."

Ronell seemed to pick it all up quickly. Whether slipping the ball into Mark's gut or pitching it out to him, the ball was always in the right spot at the right moment.

Micah took a turn, slipped. He got up, apologetic.

"It's all right," Trost said.

He told the two to switch every two plays, but Ronell soon ended up doing most of the repetitions and when Trost sent everyone away for a quick drink, Ronell confessed to Micah, "It's kind of easy." Micah wasn't so certain. He had gotten some snaps at quarterback when Dave O'Harrow had a hamstring injury and George Lasley was AWOL, but not enough to get comfortable in the spot.

Trost called them back and lined them up again.

"Micah first?" Ronell asked, still hoping for a reprieve so he could remain a receiver.

"No, you're first," Trost said, and quickly thought of an explanation, so as not to upset Micah. It was always a delicate balance to keep all of the egos and expectations in line. "You're first in alphabetical order."

This is how a position is won.

Ronell would run a play. It would take a time or two, but he'd be smooth. He would smile, laugh, joke with Trost. He'd get it. Then Micah would go. The play would be bumpy and tentative, like someone feeling his way through a darkened room. At one point, Micah made the call, barked out the count and, with the play supposed to go right, turned left instead.

"Don't worry about it Micah," Coach Smith said. "It's a learning process."

Micah lined up again. Same call. This time he dropped the ball.

"C'mon, man," said Mark, his older brother, through a disappointed scowl.

"Relax, Micah," said Coach Smith. "Relax."

It is easy to say, relax. But it is one of those things. The more you're told to relax, the harder it is to relax. It gets in your head and then it gets stuck there. You realize people are watching, watching to see if you relax. So you start to think. You think of the play: This is how it goes, a turn this way and then a step back. Then when it comes time to do it, thinking about it makes it all slower. And then it turns out even worse.

Micah nodded to Coach Smith and stepped to the side-line.

He stood near Marty Wallner, a fellow Shorewood sophomore. The two had played on the freshman team last year and, while the varsity could claim one victory, they notched two, Brown Deer and Dominican.

"I know Bull Zero Four," Micah said, repeating the called play.

"Just relax, man," said Marty, who had his own jitters before the Bay game. "You'll get there."

They watched Ronell. Smooth.

After practice, which ended at 8:45 p.m., everyone wanted to get home, especially Trost's son, Bryce, who spent the evening running around the field and was now tired and cranky. But there would be an extra stop.

Rob Wyatt, the junior from Messmer, walked into the office.

"All I'm asking him," Rob said to Trost, "is, 'Do you want to play or not?' No begging."

He said it again, to underline it.

"No begging."

He meant Dave O'Harrow, the dearly-departed quarterback. The coaches had said someone should reach out to Dave and Rob was the logical choice, since he had played with Dave at Marshall High School and was on the grade-school team coached by Dave's father. Rob tried Dave all day on Sunday, but he wouldn't come to the phone. He finally got Dave's father that afternoon and told him they were coming out after practice.

Two years earlier, when Mark Moore was a sophomore, Mr. O'Harrow took a group of the guys — Dave, Rob and

Ronell among them — to see Shorewood play. A loss, of course. Afterward, as the boys waited near the bus to talk to Mark, Mr. O'Harrow wandered up to one of the Shorewood coaches, nodded toward his guys and said Shorewood ought to get players like that on its team. The coach looked the boys over, quickly dismissing the thought — and them. "So, you guys are the ones who are going to save Shorewood football?" he scoffed. Yes. They were supposed to save Shorewood football — not then, but now. It was a perfect script for a movie, the old team, together again. The way Mr. O'Harrow saw it, the boys had their minds set on winning another championship.

And Dave, his son, would lead the way.

They went out to Dave's house as much out of duty as any expectation of success. Trost was in one car, Bryce napping on the seat next to him. Mr. Wyatt had the boys in the van — his son, Rob; his grandson, Ronell; and Mark and Micah Moore. When they got there, Mr. O'Harrow waved them into the living room. Dave was upstairs. "We're coming to get you," Rob shouted. But, when Dave came down, it became clear they could not.

The conversation was tight. Definitive.

I'm playing for the wrong reasons, Dave said.

Are you sure? Yes.

Dave and his father had already talked about all this. Mr. O'Harrow assured Dave he was proud of him, would love him no matter what, but said he wasn't proud of the way he was handling the situation. The team had only played two games. Dave had been in class at Messmer for only two days. He had made a commitment. Others were counting on him.

But, in those two days at Messmer, Dave decided, things just didn't feel right. He saw the other players at lunch, when they all found a corner of the cafeteria, but the rest of the day he felt singled out, not part of a team or a school, just a guy. Alone. He caught a few comments —

"Look at the white boy," or "We got a white boy at quarterback." The other players thought it didn't mean anything, just talk and hazing and guys messing around. He'd be accepted, in time.

The questions continued: Would you rather try a different position? One with less pressure? No. Would you come back for your dad?

No.

They slipped one of Mr. O'Harrow's old game tapes into the VCR. The picture was a bit fuzzy. A bunch of kids, small in stature, struggling to fill the bulky football pads. It was the boys, years ago, the Golden Season. Happier times. As they watched — Bryce on the floor playing with the dog, Max, a cocker spaniel — Mr. O'Harrow started to cry. It was as hard for him now as it had been for Dave. Looking at Dave's blank face, Trost realized he hadn't quit three nights ago. He was lost after the Bay game.

In football, if a player is injured, the team must go on.

Dave was done; on they went.

The week went quickly, too quickly for a team breaking in a new quarterback and relying on inexperienced receivers — Maurice Ragsdale and Marty Wallner, who would rotate in a one-receiver set. A tight end would be added to help with blocking and pass protection. The switches meant the coaches had to force-feed some of the other guys enough basics to get them into the lineup. At the end of the Lakeside Lutheran game, the guys on the field were dragging, while Lakeside kept running in new players. That was a problem last year, too — the very problem the partnership with Messmer was supposed to solve. But while there were more bodies, many weren't ready for a game, for the speed involved, the strength, the pounding.

Tuesday. The sun hot. The field dry. Dusty.

Time for Oklahomas.

"We got grass over here?" Trost asked.

"We don't need grass," Coach Carroll joked. "We should do it on concrete."

That was the mentality needed for Oklahomas. Toughness — mental and physical. When they split into the two groups, Trost promoted Justin Moore, a Messmer senior, to the top group. Nobody called Justin by his first name, not even his mother. It was J-Flex, or Flex for short, a nickname he picked up in grade school when he played football on the playground, trying to sufflex the other players World Wrestling Federation-style instead of tackling them. He was one of the Messmer seniors who waited years for a football team. He was the one, after the Lakeside loss, who lamented how he had practiced since March and didn't play. Over the weekend, Flex considered quitting, but instead came and asked Trost to give him a shot at the starting lineup. He even brought along his father, who had a day off from his job at a Coca Cola distribution center, so he couldn't back out of talking to Trost.

This was it. The chance.

Flex took the offensive line spot, dug in and got beat.

"Run it again, same group," said Trost. "J-Flex, you're holding him."

They tried again. This time it was Trawitzki: "Justin, holding, 10 yards."

Flex shook his head, lined up and did it again. Better. But still a ways to go.

The Oklahoma drill again had one linebacker going against two running backs, in addition to the two linemen. The linebacker first had to beat the fullback, who charged through as a blocker, then he had to stop the ball carrier. There was a slow start from everyone, but then Drew O'Malley busted through and brought the runner down. He got up, did it again.

Trost blew the whistle.

"I want everyone to watch this," Trost said. "He doesn't

give up until he finds a tackle."

All eyes on him, Drew stood in at linebacker, in the familiar crouch, arms set, fingers twitching with anticipation. The whistle blew. The linemen crashed and Mark Moore, at fullback, busted into Drew, who slipped past Mark and grabbed Maurice Ragsdale, dragging him to the ground.

"Here's a linebacker!" Trost shouted.

The whole team was like that, in a sense. A slashing tackle, a stutter-step run and it was as if Trost had, somehow, captured lightning in a bottle. But, on the second look, after a bungled snap or a dropped pass, it wasn't lightning at all.

Just a reflection on the glass.

Wednesday. Start of practice. Hot sun, slight breeze. As the team did its stretches, Trost walked among the players, calling out attendance. Ronell Halbert looked up from the back row.

"Hey, I can help find you a quarterback," Ronell said to Trost, who stopped, still reading the roster. "He plays on the freshman team."

That was Teddy Hanrahan, a Shorewood freshman, a natural. Strong arm. Effortless throw. He was well beyond the other freshmen and one of the team's most dedicated players. Though the team ran only a handful of plays, all modeled after the varsity, Coach Groser allowed Teddy to call them on his own. When a play went bad, Teddy had a knack for tucking the ball and running, getting positive yards.

"You brought me a quarterback before," Trost replied, "and it didn't exactly work."

"Who? Dave?" Ronell protested. "I didn't know he was coming."

"You and Rob brought me Dave."

Dave hadn't been in school at Messmer all week. No

one had heard from him, so everyone figured he was back at his old school. Ronell returned to the quarterback topic. He shrugged and glumly shook his head, lamenting his fate.

"Guess I ain't gonna be throwing this week," he said.

"Yes, you are," said Trost.

"Who'm I gonna be throwing to?" Ronell quickly looked up.

"Maurice."

"Yeah, right."

Despite the one-week stint as a captain, Maurice Ragsdale was still struggling — mightily — to gain the confidence of his teammates and the coaches. Teachers and others at Messmer thought Maurice had a problem staying focused. Even Maurice would sometimes admit he could do better, in school and in sports, but he somehow just didn't. He had quit both basketball and track. He had a scholarship, but struggled with grades. On the new scholarship application form, under career possibilities, he had written "Businessman" and "NBA player." Now, though, he was thinking about maybe joining a fire cadet program.

That afternoon, Maurice had walked into the locker room while a full-fledged ribbing session was going on, all about who had a girl and who didn't, who could play and who couldn't. It was a frequent locker room thing, jokes about how one player looked like a frog and another — one of the only black players who actually lived in Shorewood — went home to a butler. Ordinarily, Maurice would have joined in, but he was quiet, digging through his locker. "Hey Maurice," said Flex. He pointed at Maurice's T-shirt, which was more gray than white, and held up a new tennis shoe, which practically glowed in contrast. "This is white." Everyone laughed. Maurice continued to busily look for his shoulder pads, saying quietly: "I gotta buy some more."

Once, a couple weeks back, when Maurice was back to field punts and the coaches were talking to the guys on the line, Maurice inexplicably began singing, "I'm a little teapot, short and stout." He added a little spin and dance, one hand on his hip, the other pointed out to the side. When the kick came, he missed the ball, chased it back to the fence, then threaded his way through the defenders. As he did, Nate Shorter, figuring no one should get into the end zone untouched, got up from the sideline and made the tackle. After a crash that in the cartoons would have prompted birds to circle his head, Maurice got back up and set himself for another punt. "Ragsdale, you're gonna run two back this week," Trost shouted. "Uh huh," Maurice replied. "I'm gonna try three."

Maurice was resilient. But he was fragile.

Later, after the stretches, when it came time to practice punt returns, the coaches made the switch: Drew in, Maurice out. Drew was running the ball better. And Drew had surer hands. He might not bust a run, but he wouldn't blow one either.

"You don't believe in me," Maurice said. His voice was both hurt and humored.

"We do believe in you," said Trost. "We'd believe in you more if you stopped dropping the ball."

Thursday. End of practice. The team gathered and listened to the final words of the coaches. Although the Slinger game was circled on his calendar, Trost's irritability level had been about average most of the week, or at least only slightly above average. Today, Trost was on edge. At the start of the practice, he admonished everyone to pull their pants up, or they'd end up running around the field in their underwear. But Trost had to leave early for his master's degree class. And Coach Smith was with the freshmen team, up playing its game at Slinger. So it was just Coach Trawitzki and Coach Carroll. As they addressed the team, several players stood in the back with their pants low, a quiet defiance. Pertrell Mallett and Maurice Ragsdale were talking. It may have been a new season, the start of the conference schedule, but the problems were woefully old.

"Shut up and stop talking," Mark Moore said, looking at Maurice.

A moment later, it was Carroll's turn.

He looked at Pertrell.

"Is it possible you may be on defense at some point tomorrow?" Carroll asked.

In fact, it was. The coaches had begun working Pertrell with the first string at times. Trawitzki was reluctant, but Trost kept saying he's a big strong kid, just give him some basic assignments, see what he can do.

"I don't know," Pertrell said.

"I think it is," said Coach Carroll. "So pay attention."

Trawitzki turned to more important matters: Slinger.

For many years, after Messmer closed and reopened, the school played basketball in the Indian Trails Conference, a far-flung collection of small schools, from Maranatha Baptist to the Wisconsin School for the Deaf. Messmer later shifted to the Midwest Classic Conference, which had more competitive match ups, but still meant regular bus rides into the small towns of Wisconsin — Burlington, Beaver Dam, Delafield. There were remarks, of course. Hurtful moments. But the players were drilled in the need to ignore it all, to politely shake hands after the game, to shatter the stereotypes about being black and living in the central city instead of reinforcing them.

Even at Shorewood, there had been a few incidents over the years. In the mid-1980s, after a game at Grafton, a small town north of Milwaukee, several Shorewood players complained to their coach and principal about hearing the N-word. They discussed it and ultimately decided to call the Grafton athletic director, who agreed to send his team captains to Shorewood, where the two sides talked it out.

The Slinger game would be its own sort of test. If things went bad, if words were said on the field, the team had to keep its cool. They were being watched and not just by their fans. The team had already been on the front page of the daily newspaper. And all of the local TV stations, over time, made a pilgrimage to do the story. White and black, rich and poor, the underdog angle. The story had it all.

Trawitzki looked around the group. If there were problems two years ago, with a handful of black players, who knew what the welcome would be this time.

"Is there anyone here afraid of Slinger?" he asked.

No hands went up.

"Anyone at all."

Still none.

"Anyone that thinks we can't beat Slinger?"

Still none.

"Anybody here think they're a bunch of strong white boys."

A few hands were raised. Other players scanned the group and scowled.

"Strong?" said Curtis Jeffries, a Shorewood sophomore. "Oh."

He quickly lowered his hand.

"Slinger is still racist," Trawitzki told the team. "If that doesn't piss you off, I don't know what would."

He ran through a whole list of grievances.

"Slinger is still cocky," he said. "But they're not good enough to be cocky. That ought to piss you off. They're trying to play power football with a small running back. That ought to piss you off."

This time, the team had a chance, a rare chance to win on the field.

"You have to want to win it more than Slinger wants to win it," Trawitzki said. "You have to look across the line of scrimmage and say, 'Not this time.'"

Friday. Game day. Trost's office. The coaches came and went, calling out to the locker room to be sure all the players were there. The office, as always, was a mess. The desk was an avalanche of old stat sheets, rosters, newspapers, medical cards and a few letters from colleges. As always, the letters were addressed to either Mark Moore or Nathan Shorter, though Nate was getting more and more of them. There was a single bench along the wall, a box of game jerseys and game balls, which always seemed to be disappearing, making it nearly impossible to sit down.

"I had three people tell me today we ain't got a chance," said Coach Smith.

"Who were they?" asked Trost.

"I name no names."

"Were they on this team?" asked Trawitzki.

"No."

"Then who cares?" Trawitzki said. "I had 15 people call me today and say we had no chance."

The Messmer players had reported that Pertrell wasn't in class. That meant he couldn't play. Another piece of the gameplan out the window.

Trost picked up the phone and dialed Pertrell's number.

"Pertrell wasn't in school today," he said into the phone. "No, you can't bring him .... He can't play ... Because he wasn't in school today."

For Pertrell Mallett, things had settled down some at home. With divorce splitting the family, Pertrell and two brothers had moved in with their father. But the brothers had been fighting — with each other and their father. One time the police were called. And Pertrell, as the biggest person in the house, sometimes felt he had to stay home so he could break it up. The coaches knew about the divorce, but the rest was Pertrell's secret. It was what

Nate Shorter, Pertrell's friend, had tried to get across to Trost on the first day of practice, without saying it directly and violating a confidence. That it was serious stuff.

Trost tapped a foot. Rolled his eyes at the other coaches. The night before, Pertrell had found out he'd be getting a lot of playing time today.

"Can I talk to him?

To be sure, of all the coaches, Trost probably would have understood Pertrell's situation the best. When Trost was a boy, growing up in Chicago, his older brothers sometimes fought with his father. Several did drugs. There would be yelling. Screaming. And Trost, in kindergarten, would try to stop it the only way he knew. He'd find his brothers' shoes and bury them in the bottom of the laundry basket or he would slip them into his book bag and take them to school, figuring if his brothers had no shoes, they couldn't go out of the house and if they couldn't go out, they couldn't get in trouble.

Now, so many years later, Trost often wondered how he could turn out one way and a brother, who grew up in the same house, under the same circumstances, could turn out so different. He attributed it, in part, to sports, to the discipline required, the pride, to the coaches as strong role models. Studies have shown that those who participate in high school sports have a lower dropout rate, better grades and higher self-esteem. They are less likely to skip school and less likely to get involved in drugs or crime. They are more likely to go on to college, more likely to graduate and then earn more money when they do. When his brothers called him "Jim the Jock," it was meant to be derisive, but it gave Trost a positive identity. To this day, Trost does not drink or smoke.

Trost wondered, too, if he was having that kind of impact on the players, especially the more troubled ones, who seemed to drift in and out like the tide, every day a different problem crashing on the beach.

Trost had driven Nate home once over the summer, when both were working Milwaukee Brewers games at Miller Park — Trost as a beer vendor, Nate delivering food to people in the club seats behind home plate. Trost shook his head when he saw the battered houses, the people lingering on corners and stoops, aimless. Weeds and litter everywhere. The environment was similar, if less extreme, to that of his own youth. The players, though, never believed it when Trost said there was a time when he didn't know where his next dollar was coming from. He seemed more suburb than city now.

Trost may not have known the full Pertrell story. But if Mr. Wyatt was trying to catch the players before they fell, Trost, in his own way, was doing the same.

The conversation continued.

"Why can't he come to the phone?" Trost asked, and waited, finally saying: "Tell him not to miss practice tomorrow."

He hung up and reported to the others.

"He was in the bathroom."

Everyone shook their head and came to the same conclusion.

Scared.

When the bus pulled up at Slinger High School, the scene in many ways was just like Lakeside Lutheran, though the community was even more white than Lake Mills — 98% of Slinger's 3,901 residents were white, according to the 2000 census. At the stadium, about the only black face, outside of the Shorewood-Messmer contingent, was in one of the photos on a generic, mass-produced program cover, Slinger's 48-man roster printed inside. In the distance, past the field, there was a water tower and a church steeple that, once the sky darkened, was bathed in light. The band, in red, white and blue, filled an entire section of the stands. A group of cheerleaders, all pretty and perfect, ran a lap around the track, as if preparing for battle, just like the players. Every half-hour or so, a train roared past, its whistle loud, its wheels racing into the quiet country night.

A truck from one of the Milwaukee TV stations was already parked near the edge of the field and when the players did their stretching, the reporter, Jessica Jallings, interviewed Trost. She had to interview some of the players, too, so Trost produced Mark Moore and Nate Shorter, who was back as a captain this week. One Shorewood, one Messmer. Jallings asked them about the team. It's good, they allowed. It's working out. They shifted their feet. Nervous. Then Jallings asked them to sing their school song, but they quickly shook their heads. Finally, goaded into it, they both sang the start.

Nate went first. A sheepish smile.

"Messmer High School, How we love thee, To our Bishops, So we can't be beat. M-E-S-S-M-E-R."

He stopped, laughed nervously. That was enough.

Then Mark went, talking as much as singing: "U rah rah rah Shorewood red and gray, The school that's got the pep we'll say, We always show our true loyalty, and cheer you on to victory."

He, too, stopped short.

"I can't sing," Mark said, shaking his head. "That's how I say it."

Finally, Drew O'Malley, another Shorewood senior, was called over. Jallings asked about a team nickname. Messmer was the Bishops, Shorewood the Greyhounds. Trost sometimes joked they should be the "Praying Dogs." Others had said "Greyhops," or "Bishounds." At home games, the announcer implored fans, in a generic way, to welcome "Your Shorewood-Messmer team."

Drew said he didn't know.

"Maybe Soldiers," he said with a shrug. "At the end of our breakdown, we say '1-2-3, Soldiers.' So maybe we could be the Soldiers."

Before the game, Trost called the team together in the end zone. Remember last week, he said. Remember the feeling, how it twisted in your stomach, how it seemed to back up in your throat. Remember how it hurt. Remember and use it now.

The Slinger band started playing and the music stepped on Trost's words.

"This is going to be a football game tonight," he said, "and you guys came here to fight."

The night before, Trost stopped at the Slinger field on his way home, figuring he could catch the end of the freshman game. But it was already over and Trost sat in his car and stewed instead, thinking about the season and where it was headed. In many ways, the season teetered on the brink, always on the verge of coming together or falling apart. There was such a thin line between success and failure.

"We're gonna leave it on the field," Trost said, voice rising. "We're gonna fight. We're gonna bite and hit and scratch."

The band was playing an old Quiet Riot tune.

"They think you're some rag-tag group that doesn't know how to play football," Trost said. "I'm ready to go into a war. I'm ready to go into a war with you people."

A group of cheerleaders ran past, into position.

"No matter what the scoreboard says, you guys give me all you've got."

The band played on, the Slinger squad emerging from the distant school building.

"Every play," Trost shouted. Louder now: "You take no quarter, you give no quarter."

He had the players put on their helmets and stare at the Slinger squad, dressed in all red — jerseys, pants and helmets — as they ran through a line of flags held up by the cheerleaders. At Shorewood, there was no cheerleading squad at all. Cheerleaders were phased out in the mid-1980s, as the popularity of girls sports rose and there were fewer and fewer who wanted to squeeze into sweaters and skirts and cheer for the guys. Officials had discarded the notion of allowing just the Messmer cheerleaders on the sideline. The flags fluttered as the Slinger players, almost 50 of them, trotted through. It was like waiting for a train, there were so many who ran past.

Before they ran to the sideline, Rob Wyatt told everyone to bow their heads. A pre-game prayer was OK, Trost had decided, if initiated by one of the players. As Rob led the prayer, the announcer read off the names of the Shorewood-Messmer defense, no one there to run onto the field. The announcer turned to the Slinger offense, and the first player ran through a giant paper sign, held aloft by the cheerleaders.

This was not Shorewood.

In Slinger, football meant something.

"We pray through Jesus. Amen," Rob said.

Then he gathered them in and, with everyone's helmets raised, shouted out the breakdown, which seemed to get more elaborate as the season went on, each call and response:

"Are you ready?" — "Yeah."

"I said, ARE YOU READY." — "YEAH!"

"What time is it?" — "Game time!"

"What time is it? — "Game time!"

"Breakdown" — "Huh."

"Breakdown." — "Huh."

"One, two, three" — "Soldiers!"

The kickoff went to Maurice Ragsdale, who still had the kick return assignment, even though he had been removed from punts. He gathered the ball off the ground and took it out to the 25 yard line. There was some clapping on the sideline, but more uncertainty than enthusiasm. Shorewood never had much of any success against Slinger in the past. A friend of Trost's came down from the stands and stood with the players, clapping loudly and shouting, "Fire up, fire up." That picked the team up a bit.

Over on the Slinger side, mixed in with the home crowd, sat the O'Harrows — Dave, the former quarterback, his father and mother. Dave had stayed home from school all week. He wouldn't go back to class at Messmer, as his father had hoped. And his father wouldn't sign the papers to let Dave return to his old school, where he felt more comfortable. Dave had come to the game because his father insisted. Mr. O'Harrow hoped seeing the guys, seeing the team play, would rekindle Dave's enthusiasm.

On the field, Ronell Halbert settled in at quarterback. He wore the wristband now. He had won the spot, as if there was ever much doubt, at least until the coaches could bring Micah along and get Ronell back over to receiver. First play, a handoff to fullback Evan Rivera, who plunged forward for a few yards. A safe call. The next play, a pitch, went to Mark Moore. Another safe call. But Mark was knocked backwards, caught behind the line, and the ball was sent tumbling to the grass. A Slinger player fell on it, to a loud cheer from the stands. One play later and Slinger was in the end zone, 7-0.

"Let's go," Trost yelled. "We gotta fight."

Maurice returned the kick to the 26 yard line this time, brought down by a mass of red jerseys, five, maybe six guys. Was anyone blocking at all? Evan got the ball again, up the middle, three yards. Now Mark took the toss and ran toward the right sideline, following Ronell, who became a blocker on the play. Mark's hand was almost on Ronell's hip, as if reaching out for balance. Then, in an instant, Mark sliced through a gap and turned up the wide open field, Slinger players lunging after him.

"Go baby!" Trost yelled.

The players jumped and shouted, slapped hands. Mark slipped into the end zone.

Punch.

Counter punch.

"Yeah, we're in a war," Trost shouted. "Let's go."

On the field, the two-point attempt failed, so the score was 7-6.

Drew O'Malley kicked off and the ball sailed, driving the Slinger player back toward his own goal line. He caught it, paused to shift his weight forward and then sprinted up the field, past one defender, past another and another.

Touchdown, 14-6.

Another cheer from the Slinger side.

In the distance, there was the dull rumble of thunder.

This time, though, there was no counter punch. Just one punch after another. A blocked punt was returned for a Slinger score. Then Slinger had a long drive for a touchdown. Then Shorewood-Messmer punted and the punt was returned for a touchdown. At the end of the first quarter, the score was 35-6. The offense was moving the ball, moving it, moving it and then throwing it away. The defense had barely been on the field, the Slinger scores came so fast and so furious.

There was more thunder, lightning, everything growing more intense.

In the second quarter, Slinger finally was stopped. This time, Trost sent Ronell back to receive the punt. He shook his head. Waved Trost off. Too tired.

"You can do it," said Coach Smith. "You gotta believe. Quit shaking your head."

Ronell went out to get the punt, but continued to shake his head, confidence replaced by fatigue. The ball sailed through the air and Ronell raised his hand and waved his arm, signaling for a fair catch. The ball tumbled closer, struck him in the chest and the ball bounced to the ground.

Another fumble. Ronell dove forward, the ball rolling just beyond his fingers. Several Slinger players thundered closer and slid to the ground, arms outstretched, grasping for the same ball.

"We got it," Smith said.

"No, we don't," said Trost, disgusted.

The Slinger players jumped up, pointed toward the end zone. Finally, the referees did the same. Slinger ball. Two plays this time.

Another touchdown.

At halftime, they gathered under the goal post again. The Slinger band marched onto the field, where it played a Van Halen song, as if the school was stuck somewhere in the 1980s, and the Slinger team lined up in front of the stands to be introduced. It was parents night and many parents wore buttons that held photographs of their sons. Everyone seemed to know everyone. Friends, neighbors, family.

The players sat on the ground, sapped of enthusiasm, if not strength. There were no reports of bad blood or bad words on the field, but who had time to say anything, with all the interceptions and fumbles? No one wanted to look at Trost.

"We gave them everything they got," said Trost, angry, pacing.

The team sat just beyond the edge of the light and, though the field was bright with Slinger pride, they sat in the dimness. Evan Rivera and Drew O'Malley stepped back in the shadows, behind the scoreboard, and took a leak. Mr. Wyatt had brought Gatorade again and empty plastic bottles were everywhere. The coaches talked about changing the formation, maybe putting two tight ends in, giving up on the pass all together.

The storm was closer now. It seemed to close in from every direction. Thunder was overhead. Lightning licked the edge of the sky. A Slinger official said they may call the game.

"They cancel, does that mean we get to play again?" asked Sebastian Negron, a Messmer senior, who was getting some time at safety.

It was an innocent question, but one that got other players excited. Maybe they could go back. Yes. Start everything over. A second chance. But the thought was quickly nixed by the coaches. If anything, they'd have to come back next week and play the second half from where the first one ended — 42-6.

There was silence now. The band was done.

The team returned to the sideline and, in a moment, there was the squawk of the announcer saying the game has been cancelled and fans should head home. The team stopped its warm ups and prepared to go find the bus. Then the announcer said the game was only delayed and they trudged across the field to the school building to wait out the storm.

Lightning again.

"Whoooaaa." Several said it at once.

"Way out here in Slinger, they have tornados out here," said Jonathan Williams, as if the team had somehow wound up in Kansas rather than Washington County.

It started to rain, slowly at first.

Dave O'Harrow and his family were already headed to their car. They drove back to Milwaukee, windshield wipers slicing through the rain. There was no rekindled enthusiasm for Dave. A game like that, how could there be? What a disaster it all had been, the transfer, the team. Maybe if it wasn't his senior year, Dave thought. Maybe if there was more time to make friends. Maybe if he felt more at home at Messmer. Maybe if it all was different. On Monday, Mr. O'Harrow would sign the paperwork and Dave would go back to his old school.

Football, it turned out, didn't fill a void for Dave. It

left him empty.

As the team sat in a second-floor locker room — the girls' locker room again, this time complete with a tampon machine and curling iron — the coaches waited at the bottom of the steps, Trost standing in the open doorway.

"I wish the rain had come right after we scored," he said, dejected.

The other coaches sat on the stairs. Outside, the field still glowed in the distance. The rain came down harder. Not in sheets, but steady streaks, the drops almost twinkling in the overhead lights. Lighting stabbed the horizon and lit the sky.

"Three times she said we were playing for next year," said Trawitzki.

He meant Cindy Wilburth, the Shorewood athletic director. He was recounting a conversation from a few days earlier. And, truth be told, they were playing for next year. For next year and the year after that. There were 28 players on the freshman squad, the most in years. They'd arrive at the varsity level with experience, perhaps even more commitment, having gone through a season once. And there was a lot of talent among the juniors and sophomores — Nate, Rob, Ronell, Marty, even Pertrell, when he showed up.

"She may be playing for next year," said Coach Carroll.

"We won't have a No. 22 next year," said Trost.

Mark.

The Slinger athletic director stopped by and told them the storm was expected to last another hour. Trost assured him they wanted to play. If not tonight, next week.

"I'm not a quitter," he said. The guy left and Trost turned to the other coaches: "A hundred dollars says we're done."

A cool breeze drifted in through the door, blowing some drops inside. They talked about the game, the irony of the

team losing a quarterback, barely getting the offense together and then running the ball up and down the field
— 129 yards for Mark, 55 for Evan — while the special
teams, which got extra practice time, suffered the meltdown. The team seemed to have a mental block with
Slinger, just like with Whitefish Bay, defeated before the
bus even pulled into the parking lot. They talked about
how they were asking too much of the cornerbacks on
defense, putting everything on Mark on offense, who still
didn't seem ready to carry the team.

"Half the time Mark was going about 40%," said Coach
Carroll. "The other half about 80%."

"It was 100% when he broke that one open," said Trost.

After a few minutes, the game was officially postponed.
The players climbed on the bus and the windows fogged
up. Trost pulled off his shirt and wiped the front window
clear. The headlights cut through the rain.

"See, I even give the shirt off my back for this team,"
Trost declared.

Forced humor. No one laughed. The players were unsure if they were supposed to.

As they drove away, the lights on the field were still
on. The truck from the TV station was still parked there,
its radar dish pointed toward the sky, ready to transmit a
story back to Milwaukee. It would focus on all the posi-
tives of the partnership, the camaraderie, the song-sing-
ing, the jokes about the nickname.

And, of course, it would mention the score.

Chapter 7
"Are we at war?"

The whistle blew and Martin Wallner got up from the ground and shook his head. He had hit the guy, hit him square and hit him hard, but the runner spun out of it, half-dancing past him and into the clear. It wasn't the first time.

"Lemme get one more shot," Marty said. "One more shot."

There was sweat running down his face. The afternoon was hot and the ground was raw, the grass in the spot long trampled away. And they had been at the Oklahomas for what seemed like hours. Pounding. Grinding. Pounding. This was the payback for the pitiful performance against Slinger. There had been no day-after practice on Saturday, so today, Monday, was the first chance the coaches had with the team and Trost had decided there was only one way to make them tougher — to have them do Oklahomas over and over until they were so mad they did them hard and did them right. It was meant to toughen the team up, but it was more like tenderizing, all the pounding and pounding. "We're gonna hit for two hours out here," Trost declared at the start, to groans from the players. Trost had replayed the game in his head all weekend and it always came back to this: Slinger was the bully on the beach and Shorewood-Messmer was the pipsqueak who had sand kicked in his face, yet refused to get mad, let alone get even.

Now Marty, the smallest player on the team, was up,

fists clenched.

"C'mon," Marty said.

There was a day years ago, back when Marty was playing youth soccer, that the coach made the team do sprints
at the end of practice. They ran, two players at a time,
down and back, with the winner getting to sit out while
the loser ran again against the next guy and the next, until
he won a match up. Marty, playing on a higher age group
team, ran the first sprint and lost. He ran the second one,
but was so far behind at the turning point, he threw his
cap to the ground and walked back. The moment would
have been unimportant, but with his father watching, it
became a lesson instead. Mark Wallner, a sales manager
for an employee benefits company, had arrived early to
pick Marty up. He was appalled. "Don't ever let me see
you do that again," he told his son.

At various times, Mr. Wallner felt he might be pushing Marty too hard, or coming close to it. With his own
bad legs, Mr. Wallner was never able to play organized
sports, but two brothers were stars on the Shorewood football team and he sometimes wondered what kind of athlete he would have been, if not for the polio. He knew the
best chance Marty had in organized sports would come
from working hard, though Marty would say he never felt
any pressure to be an athlete. In any case, like the times
when 5-year-old Marty tried to run past his father on the
living room floor — never stop moving the feet — the
new message stuck: Never, *ever*, give up.

Marty waited for Trost.

Trost nodded.

Marty was in as the linebacker, but needed another six
inches and 40 pounds to truly look the part. Strips of
athletic tape were wrapped around the bottom of his pant
legs to keep the kneepads from slipping out. Marty buckled his helmet and rolled his head, like a boxer trying to
get his neck loose. He set himself again in the familiar

crouch, hands ready. Now. The linemen crashed together and the runner dodged past, legs high and — now — Marty was on him, shoulder into the guy's gut, driving him back, dislodging the ball. It bounced to the grass and the runner was driven to the ground. And now Marty was up, scrambling over the fallen body, landing on the ball, clutching it hard to his chest.

"Yeah, yeah, yeah!"

It was Coach Carroll shouting. But he was shouting in response to a play with the other group of players, where Rob Wyatt, on the line, had driven Justin Moore — Flex — up and back, his feet peddling, until Flex tumbled backwards. A pancake.

It tasted good.

"There it is, Marty!" shouted Trost.

He turned, saw Flex getting up and blew his whistle.

"I have four guys not quitting," Trost shouted. "I love you all."

He could have kissed them.

All was not perfect, of course. It still took too long to get the team going each day. Trost had been on Rob from almost the start of practice, calling for harder hits, pleading for them and then screaming with joy when they came. But, slowly, it was working. Even Flex, the victim on several of the match ups with Rob, had better form. He was staying low on defense, not committing to one side or the other, which allowed the runner to skirt past.

"Nice job, Justin Moore," Trost shouted a few minutes later, after another good play. "Oh my God, a football player showed up."

And then Flex was into it, too, slipping past his opponent to make a tackle, driving hard even if he couldn't get there, pounding the ground if he missed a play. At one point, Trost told him to get a drink if he needed one. Flex shook his head.

"I can get him, Coach," he said, lining up again. "I can

get him."

Confidence is a funny thing. It is there one moment, gone the next. It can take days, weeks, to build up, as delicate as a house of cards. But pull a single card away and it all collapses into nothing. The team had been like that last year. They'd do great in practice, come storming out of the locker room, all piss and vinegar, and then freeze up on the field. It was like they went into brainlock or something, one bad play leading to another, leading to another, leading to disaster, then defeat.

It got so bad, Trost finally called in a psychology professor from the University of Wisconsin-Milwaukee to talk with the team. They met, just the players and the shrink, who urged them to focus on themselves, not how their teammates were playing. To focus on having fun, not getting down when the first thing went wrong. The episode prompted a story in the daily newspaper — the biggest mention of Shorewood football in years. Trost sometimes chuckled about it, the idea of turning the locker room benches into a bunch of psychiatrist couches. Only in Shorewood, he thought, would it work. And the team had, in fact, won the game against Brown Deer.

If there was ever a time that confidence was critical, it was this week. Next up, on Saturday, was Watertown Luther Prep, the toughest team on the schedule. Tougher, even, than Whitefish Bay. Luther Prep was ranked sixth among all teams in the Milwaukee area, third among schools its size statewide. In more than three seasons in the Parkland Conference, Prep hadn't lost a single football game. The school, with about 560 students, is affiliated with the Wisconsin Evangelical Lutheran Synod, aimed at training students for pastoral or teaching work. The students, from 28 states and eight foreign countries, live in dorms on a sprawling campus. As far as opponents were concerned, Luther Prep was a burgeoning athletic powerhouse, a jock factory, able to lure good athletes from across the country.

The Luther Prep game Saturday would be the last of the toughest games on the schedule and the last of the long road trips. The next two teams — Pewaukee and St. Francis — were good, but at least they were home games. If Shorewood-Messmer somehow could steal one, the final three could still be the playoff run.

Another group lined up for Oklahomas.

Another hit, another whistle and another shout of excitement.

Another card carefully put into place.

The first plane struck the first building at 7:46 a.m. Milwaukee time, sending smoke billowing into the New York City skyline. Then came the second plane, this one on live television, slicing in like a bullet. Word spread quickly at both schools and TVs were clicked on. And then the twin towers of the World Trade Center fell, crumbling into a heap of devastation.

First one and then the other, they fell.

Practice was cancelled.

They returned to practice the next day, of course, because they had to. Life went on. Somehow, life went on and so, somehow, the season went on. This time, though, all of the players — Shorewood and Messmer alike — carried some of those adult worries with them. It was as if the ball was somehow heavier, the ground uneven.

"Are we at war?" asked Jason Davis, a Messmer sophomore, as the first players stood outside, waiting for the stragglers to get dressed.

The last time the nation had been at war, in the Persian Gulf, none of the guys on the team was past the third grade.

"They don't draft you if you're not 18 and still in high school do they?" asked Mark Moore, to no one in particular.

No one was sure. No one answered.

It is rare that you can cite a single day, an instant in which everything changes and everything that follows is different from everything that went before. They say high school graduation is such a moment, when you walk across the stage, when you take the diploma in your hand and move the tassel over, left to right. Youth to adulthood. But that walk across the stage is more about symbolism than anything. In truth, the shift to adulthood comes gradually — in the loss of a parent, in getting a job to help pay the bills, in the struggle to make the right choices and avoid drugs and violence. The shift comes here and there. And then, one day, it is no longer the burdens of adulthood that intrude upon youth, but the reverse. It is the pure moments that come in flashes, each a glimpse of the youth that was there before.

Trost wanted the football field, for this team especially, if only for two hours a day, to be a place of youth. If he could have, he would have drawn a line around the field and kept all of the problems out. Kept the team back where it was in July, on the last day of summer camp, just running around in the sun, the laughter as easy as the evening breeze. Problems, adult problems, had already cost the team George Lasley. They had cost the team Dave O'Harrow. They made Pertrell Mallett a constant question mark. The same for Maurice Ragsdale, who seemed to veer back and forth between commitment and cashing it all in. They were a test for Mark Moore and his brother, Micah. The team had so much baggage, Trost could have been the bellhop as easily as the coach.

Now he gathered them in.

"You know, we lost more people yesterday than in some wars," Trost said, shaking his head. "The thing about terrorism is it can happen anyplace, anywhere, anytime."

The players looked at him, waiting, perhaps, for something more, some insight to put it all into perspective, some assurance that things would continue on as normal, something else, something more. The way a father, a mother, would always find the right and perfect words. Instead, Trost blew his whistle.

"Let's go."

The stretching began. Trost took attendance.

Drew O'Malley was missing, but excused. He had the internship at the fire station and was stuck out on a late call. Drew had always wanted to be a firefighter, at least since he was in the sixth grade at St. Robert Elementary School and wrote a report on what firefighters do, even getting to go to the fire house to see the giant trucks and the helmets and the heavy coats and the big boots lined up for the next emergency. The station was about a block away from Drew's house and he would often hear the trucks racing past. When the word of the terrorist attacks first spread, Drew was in class and watched as the World Trade Center towers fell and the sirens screamed and the death toll rose and the whole world changed. And then, when he went to the firehouse that afternoon, as everyone sat in front of the TV and watched the devastation come into focus, Drew decided he didn't want to be a firefighter any less. If anything, he wanted to be one even more. It soon became a high compliment from the coaches: "That Drew, he's a fireman."

On offense, the team worked on a new play, hoping it would catch Luther Prep off guard. It wasn't a traditional option, in which the quarterback could run, pitch to the fullback or pitch to the running back, but it had an option feel to it. Ronell, still at quarterback, handed off to Mark who, as he reached the edge of the line could tuck the ball and go for it or pitch it to fullback Evan Rivera who would take a wider path to the outside. They ran it a few times, but there was little enthusiasm.

It was a perfect fall day. Sunny. A slight breeze. Some clouds in the distance, the sky a deep, clear blue. There was a junior varsity soccer game going on down on the big field, Shorewood vs. Slinger. If anyone at Shorewood cared much about the football rivalry or Friday night's debacle, the soccer match would have been a chance for a measure of revenge. But that got barely a thought. It had been decided, even before the terrorist attacks, that they wouldn't go back to finish the game, which ended with the half-time rain. In the stands, the crowd was sparse, but there was something normal about the scene, kids running through pre-game drills, parents watching in the stands. It was as if at least one thing hadn't changed.

Then there was a squeak and a voice echoed over the public address system: "Could we please have a moment of silence for the events that happened yesterday?"

"Helmets off," Trost said to the guys on the practice field.

The players stared at the ground for a moment.

"Helmets on."

And it was back to work.

A few minutes later, as Trost called out another play, he looked around at the group. Several guys were standing near the back. One had an ice bag on his shoulder, held in place with plastic wrap. Another held an ice pack to his elbow. Another had a jammed finger. Yet another was walking from the direction of the trainer's room, more ice.

"This is like a M*A*S*H unit," Trost said loudly. "Here comes another one."

His voice was filled with disbelief.

On the shorthanded scout defense, Maurice Ragsdale, usually a safety or cornerback, put himself in at lineman, just so they'd have a four-man front. As the offense got set, he'd start in one gap, make a 360-degree turn and jump into another gap. Players rolled their eyes. Typical Maurice. There were only seven guys on defense, and yet on the snap Maurice would snake through, ending up in the backfield. Once the play was over, he would pounce back across the line, scoot into place and do it again.

"Dude, what is up with Maurice?" asked Mark Williams, a Messmer senior who was getting some time on the offensive and defensive line. He stood holding an ice pack to his elbow.

"Don't laugh at him," Coach Trawitzki said. "He's taking your position."

"Let's go line," Maurice shouted.

Trost walked over to Mark Williams.

Mark lived, literally, across the freeway from Messmer. He lived with his grandmother, who brought him to Milwaukee from Philadelphia when he was 10 and, after two years in the public high schools, sent him to Messmer. His grandmother always told him not to quit and Mark had promised himself, no matter how hard it got, he never would.

"What happened to you?" Trost asked.

"Elbow," Mark said simply.

Trost pretended to kiss it.

"There. All better. Who else?"

The jammed finger. Kiss. All better. The sore shoulder. Kiss. All better. Feet shuffled in embarrassment. In football, there is an ethic. You play hurt. Trost harped on it over and over: There is a difference between being hurt and being injured. Being injured was a broken bone, a torn ligament, a concussion. Tight muscles? Sore shoulder? Jammed finger? That was hurt.

"At this point in the season, we're all hurt," said Trost, who quarterbacked the scout offense every day. "Hell, I'm hurt."

They tried another play and this time there was a shout: "Ow, ow, ow."

It was Blake Comer, a Messmer junior who was rotating with Nate Shorter and Rob Wyatt at offensive tackle. His elbow had hit a helmet. The loud bang startled everyone.

"Where does it hurt?" asked Coach Trawitzki, rushing

over. "Let me see it."

Blake waved him off. Mark Williams dropped his ice pack.

"I'm ready to go," Mark said.

As players got to Shorewood on Saturday morning, they passed workers hanging red, white and blue bunting from the street lights along Capitol Drive. A large "Peace on Earth" sign was displayed on the lawn in front of the school, a Christmas decoration brought out of storage. Like the bunting, used on the Fourth of July, it was instant patriotism, but with a Shorewood twist.

The day before, Sept. 14, was the day William Rehnquist, chief justice of the U.S. Supreme Court and a 1942 Shorewood graduate, was to be recognized at a special program at the high school. His trip was cancelled in the wake of the terrorist attacks, but about 70 protesters from a loose coalition of liberal groups came to the school anyway. While most people in the country were fixated on revenge, the event in Shorewood became an anti-war protest, complete with everyone singing "We Shall Overcome" and holding hands in a giant circle. In the evening, there was a community prayer service at an area church and many residents set out candles on their porches and steps, which were left to burn until morning.

In the locker room, the players got dressed, but it was as if their energy was already sapped. As the coaches wandered in and out, there was some talk, mostly idle. The music was quieter, no longer the soundtrack for the season. In the office, Trost reported to the other coaches about the trip he and Trawitzki took to scout Pewaukee vs. Dominican, two upcoming opponents. Dominican doesn't want to hit, Trost said, and Pewaukee, though precise and disciplined, was beatable.

Meanwhile, Ronell Halbert and Rob Wyatt had gone to see Rufus King play against Marshall, their old team. It

Milwaukee Journal Sentinel photo by Benny Sieu

Head coach Jim Trost criticizes the team's lackluster first-half performance in the locker room at Watertown Luther Prep, a 52-0 loss. The incident nearly lead to Trost's dismissal during the season.

was a match up between two City Conference schools, which meant tight security at the games. They talked about the game in the locker room.

"Guess who had the nerve to show up?" Rob asked, loud enough so everyone would hear.

Dave O'Harrow.

"You talk to him?" someone asked.

"Naw, he was on the other side," said Rob. "He came there with his friends."

"White friends?" asked Flex, looking up.

That had long been a question among the players about Dave. Did he leave Messmer because he was white and almost everyone else was black? Those on the team thought so. One reported hearing Dave say something about feeling "outnumbered." Others saw Dave in the hallway, walking by himself, isolating himself. The players felt like they had given Dave a chance, but he hadn't given them one.

Dave didn't see it that way. For him, it was more of an issue of feeling comfortable. He was comfortable at his old school, where his friends helped him deal with his father's health problems. It was his senior year and he didn't want to make an adjustment to all new classes, all new teachers and all new faces. It wasn't worth it just to play football, when he didn't really want to play football.

"Yeah," said Rob.

Dave was with white friends.

Players nodded. It confirmed what many had suspected. And it was suddenly as if Dave was inauthentic, a fraud, never really one of them at all.

Race was rarely discussed in the locker room, but it was always there, in the background, like a shadow. In that sense, it was like the Milwaukee area's silent conversation. It was there in the hip-hop music that normally pulsated from the CD player, though some took refuge with headsets and Metallica or Limp Bizkit. It was there in the fashion trend of the day — pants slung low, boxers peeking out at the waist — something several of the white players emulated. It was there when an opposing player was referred to as "that white guy," a phrase that would never be tolerated in reverse.

In every instance, it seemed, a subtle line was being drawn. Black was here, white was there. Poor was here, rich was there. You may be allowed to step across the line sometimes, but it remained a line.

"Dave tried to act all hard," Ronell said, laughing. He meant tough.

Drew O'Malley announced that he, too, had been at the King vs. Marshall game. Drew seemed to cross the line more easily than Dave ever had. He stood now, relaxed, jeans pulled low, the top of his boxers showing, hands in pockets.

"Where were you at?" asked Ronell.

Under the scoreboard, Drew said. Not in the stands.

Over where that big dog kept barking.

"You didn't see us?" Ronell asked. "Everybody got up in the fourth quarter."

Drew shook his head.

There was nearly a fight between guys from the two schools and Ronell told the story. He enjoyed telling it, because telling it made him seem tougher for having been there. Ronell wore his time at Marshall as a badge of honor. Ready-made street credentials. One guy almost got "banged," Ronell said, and people called for backup on their cell phones and all of a sudden extra cars pulled into the parking lot and the guy who was the target kept saying, "Ain't no drama, ain't no drama," trying desperately to make the excitement die down.

Everyone stopped and listened.

After a moment, Ronell asked Jay White where he lived, joking someone told him it was in Milwaukee, over on 19th St. No one needed to be told that was a tough area. Tough and dangerous. Tough and dangerous and black.

"Naw," Jay said. "I stay in Shorewood."

Jay, a senior, had moved to Shorewood from Raleigh, North Carolina, before his freshman year, when his father got a high-level job with Wisconsin Electric. Before they arrived, Jay checked out several area high schools — Mequon, Homestead, Whitefish Bay — but settled on Shorewood, where he found he had a tough time fitting in with all the cliques and circles of friends that had formed back in grade school. He didn't like the gossipy nature of the school, everybody in everyone's business, talking about who had what and who was dating who. Last year, Jay White found a comfortable spot when he joined the football team, though he sometimes felt out of sorts and unsure on the field. He had written "White Boy" on the tape above his locker — ironically, of course, though it took a while for some to get it.

"You live on Lake Drive," Rob said, piping up. "Like

Drew here."

It was an accusation, not a statement.

Another line. Stronger this time. A little deeper.

The bus ride seemed to go faster since the sun was bright, not disappearing on the evening horizon. The city slipped into suburbs and then into farmland, the farmland gave rise to small towns. There were flags on porches, flags from light posts, flags flying from the roofs of passing cars, flags spray painted in the grass.

There was more room on the bus this week. After the losses to Lakeside Lutheran and Slinger, several players — including Abdul the running back — stopped coming. The coaches, as usual, sat in the front. They had succeeded in getting more players into the lineup — only five now were starting both ways, down from nine in the first week. It could be three next week, once Micah Moore and Jerrel Jackson, a Messmer sophomore, were plugged in somewhere on defense. Both were out today, Micah with a tight back, Jerrel with neck problems. But Pertrell Mallett, who the coaches had scorned as afraid when he missed the Slinger game, was back and after a strong performance Wednesday in the Oklahoma drills was starting on defense. Pertrell was a machine that day, smashing into the ball carrier at the line, chasing him down the field, never stopping, never quitting. But he still was a wildcard. Later in the same practice, when he was supposed to be blocking for the returner on the punt squad, Pertrell got turned around and tried to tackle him instead.

"Who are the cornerbacks?" asked Coach Smith.

He had missed the run-through practice the night before, while working the late shift at an Open Pantry convenience store.

"Mark and Timmy," said Coach Trawitzki.

There was a pause.

"How's that gonna go?" Smith asked.

He meant Timmy Lathrop, who usually played line or linebacker.

Trawitzki slowly made the sign of the cross.

On the other side of the aisle, Coach Carroll and Trost talked about the need for the team to start hitting from the opening kickoff. Trost said they'd do Oklahomas during warm ups to get the players fired up.

"Never saw that before," said Coach Carroll.

"You're gonna see it today."

Indeed, of the hundreds of high school football teams in Wisconsin, Shorewood-Messmer may have been the only one still doing so much hitting in practice. Most schools stopped after the first game of the season. In five years on the staff at Marquette High School, one of the perennial football powers in the Milwaukee area, trainer Steve Wittemann had seen the Oklahoma drill only one time. Wittemann was uncomfortable with the amount of hitting and, after that early-season blowup between the coaches, had begun to separate himself from Trost and his hard-line approach, keeping notes on some of the confrontations over player safety.

The trip to Watertown, about 50 miles west of Milwaukee, took less than an hour and once the bus pulled off the main street there was Luther Prep. It looked like a college campus, the lawn manicured, only a few fallen leaves here and there. There were tennis courts, a softball diamond, a soccer field with a track around it, a sand volleyball pit and, of course, the football field, lines fresh and grass cut perfect.

"So that is how they get all the good athletes," marveled Mr. Wyatt, who pulled into the lot about the same time the bus did and had walked over to the coaches.

"They recruit 'em from all over the country," said Trost.

The trip to the locker room was like being led through a maze, turn after turn, past the Uniform Drying Room, the Training Room, the Wrestling Room, the Referee's

Room — all helpfully labeled for visitors — and into a small locker room, which had a garage-style door that was lifted to reveal an even larger locker room. There was even a separate Towel Room. The green chalkboard in the small locker room had pictures of volleyballs and the words "Go Mariners" on it — St. Francis must have been a recent guest. As the coaches talked strategy, the players quickly got dressed in the other room. One forgot his cleats and checked to see if anyone had extras. Jonathan Williams pulled on a pair of white socks with fat red stripes down the side. Evan Rivera and Drew O'Malley, the Shorewood seniors, put on black socks. Everyone was doing their own thing.

Trawitzki called the team together, drew up a Luther Prep play that had been seen the night before in the freshman game, explained how to defend against it and then, no eraser to be found, wiped the board clean with his palm. The coaches issued basic instructions: Play hard. Have fun. Fly to the football.

"Hit hard," said Trost. "Tackle low. If nothing else, do that."

They walked out, cleats clicking on the floor, one turn, then another, then another, past the Referee's Room, the Wrestling Room, the Training Room, the Uniform Drying Room and stepped outside at the edge of the field. They ran along the end line, up the sideline to the opposite end zone and then out in their pattern to start stretching. It took Trost all of about a minute to see Jonathan had the wrong socks on.

"We're wearing all white," he said, voice angry.

Then Trost spotted Drew and Evan, up at the front as captains, both in black socks. In theory, the team could be penalized for not having consistent uniforms. Players already had been penalized several times for not having mouthguards in or for tying knots in the armpits of their jerseys, so the big floppy sleeves disappeared and they

looked stronger and sleeker. Drew and Evan were also missing the blue M's for Messmer on their helmets.

"Pull the socks down," Trost said.

He was more irritated because it was Drew and Evan.

"We're a team," he said.

On the other side of field, Luther Prep ran out in a
single-file line and high-stepped it across the end zone, no
wasted time, no wasted steps. Forty-four players in uniform. They each wore gold pants with blue and white
stripes, navy blue socks, a navy blue jersey with white
numbers and gold trim, plus gold helmets — the metallic
kind of gold worn by the University of Notre Dame. They
clapped rhythmically, over periodic, piercing shouts —
"Aieeee" — the kind that in a Western movie would have
instilled fear of an ambush.

"We're gonna do Oklahomas to send a message," Coach
Trawitzki told the team, over the din from the other end
of the field.

The only fans in the Shorewood-Messmer stands were
Mr. Wyatt and his daughter — Ronell's mother, Rob's
sister. Only a handful of others would make it before game
time, all parents or family.

"Let's do it, man," said Nate Shorter, his voice com-
manding, intent.

"Don't play like it's Luther Prep," said Rob Wyatt, offering his own advice. "Just play like you're in the back
yard — street ball. And have fun."

He called them in. They raised their helmets over his
head.

"1-2-3," Rob said.

"Hit," came the response.

Everyone took someone else's hand and then they
walked backward as far as they could go until they were in
a circle. Four guys were called to the middle, gladiator
style. The team started clapping, slowly at first and then
louder. There was the clash of pads, grunts of effort, cheers

from those forming the circle.

"Good hitting, y'all," said Drew O'Malley.

A few players from Luther Prep glanced over their shoulders and shook their heads, more out of bemusement than fear. They had never seen such a thing either.

Before the game, both teams lined up along the sideline for the National Anthem, held their helmets at their hips, and looked at the American flag set at half-staff above the scoreboard, limp for lack of a breeze. Major League Baseball had cancelled its games that week, which would end up pushing back the World Series. The Saturday college football games had been cancelled. So had the Sunday NFL games. There were concerns about airline travel, about stadiums becoming targets.

But high school football went on.

That was appropriate, of course. High school is small, it is local, it is intimate. And it is innocent. So, across the country they played on Friday night, on the plains and in the mountains, down south and up north, in the big cities and the small towns. At some schools, there was a prayer over the public address system, at others a request for silence. In some places, teams shook hands before the game, not after. Or they followed their captain, who carried a flag, onto the field or stood silent as Taps was played before kick off, the mournful notes hanging in the night air.

High school is rooted close to home, to a place where the head cheerleader may be the baby sitter, the quarterback may deliver the morning newspaper and the tuba player may be the kid bagging groceries at the Mini-Mart. So, on Friday night, like the candles left out on the Shorewood porches, the lights went on. And in the darkness everywhere, high school football stadiums glowed with comfort and defiance.

Now, on Saturday, the final games of the week would be played. Luther Prep played most of its home games on

Saturdays since, despite its rambling facilities, the football field had no lights. The players squinted in the afternoon sun, some mouthing the words to the National Anthem, others silent. Then they pulled on their helmets,
faces disappearing from view. They buckled their chin
straps, adjusted shoulder pads.

Ready for this week's war.

There was a tradition at Luther Prep. Every time the
team scored, several students ran down from the stands,
arms waving. They ran past the bleachers, dropped for
pushups — one for each point — then ran back to their
seats.

They did seven pushups with 11:09 left in the first
quarter, when Prep scored on its first play, after recovering
a fumbled Shorewood-Messmer snap. JoJo Moore, the
team's star running back, took it in from 22 yards out.
They did seven more pushups with 8:01 left, after Moore
scored on a pitch to the outside, 24 yards this time. Three
more with 2:48 left in the first quarter, after Shorewood-
Messmer stopped Luther Prep on the three yard line and
Prep settled for a field goal. Seven more after a touchdown
with 8:09 left before the half. And seven more with 1:05
left, after Prep's first string returned to the field and scored
on a pass play.

The halftime tally: 31-0.

It was all too familiar. There was no fight, no life, no
anything. Even Nate Shorter, one of the most dependable
players, at one point limped to the sideline, dropped his
helmet and grimaced in pain. He rubbed his bad knee.

"It hurts like crap," he told Steve Wittemann, the
trainer.

With scarcely a minute left, Mark Moore and Drew
O'Malley went back to receive the kickoff. Drew had now
replaced Maurice Ragsdale in the kick return spot, since
Maurice had missed practice and arrived that morning

head-hanging sick. Drew took the ball near the right sideline, but when he looked up there were three, no four,
Luther Prep players closing in. No one had blocked, or if
they tried to, they had wound up on the ground, and now
a Prep player pounded into Drew, a brutal hit that stunned
the coaches.

A play or two later, the half mercifully ended.

"Sprint to the locker room," Trost said, unable to hide
his disgust. He ran ahead of the team. "Let's go."

The team jogged along behind him instead, all way-
ward and half-assed. No pride. Trost paced in the locker
room as he waited for the others to arrive. The players
hung their heads and slumped on the benches or against
the lockers. As Coach Trawitzki stood at the chalkboard,
drawing out defensive adjustments, Trost looked around
and seethed. *Unbelievable*, he thought. Trost didn't expect
to win. Truly didn't. Effort. That is what he wanted. They
talked about it all week. Effort. How many times had he
said it? Effort, effort, effort.

Instead, there was no pride. The players hadn't even
mastered the concept that they all wore white socks because they were one team. Not Shorewood. Not Messmer.
Red and blue make purple. Jogging off the field underlined all of the problems.

Now Trost spoke.

"Turnovers on offense, guys standing all over the field,"
he said. "What do you think this is? What do you think
this is?"

His voice rose, raked with emotion.

"You're afraid, you're cowards, you're afraid."

He pounded the chalkboard, face red, veins in his forehead bulging. He pounded the board and swept Trawitzki's
diagram away with his fist.

"Nothing on that board is going to do you any good,"
Trost declared and pointed at his chest. "If you don't have
it in here, you'll never have it."

He stormed out, the door slamming behind him.

Some players sat with helmets at their feet, others held their helmets in their lap. No one looked at each other, instead staring holes into the floor, the wall, staring right through Coach Trawitzki. In the outer room, Coach Groser, who kept statistics for the varsity games stood quietly. Wittemann taped an ice bag to Nate's knee and slipped out. Mr. Wyatt, having passed out the Gatorade, went outside and back to the sideline, where he paced, shocked at what he had witnessed and unsure what, if anything, to do about it.

It hurt to watch.

"Heads up," Trawitzki said.

He had to tone down Trost's blow torch message. In the second half the team had to do something — any-thing — positive.

"The season is salvageable," he assured them, then added: "I didn't want to bring this up. But think about the firemen in New York. They're working 24 hours straight. Don't you think they're tired?"

There was no answer.

"Guys, suck it up," Trawitzki said. "There's people more tired than you'll ever know."

The team ran back out to the field, quiet, back through the maze. Nate was near the back. He limped up the stairs, a pack of ice wrapped around his left knee, the water soak-ing into his pant leg. Someone asked if he was going to play. Nate nodded.

"Yeah."

On the ride home, the bus was quiet and deflated. The coaches stewing up front, the players bruised and burning in back. The words echoed with them all, like the slam of a locker.

"*You're cowards. You're afraid.*"

In the second half, the team had stopped Luther Prep

a few times, but it was Prep's second string, third string. And the points kept climbing higher, until it was 52-0. Shorewood-Messmer ended with 39 yards of offense — 44 for fullback Evan Rivera, minus-12 for Mark, the rest by Ronell Halbert at quarterback, from when he ran by design or desperation. They had a single first down. Not one pass was attempted. The tackles were brutal and bone-crunching, heads jolted back, the ball jarred loose, players sledgehammered to the hard and dry ground. By the end of the game, it was like Nintendo football. Try a play. Any play. Everything Luther Prep did worked to perfection.

Nate never did get back in. No sense in getting hurt worse. Instead, he sat on the bench, left leg straight out, right leg pumping with anger. His faith in the team, in the season, was fading. Toward the end, on the sideline, Mark Moore shook his head, muttering his frustration. "I'm through with this," he said to Drew.

On the way home, as the bus turned onto the highway, it passed a tidy farm house with a "For Sale" sign in front.

"Hey coach, see that house?" Coach Groser said to Trost. "You win four games and I'll buy it for you."

"What about three wins?" Trost asked. "Do I get half the house?"

"Outhouse," said Groser.

The bus rumbled past the farms and the fields, the small towns, through the suburbs and back toward the city. As they rode, Trost took his clipboard, drew a line down the middle of a sheet of paper and wrote at the top of the left side: "I am committed to becoming a better football player over the next five weeks — coaches included." He signed it, stood up and told the team to read it and sign it, one side or the other.

"Remember," Trost said, "tough times don't last — tough people do."

The phrase had become a bona fide Trost-ism. Like

"take off the dress" and "perfume on a pig," which the coaches sometimes joked should be the unofficial theme for the season.

Montreal Miller, a seldom-used senior from Messmer, was first. He signed and wrote "For sure" in parentheses. Then came Marty, who wrote out, in formal fashion, Martin Wallner. The clipboard was passed to the back, one seat at a time.

The bus driver took Capitol Drive through Milwaukee's western suburbs, then its gritty city stretches, then past Messmer, across the river and back to Shorewood. The ride was hot and stuffy. When the bus arrived, Curtis Jeffries handed the clipboard back to Trost. Curtis didn't say anything. He just glared and turned away.

"Better be 25 names on there," Trost said loudly.

He and Coach Carroll looked over the clipboard and counted. On the "Not Committed" side, someone had written down two names that were later crossed out — George Lasley and Dave O'Harrow. A final indignity for the two who left so early, so much promise unfulfilled. Trost and Carroll counted the rest, evaluating scratches and poor penmanship, some names almost entirely illegible. Trost finally tapped the board.

"There's 25," he said, forgetting the first signature was his.

Later, as Trost drove home to Hartford, following the same route they had just taken, the city giving way again to open fields, he thought about the game and the locker room, all of the anger, all the rage. His anger and his rage. At the first team meeting in August, in addition to victories, he had promised the players one thing: The coaches, no matter what happened, would always be positive.

Man, Trost thought, *I really lost it in there.*

Chapter 8
"Don't put your heads down."

When Coach Trost arrived Monday, the players were all in the locker room, book bags at their feet, sitting on the benches, leaning in doorways, still in street clothes. The events of Saturday had stuck with them, too. Not what happened on the field, for deep down that was expected. But the locker room.

"Let's go," Trost said.

Nothing.

"C'mon."

Still nothing.

"We want to have a meeting," Rob Wyatt told him.

Behind him, others nodded.

There was a chalkboard in the center of the room, the one they had dragged out on the first day of practice to draw up the basic formations. On it, Rob — one of the guys Trost had designated a captain from the start — had written the dictionary definitions for two words:

"**Coward**: One who lacks courage or who is shamefully afraid."

"**Encouragement**: To give courage, to give hope or to give confidence to someone or somebody."

Below the words were six questions: "Are we as a team ready to play? Are the coaches ready to coach? Do the players listen to the coaches? Do the coaches listen to the players? Do the players listen to the players? Do the coaches listen to the coaches?"

The words and questions were Rob's idea, though others had been thinking many of the same things. Rob, searching for the right way to address the problems, had looked up the definitions at home Sunday, wrote the questions out and showed them to the Messmer players in the hallway during the school day, then to the Shorewood players out in the parking lot. Everyone nodded. As they waited, the room felt more crowded than normal, hotter, stuffier. Trost stood in the middle, angry to see everything he was doing questioned. He did a mental count, scanning the room.

"Where's Mark?" Trost asked.

Indeed, Mark Moore was missing. He had gone home after school and his brother, Micah, said he didn't know what was going on. The word among the players was Mark was quitting. Another player lost. How many names had already been stripped from above the lockers?

Not Mark, Trost thought.

With the locker room doors closed, the bad blood spilled out — everywhere. All of the hurt, all of the anger, all of the frustration. All of the ego, the pride, the pressure. Some players complained about practicing every day and sitting the bench on Friday nights. Others challenged the play calling — not a single pass against Luther Prep. One asked why Marty never got a real chance, when he was the hardest worker of all. On it went. Justin Owen, a sophomore who moved to Shorewood from Indiana over the summer, apologized for being hurt so often. He had been penciled in as the starting center, but back problems had kept him on the sideline all season. He looked at Trost and said he was truly in pain. Trost nodded. They talked for about 90 minutes, offering apologies and acknowledging shortfalls, coaches and players alike.

Rob, standing in the middle like a teacher, admitted he hadn't always practiced as hard as he could have, but promised he would now give his all, every day.

"Time to walk the talk," Rob said.

"We have to stay together," declared Drew O'Malley.

"I want to prove the doubters wrong who said we wouldn't be nothing," said Maurice Ragsdale. "I'm tired of hearing that shit at school."

"It's all about winning them four games," said Flex.

He meant the playoffs. The team was still talking about the playoffs, something the coaches had all but promised them from the start. To an outside observer, though, it was plainly ridiculous. In four games, the team had scored exactly twice. They had given up an astonishing 179 points — more than a season's worth for even a bad team. In some games, a first down was a worthy achievement. The team was already on its second starting quarterback and now its star running back was missing.

Trost assured the players the coaches wanted to win. They obsessed over it. Trost and Trawitzki would sometimes talk for hours after practice, go home, and talk more by phone. If the coaches went to the bar, about all they talked about was who was playing well and who wasn't, who needed a nudge, who needed a push and how to get the team past the brutal front-end of the schedule. As they stood in the room, it galled them to be lectured to by the players, some of whom were regular no-shows at practice, to hear them preach the gospel of commitment.

The talk returned to Mark Moore, with Maurice Ragsdale saying maybe they shouldn't go after him if he had made up his mind to quit. But the coaches had gone after George Lasley when he quit the first time. The players went after Drew O'Malley, who returned, and Dave O'Harrow, who would not.

"Raise your hand if you want him back," Trost said, and nearly every hand went up. "OK, if he's here tomorrow, he's back on the team."

Trost didn't waste any time.

"Get dressed," he said. "No pads. Just shorts."

Trost followed the coaches into the office, banged the

door shut and they all vented. It was a near repeat of the meeting back at the start of two-a-days, but even more angry. "Your ego is out of control," shouted Coach Larsen. But Trost couldn't abide that criticism, not from him. In Trost's mind, Larsen ratted everyone out over the disagreement about player safety and the Oklahoma drills. "What happens in the locker room, should stay in the locker room," Trost would often say. "The locker room is sacred." There were questions, too, about Coach Smith — maybe he was getting too close to the players, Mark especially, trying to be a pal when a sterner approach was needed. The coaches questioned whether the team was sincere, or if the meeting was just about guys being lazy. And Rob as the ringleader? The next sprint he ran hard would be the first.

In the locker room, the players pulled on their shorts and prepared for the inevitable sprints.

"If he doesn't come back, we're through," said Flex. He meant Mark.

"He's coming back," said Jason Davis, a Messmer sophomore.

As they talked, Nate Shorter looked at the chalkboard with all the questions and spun it over to see the other side. As the chalkboard flipped, the frame broke loose and the green board banged to the floor. Heads spun and, after a moment, Drew broke the tension.

"Dang, we had that for 25 years," he declared. "Do you know how many losing game plans have been drawn up on that blackboard?"

Finally, the coaches walked out of the office and up the stairs to the practice field. The players followed, looking at each other, unsure how bad it would be.

"We're gonna run like *Amistad*," said Flex, referring to the movie from a few years back about African slaves who mutinied only to be imprisoned again when their ship

Milwaukee Journal Sentinel photo by Benny Sieu

Head coach Jim Trost and assistant Joe Trawitzki show looks of disgust after a loss. Throughout the season, the coaches tried to find ways to motivate the team — and themselves.

was captured. "They're gonna run us like Negro slaves."

Outside, the freshman team was finishing practice by running its own sprints. The team was lined up in the distance and with each sprint, Coach Groser shouted "Messwood!" The players shouted it back and ran to the end, turned and eagerly lined up for another one. While there were some problems with commitment on the freshman team, Groser had convinced most of his rag-tag bunch to buy into his approach, in which the season was a journey from youth into adulthood. Before the games, Groser would sometimes call the players together and ask them a series of questions. Among them: "What do your parents and coaches want from you? Yes. To do your best."

The shout came again.

"Messwood!"

The varsity lined up and the whistle blew and the team ran. And ran. One sprint, another, another. On and on. There were no shouts, no demands from the coaches. It was all up to the players, to show the newly-declared commitment was real.

"How many more of these we running?" Ronell Halbert gasped at one point.

"A lot," Drew said, taking a deep breath, before finishing, "more than this."

The day after the Whitefish Bay game, the team had been at a similar crisis point. It was a point when the coaches could have lost the team as easily as held it together. On that day, the first worst day, the coaches expected three things of the players: Run without complaint, hit without fear and believe without question.

Now, for perhaps the first time in the three weeks since, the first time really since the start of practice, the team ran without complaint.

After the sprints, Trost lined up the offense in a new formation — the fullback behind the quarterback and the running back behind the fullback. They walked through a couple plays, a preview of what to expect tomorrow with Mark gone. Simple stuff. Fullback up the middle. Running back around the corner. The players had been talking among themselves for weeks about using the I-formation to keep the defense off-balance, since Mark could easily go either way with the ball, instead of the looping sprint to the opposite side that had become a fixture of the offense. But Mark was gone and no one showed much enthusiasm.

At the end, Trost called everyone together. About 20 players knelt or stood around him, fewer, even, than the 24 who signed the clipboard on the bus back from the Luther Prep game.

"We're out here as one," Trost told them. "The guys we have here are the ones who are gonna be with us. You're the guys we're gonna end the season with."

He paused.

"And we're still gonna win some games."

Afterward, the sun setting and the shadows long, the coaches stood in a small knot on the field. Everyone had cooler heads now. They talked over the meeting. Some issues, they figured, were legitimate, others just a bunch of talk. In any case, they had to pull the team together — and fast. Pewaukee High School, the opponent Friday, was big and strong and disciplined. They broke the huddle quickly, pounding out plays as if beating a drum. And with no Mark Moore, all the opponents would be salivating. His number — 22 — was the one that went up every week on the opponent's chalkboard. He was the one, virtually the only one, teams had to account for and stop.

"Did he ever really say he quit?" asked Coach Carroll.

They kicked around the idea of someone calling Mark's aunt, or else his girlfriend, Leslie, who was away at college. Last season, the coaches had labeled Leslie the savior of the football team, for helping Mark get focused in the classroom. The coaches wondered what would happen to Mark Moore without football. They knew his twin brother, Matt, had left Shorewood after a drug arrest — a living example, they thought, of what happened when the wrong path was taken. To the coaches, football was what kept Mark working in school. It filled his time and gave him a dream. To play in college.

"Coulda been a great running back," Carroll said at one point.

"We're gonna be saying that 20 years from now," said Trost.

As they talked, Cindy Wilburth, the Shorewood athletic director, appeared in the doorway. The coaches didn't like her, didn't trust her or, in some cases, both. They thought Shorewood was too much about cross country and volleyball and — worse — soccer. It bugged them that most nights the soccer team, not the football team, practiced on the main field. And they'd often talk about how the school, even though it was second largest in the conference, was hopeless in football, basketball and baseball, the traditional big three sports of high school. One of the coaches nodded toward Wilburth. Trost, hands in pocket, turned to look.

"What's this about?" he wondered aloud.

The others shrugged.

Trost walked over and the two began talking. The other coaches tried to resist the urge to turn and look, but they kept stealing glances, like kids at a high school dance. Every time they did, they tried to decipher the body language, the crossed arms and animated gestures. Whatever it was, it couldn't be good. Eventually they gave up and left, walking past the two and out through the empty locker room. The floor had been freshly mopped, but the smell of detergent couldn't push out the lingering staleness.

On Tuesday, Mark was back. Nothing was said about why he was gone, but it was a relief to see him there. After practice the night before, Coach Smith had Micah Moore call home, then took the phone and told Mark about the new offense Trost was putting in. The I-formation. That seemed to perk Mark up.

But now there was no sign of Trost.

In his office, the desk was empty. After talking to Wilburth until nearly 11 p.m., Trost had cleaned everything out. It turned out someone had called Rick Monroe, the Shorewood principal, to complain about Saturday's locker room tirade, calling the kids cowards, comparing a football game to the terrorist attacks at the World Trade Center. It was all outrageous. Wilburth told Trost he would have to meet with Monroe before practice the next day. Trost drove home expecting to be fired.

To be sure, Trost felt like he had been at odds with the Shorewood administration from the start, never convinced they truly bought into the partnership with Messmer. He remembered how the team, after so many blacks from Messmer showed up for the spring workouts, was sent to Estabrook Park. And during one meeting, when Trost asked about getting matching shirts for the coaching staff, he was told his head was in the wrong place. Trost wound up buying the shirts and caps himself.

As the coaches waited for Trost, Mark sat on the hallway stairs by himself, staring at the floor and chewing on a red mouthguard. It was a time to assess his own season, half gone. At a recent practice, Trost sidled up to Mark while he was stretching and asked him if he was going to break the Shorewood rushing record, which stood at 1,203 yards. "I don't know if that's possible," Mark said, shaking his head. "Yeah it is," said Trost. "You're gonna get 600 against Martin Luther." Trost had a way of planting a seed in a player's mind, getting the player to see his potential and set a goal. After the first three games, Mark had about 260 yards, a respectable number. But against Luther Prep, he literally went backwards — minus 12. In the game, Mark had been pounded time and again, so battered he went home and took a nap Saturday evening.

Mark never really wanted to quit, of course, but when the clipboard was handed back to him, he couldn't bring himself to sign the sheet. It was an insult to call into question his commitment, on this team especially. He rarely missed practice. He lined up every play, took all the shots. He had stayed at Shorewood, even after his mother died and he thought about moving away. And now they wanted his name on a stupid piece of paper?

As Mark sat, watching the other players warming up outside, there was a whistle from the bottom of the stairs. Then another, a sharp blast. Trost jogged up the steps and out the door.

"Let's go."

It turned out Trost hadn't met with Monroe. Instead, when Trost got to Shorewood, Wilbuth called him into her office. She still wouldn't say who had complained about the locker room meltdown, though Trost had his suspicions. But something definitely had changed overnight. Now Wilburth wanted him to stay, at least until the end of the season, when everything would be re-evaluated. Trost figured it had become clear they couldn't dump him based only on the word of a player or a parent, without hearing his side of the story. And they would have trouble finding any coach, especially at mid-season. Trost was the eighth at Shorewood in the past 12 years.

So Trost walked out onto the field with a new life, or at least one that lasted five more games. Trost wasn't sure he wanted to stay and coach next year, even if the administration would have him back. He told the other coaches as much in a brief meeting before the start of practice. And, in the room, the door pulled closed again, the coaches made their own vow to each other: You go, we all go.

But we go down with some wins.

Once practice started, there were the usual grumbles from the players. So much for a change of attitude. When it was time for offense, there was indeed a switch, but not to the I-formation they had tested the day before.

"Drew O'Malley, you're with me today," Trost announced.

That meant the running backs. No more grunt work on the line. Time for a little glory. Drew shrugged his shoulders, smiled and followed the group.

All season, Trost had looked for someone to put opposite Mark in their triangular backfield. They had tried Jonathan Williams, Ronell Halbert, George Lasley, even Maurice Ragsdale. Now Drew. Trost lined them up. It was now an all-Shorewood backfield, no more searching for Messmer athletes.

"I thought we were putting in a new formation today," said Ronell, still in at quarterback.

"No," said Trost, nodding toward Mark. "We got our running-back back."

They did put in some new plays, including one where Ronell could choose between two receivers, both on the same side of the field, one running short, the other a bit deeper. Or Ronell could dump the ball off to Mark, who would slide out to a hole behind the line of scrimmage. Trost knew he had to work more passes into the offense. But his best receiver was at quarterback, he didn't trust Maurice Ragsdale and thought Marty Wallner was too small. So the answer, he felt, could still be in the running game. Another threat in the backfield would make Mark even more dangerous.

"Drew is gonna get 40 carries," Trost declared, then looked at him. "You ready for 40 carries?"

He always exaggerated that way. It was about boosting confidence, managing and massaging egos. But sometimes pumping up one player ended up deflating another.

"Five yards a pop," Drew replied confidently.

Mark Moore stood nearby, mouth tight. Hadn't Trost just talked to him about the rushing record? For Mark, fewer carries meant fewer yards.

And the record, the college scholarship, everything, seemed further away.

After the practice-ending sprints, Trost told the team he wouldn't go easy on them the rest of the season. They could win games, but they had to want to win games, believe they could win games.

For everyone, emotions were still raw.

Coach Smith told the team if they were mad and wanted to prove a point, they should do it on the field.

"Maximum intensity," he said. "That's how I live my life. That's how I play this game. If the coach says 100 sprints, so what? I can take it. I'm tougher than he is."

Smith wanted the team to see what he didn't know at their age, couldn't know, to understand the chance they had, how beautiful and rare it was, how soon it would be gone and how impossible it was to ever get it back.

His older brother, Robert, had played football, offensive line, first at Hines Community College, where as a freshman he got some looks from Texas A&M and Kansas State, then at Southwest Baptist University in Springfield, Missouri. When their parents split up, when Smith was about 10, it was Robert who took him under his wing, taking him for long walks, talking sports, talking life. They stayed close even after Robert moved away. Smith followed in Robert's footsteps to Hines, in their hometown of Jackson, Mississippi.

Then came the spring day when Smith returned home after lifting weights and saw all the cars parked outside his mother's house, saw his aunts and uncles in the living room, the ones who shouldn't be there, grief stained on their faces. His father was there, too, and in his role as minister stepped forward and said Robert, was in a car accident.

Robert was dead.

Smith now had a tattoo on his left shoulder, one based on a photo of him and Robert, when the two were boys. Smith went on to play a year at Jackson State University, before his own dream slipped away. Now he lived his football dreams through a younger brother, who was getting some interest from colleges — and, of course, through the players on the team.

Why couldn't they see everything they had?

"You gotta come ready to work," Smith told them. "I can't stand anyone working harder than me. You can be better than me, but you can never outwork me. Can we really say, honest to God, we outworked them?"

Players shook their heads.

"Let's raise 'em up," Trost said.

He meant the helmets. The school songs. Rob Wyatt, who usually called out the breakdown, glowered instead. There was a long pause. Smith looked into Rob's eyes, finally turning away and shaking his head. There was no enthusiasm as Rob called it out:

"What time is it?" — "Game time."

"What time is it?" — "Game time."

"Let's take it to the house." — "Whooo-ooo-oooh."

In the locker room, Trost called for Mark to come into the office. He wanted an apology for Monday, an explanation, something. The two had a pretty good relationship, coach and star player, and Trost had already contacted several colleges on Mark's behalf. In the office, Trost rehashed his meeting with Wilburth. All the coaches were to meet with her tomorrow, to get some things out on the table.

As they talked, it wasn't Mark who walked in, but Maurice Ragsdale.

Maurice had missed a few days of practice without excuse, and when he was there, he seemed out of it. No laughs, no jokes, no funny voices. The coaches knew Maurice was drifting, but didn't know how far. They missed it when he'd slip into the back room after practice, palm an old bagel from the refrigerator and head out to the bus stop. And they missed the exchange in the locker room when Flex had called attention to how gray and worn Maurice's white T-shirt was. But now Maurice asked if he could come early tomorrow and practice catching punts. He knew he had to catch the ball better if he was going to get his job back.

"Is everything all right?" Trost asked him.

"Yeah," Maurice said, quietly.

"What was going on?"

"My moms wanted me to work at a gas station," Maurice said.

He meant now, before the season was over. No more

football. Maurice was grown and grown people helped pay the bills. It was that simple.

"But I don't want to work at no gas station," Maurice said. "People be getting shot in there every day. They got Plexiglass at the counter."

"Come early tomorrow," Coach Carroll said. "We'll get someone to work on those punts."

It was Thursday again. And the team was still operating on two levels — coaches here, players there. Throughout the practice, there was an undercurrent of frustration, but the coaches didn't really sense it.

It centered on Rob Wyatt, who had led Monday's locker-room meeting. From the start of the season, the coaches had been on Rob to be a leader. He seemed to be a natural. Back during two-a-days, Rob once sat and ate dinner with the coaches, laying out in great detail his plan for one day owning a Nissan car dealership. The coaches walked away marveling at his salesmanship, with Coach Groser remarking, "He'll sell you a swing set and your kids are 18, 21 and 23 years old." Now, with more of the same old attitude on the field, the coaches wondered if they had been bamboozled all along.

The day before, on Wednesday, as the coaches continued to try to get more guys into the starting lineup, Rob had been replaced on the defensive line. Once the coaches went to their meeting with the athletic director, Rob dropped his pads outside Trost's office door, cleaned out his locker and peeled off the tape with the nickname — "Big Dub" — he had written out in July. "That's what they want you to do, man," said Flex. Others joined in. "You'll be no better than Dave," said Drew. "You just had a meeting about staying together," said Ronell. Finally, Rob collected his things, returned them to his locker and made this vow, loudly, so everyone in the room could hear it: "I'm telling you right now, I'm coming tomorrow and if I'm not in the starting lineup on defense, I'm walking off the field."

Now it was tomorrow.

Trawitzki called out the first-team defense. No Rob. Trost tried to steer him to the fullback slot on the scout offense, but he wouldn't budge. Players cast a wary eye toward it all. But Rob remained on the field, quiet and sullen.

"Hey, Coach," he said finally. "Ain't I playing tomorrow?"

"Yeah," Trost said. "You're playing offense."

"What about defense?"

"We want to get as many guys going one way as possible."

"I want defense more than offense."

"Well, the coaches feel you're better on offense right now," said Trost. "You don't want to play offense, OK."

Trost saw it this way: Football is a team sport, but it is not a democracy. Players don't decide who plays where, the formation to use or the plays to run. The coach decides. A coach tells the players what to do and the players do it.

"Rob, you want to go to right tackle?" Trost asked. "There, I just empowered you."

Rob saw it this way: He was being singled out and punished for organizing the meeting, for handling everything the right way. Forget the talk about getting more guys into the lineup, what really stuck was the continued jibes about not running hard, coaches calling him out in front of the team every week.

"You're waiting too long to decide," snapped Trost. "Blake go to tackle."

Blake Comer, a Messmer junior, pulled on his helmet and stepped in. Ronell Halbert, Rob's nephew, mumbled something. He was in at quarterback.

The pot was boiling.

"Is there a problem?" Trost asked loudly.

Ronell saw it this way: The coaches were mad at Rob and if the coaches were mad at Rob, they were mad at him, since he and Rob were always linked. And if the coaches disrespected Rob, well, they disrespected him, too.

Ronell shook his head, waved an arm.

"Naw."

All week long, Trost had preached discipline. That was the key to Pewaukee's success. They ran to the huddle, took the call from the sideline, ran to the line of scrimmage, executed the play. Trost wanted his team to break the huddle with authority, a unified clap, then hustle to the line of scrimmage, ready to go.

Now Ronell broke the huddle. The clap sounded like popcorn.

Trost groaned.

Of course, there were other problems with the way Ronell was running the plays. Subtle things, fakes and footwork. The details. Take the snap count — "999-999 Set-Red-Hit." Trost's plays depended on timing. On some, Trost would tell players to go in motion on "Rrrrr." On others it was on "dddd." Ronell was saying it all too fast.

"Say 'Set Red Hit,' not 'SetRedHit.' Put a little space in there," Trost said, then added this admonition for everyone: "If I see guys walk to the line one more time, 100 updowns."

Ronell broke the huddle. He walked.

The lid was off.

"I'm sick of this," Trost shouted, "watching you walk to the line."

"Man, don't yell at me," said Ronell, twisting away.

There is so much caught up in a moment, any moment. There is the emotion of the instant, the surge of anger, the humiliation of being singled out. There are past slights, past disputes, seemingly forgotten, that resurface in an instant.

"Step out of the huddle," Trost said. "Step out of the huddle."

Eyes wide and angry, Ronell tossed his helmet to the ground at Trost's feet.

"You're through," Trost said and pointed toward the locker room.

Ronell walked toward the building, shrugging his shoulders. Another quarterback gone. Rob Wyatt turned and followed, saying nothing. At the doorway, Ronell turned.

"Suck my black dick," he shouted.

Trost didn't look back at him.

"I don't want any coaches going in there talking to them," he said, facing the team. "They're through."

The players were stunned, silent.

"Doesn't matter," Maurice Ragsdale said after a moment. "We're still a team."

"Micah, get in there," said Trost.

There were some shouts of encouragement. Micah Moore, Mark's younger brother, who never much seemed to want the pressure of being quarterback, was in the spot now. He stepped to the middle of the group. There were 22 guys left on the field.

"All right Micah, it's yours now," said Drew.

They ran some more plays and Micah slid into the role, tentatively at first, then a bit easier. Afterward, the coaches called the team over. They talked about the need to be ready, the need to stay together, the need to be angry — angry about what happened the week before against Luther Prep, angry even at the coaches.

"If you're angry at us, take it out on the field," said Coach Carroll. "It's a team game, but it's really just a game between you and the guy across from you. A personal confrontation. Whoever is across from you, get violent with him. Do what you can, within the rules of football, to knock him in the dirt. It's a war. It's a struggle. It's a fight. You guys have fight in you. It's time to find it and fight with someone else.

"I'm sick of us fighting ourselves."

Trost had followed Rob and Ronell down to the locker room to be sure they left. He returned with the quarterback wristband, the one with all the plays on it, the one that carried as much symbolism as responsibility, and flipped it to Micah.

"All right, Micah," Maurice said, and the others clapped.

Micah looked at the wristband in his hand.

"You can smile," Maurice said.

And Micah finally did.

On Friday, Ronell Halbert was already waiting for Trost when he arrived. Ronell knew he had screwed up. Big time. Maybe tossed his junior season away in one stupid moment. And for a kid who held dreams of playing Division One football in college, he couldn't afford to get the tag of "underachiever" or "discipline problem." He left Shorewood sniffing back tears, then called Trost from home to apologize. Mr. Wyatt, his grandfather, ordered him to apologize again in person and take whatever punishment he had coming.

"These boys weren't raised that way," Mr. Wyatt had told Trost. "They were raised to respect adults."

And these boys needed football.

On Trost's own high school team, there had never been such brazen disrespect. St. Pat's, like Trost's elementary school, was run by the Christian Brothers order and the discipline started in the classroom. In high school, Trost sometimes would say, he was "systematically late" — that is, he had a system in which if there was a test in second period, he would get to school in time for third. Trost's senior year coincided with the Super Bowl season for the Chicago Bears, which meant weekly visits to the neighborhood bookie and a wad of cash by January, since the

Bears only missed covering the spread once. Over the years, Trost had been whacked. Punished. He almost didn't graduate, earning mostly Cs and Ds.

But Trost would never have dreamed of walking off a football field. During the summers, Trost sometimes would go down to Hansen Stadium, jump the barbed wire fence and conduct his own workouts, running up and down the stadium stairs, sprinting across the artificial turf, newly installed from Soldier Field, imagining he was Walter Payton, running on the hallowed ground. Sometimes the St. Pat's fight song would ring in his head — *"You're a grand old school and our one golden rule, which we'll cherish as years go by."* Trost would think about wearing the golden helmets, the green jerseys, bursting onto the field on Friday nights. *"Every heart grows bold, 'neath the green and gold. Keep your eyes on St. Patrick High."* How could anyone one throw that away?

Or, now, take it away?

Trost asked Ronell what he thought the punishment should be. Ronell said to not start the game. Trost thought about it, finally telling Ronell he could suit up, but warned that he might not play at all. Rob, meanwhile, had told Trost he wasn't trying to quit — he was only going after Ronell to calm him down. He, too, would start on the bench.

Trost walked down to the cafeteria where the team was eating and sat down with the other coaches. They were off by themselves, huddled over a table.

"I may have to suit up the freshman QB," Trost said and nodded to Coach Trawitzki. "The one you think is so great."

"Potential is the word," said Trawitzki, swallowing a bite.

He had watched the freshman game the night before, a 35-0 loss for Shorewood-Messmer. The kid, Teddy Hanrahan, had a great arm. A good attitude. On one play, he avoided a sack and shoveled the pass to a receiver. Indeed, he was the quarterback Ronell Halbert had told Trost to seek out when Dave O'Harrow quit so many meltdowns ago.

"Better than Micah?" Trost asked.

Trawitzki shrugged, then nodded.

Trost went outside where the freshmen were practicing and found Coach Groser. He didn't want to play Teddy, but wanted him available if Micah got hurt, to show Ronell that actions carried consequences. To be sure, if this was a bigger team, such threats would hold more weight. Ronell would have been kicked off most teams. If he had made the same comment in the hallways at Messmer, he would have been expelled. Trost and Groser talked for a few minutes. Groser was amazed Trost even brought up the idea.

Groser saw it this way: When you give ultimatums to kids, you always lose. Put your ego against that of a 16-year-old and you're on his level. You've already lost.

Trost returned to the cafeteria.

"Groser thought I was nuts," he said, reporting back to the others.

They ate for a few minutes.

Micah wandered over. He wore a pair of boots, laces untied, red shorts, a gray T-shirt that said "Shorewood Baseball" and the quarterback wristband. He had told Trost his hands were shaking a bit in school, but assured the players starting at quarterback was no big thing. Micah asked about a couple plays. Trost got up and demonstrated the footwork. Micah watched, running through the plays in his mind, moving his arms and handing off the imaginary football to the imaginary runner.

"Are we doing any pass plays?" Micah asked.

"Yeah."

"All right." His face lit up.

As the coaches sat in the cafeteria wrestling with Ronell's fate, Ronell was in the locker room, arms folded across his chest, bopping to the loud music, a smile like the mouse that had gotten one over on the cat. He even put the black streaks under his eyes, the mark of the quarterback.

Yeah, he would play. He knew it. Everyone knew it.

After warm ups, they all waited in the locker room for the last words. It was their first home game since opening night and there were more friends and family in the stands now, since the Whitefish Bay game had come before the school year started.

The coaches had already talked about the strategy for the first time Pewaukee kicked off. Pewaukee's best running back, Matt Eales, was also the team's kicker. So they structured the kick return team to put Big Nate on the front line, right in the middle. But instead of dropping back to block, Nate was supposed to knock Eales on his butt. And if Eales got up, to knock him down again. That would set the tone. "Just keep jacking him and jacking him," Coach Carroll said. "Do not stop until the whistle. That is our theme tonight." Nate liked that idea. Pewaukee, a large suburban school, may have had some 40 players on the team, but it didn't have the aura of a Luther Prep, or the psychological hold of Slinger.

After the prayer, led by Coach Smith, Trost stepped to the middle.

"We've been through more this season than any other football team in the state," he said. "I guarantee you that. Football is about going through a lot of trials and tribulations. Basically, we've been to hell and back."

He paused.

"And we're back."

Maybe Trost believed they could win, maybe he didn't. But it didn't matter. The players had to believe. Fire and brimstone speeches wouldn't get them there. Bible stories wouldn't get them there — some had tossed the mustard seeds in the garbage long ago. Even the coaches couldn't get them there. The players had to get there themselves.

Trost said it again.

"We're back."

"Let's go," Nate shouted, the first to his feet.

Others followed and Nate pounded their shoulder pads, strong thunderous pounds, each one accompanied by an ever louder "Let's go," until everyone was screaming. As they ran out, the band was already in position in the distance, spread evenly across the field. The band was in full uniform now, not the polo shirts from the Whitefish Bay game: Caps low on their eyes, jackets pressed and perfect, jaws stiff, instruments polished and gleaming. Everything seemed more official.

After a moment of silence for the victims of the terrorist attacks, the band played the national anthem. The players faced the flagpole, to the north, the flag still lowered to half staff. The players had small American flag decals on the back of their helmets, added that week, just like the NFL players. Drew O'Malley, the would-be firefighter, pasted two on his helmet. A majorette stood on one of the benches, directing the band. Up close, the music had a distorted quality, some instruments coming in more prominently than others — the high pitch of the flutes, the low oomph of the tubas. When the band reached the "Land of the free" line, someone shouted, "Helmets up," and the players lifted their helmets into the air. All except Mark Moore, who was busy strapping his on.

Drew O'Malley kicked off and the team raced down the field, the red jerseys flashing among the silver and white of Pewaukee. After a short runback, Pewaukee took over on the 20 yard line. The first play was a pitch, 14 yards. The next play, the same pitch, 12 yards.

Trost was already impatient.

"Rob, get in, let's go," he shouted.

So much for being benched. And so much for not using Rob on defense. Rob pulled on his helmet and ran out to the huddle.

Third play, again the pitch. Seven more yards. This time, tackle by Rob. Pewaukee's pace, as predicted, was quick, precise. Gash, gash, gash. Through the line, around the end. Coaches screamed, players screamed and still Pewaukee rumbled down the field, scoring with 7:41 showing on the clock. After the extra point, Nate limped off the field.

His knee had been sore from the start of the season, from even before practice began. The trainer was now concerned about fluid on the knee or possibly tendinitis. But if the fluid was drained now, Nate's season would be over.

"Rob, Rob Wyatt," Trost shouted. The kick return unit was already on the field. "Go right in there in the center and hit No. 20."

The kick went to Mark Moore, who returned it 17 yards to the 30, but on the sideline all eyes were on Rob, who slammed into Matt Eales, knocking him down. Eales leaped up and Rob banged into him again. And again.

The whistle blew.

The tone was set.

The team lined up on offense, Nate back in at tackle. Drew O'Malley was in the backfield for the first time, which meant three Shorewood seniors. Drew had switched to the No. 11 jersey, to play off Mark's 22 and Evan's 33. But before they snapped the ball, there was a flag. Someone moved. False start. Back five yards. They lined up again. And again someone moved, false start, five yards more. First and long.

Indeed, the tone was set.

After three plays, Shorewood-Messmer punted and Nate again limped to the sideline.

"Nate can't walk," Trost said.

Coach Smith walked over to Nate, who was never one to sit out a play, never one to complain. "Do you need the trainer?"

Nate shook his head.

Nate, whose father had played high school football in Mississippi, had begun getting recruiting letters from the University of Wisconsin, where he had attended a summer football camp. Nate was amazed anyone would notice him on such a losing team. His mother would often take the letters to church and mention them when it was time for announcements — who had a new job, who got a good report card, who had a birthday. Nate found it embarrassing, like a public pinch on the cheek, and started throwing most of the letters away, so she couldn't find them. Truth be told, they were mainly form letters. But they meant something. They meant he had something to prove.

Indeed, Nate's father had drawn some college interest, back in the day, or so the story went. But he blew out a knee and his dream was lost with it. Nate's parents had divorced and his mother had remarried, but his father still came to some games, usually leaving early to make it to his third-shift job at a meat-packing plant. During the games, Nate sometimes imagined his father there watching, somewhere near the fence. It was comforting to imagine it.

In a way that Mark Moore wasn't on the Shorewood side, Nate was the undisputed leader of the Messmer kids, which itself was a burden for someone so quiet. Nate never joined in the locker-room ribbing sessions, speaking only when he had something to add. As a junior deacon at his church, Nate was sometimes allowed to preach. The first time he did, his voice a mumbled bunch of nerves, Nate talked about phonies, those who drank and carried on during the week and then showed up in church on Sunday, all pious. Nate didn't go out much, instead playing games at home on the computer or just writing stuff. Maybe something scary if he had just watched a scary movie. Maybe some poetry. He didn't share it with anyone. It was just for himself.

As the season wore on, Nate would come home after games, plop onto a couch in the basement and idly click from channel to channel on the TV, searching for football, all to avoid hearing his mother say, "One of the teams has to win and one of the teams has to lose and what matters is you did your best." He couldn't bear to hear it any more. But Nate recognized what his example meant to the others.

And, in a moment, he ran back onto the field.

The quarter ended 7-0. The half ended 21-0.

The game: 41-0.

By the end, Nate's jersey and pants were completely muddy. He made tackle after tackle, swooping onto runners from behind, grabbing their feet, stuffing them at the line, driving them hard to the ground, the thud audible on the sideline. The public address announcer was almost redundant: Shorter, Shorter, Shorter.

To the casual eye, the game looked much like all the others. Indeed, as the band lined up on the track and the announcer read the final score, one of the band members remarked: "How unsurprising."

On the field, the attitude was different.

"It doesn't even feel like we lost," Rob Wyatt said to his father.

"Don't put your heads down," said Nate.

Of course, Ronell had gotten in, first as a receiver and then near the end at quarterback. Micah had done pretty well, all things considered, connecting with Ronell a couple times on passes. The whole team had more fight. More pride. More anger. In the second half, Evan Rivera was ejected after taking a swing at a Pewaukee player who, Evan reported, had swung first. On the next play, after tackling the same Pewaukee player along the sideline, Drew was penalized when he let out a loud whoop. And at the very end, Timmy Lathrop, drew a flag for hitting a player in the back. Indeed, throughout the game, the whole team, after the example from Rob, hit hard.

They hit without fear.

That was part of what the coaches had long demanded — Run without complaint, hit without fear and, the last step, believe without question.

The coaches were stoked by the emotion, but wanted to be sure the team channeled it properly. Play hard, but play smart, they said at midfield. Great physical effort, but give a better mental effort next week against St. Francis. Four games left. We can get them. Four wins.

"In our hearts, we won," Rob declared to everyone, comfortable again in a leadership role. "When you look in the mirror, you gave 100%. You know we won."

On the way back to the locker room, Coach Smith fell in next to Mark Moore, who carried his shoulder pads at his side. Mark had come back, if he had ever quit, but he was still a marked man. That much hadn't changed. Every week, Mark ran with a bullseye on his back. He had finished with about 70 yards rushing, up to 330 for the season. He'd need more than 200 a game the rest of the way to break the Shorewood rushing record.

"You're gonna play in college either way," Coach Smith said.

"Hopefully," Mark said quietly.

Mark was still getting letters from colleges, but when Trost gave them to him, he slipped them into his locker with barely a glance. He had taken the ACT in the spring and fell a couple points short of qualifying. Sometimes he joked he'd send Matt, his twin, to take it for him when the season was over.

"Hopefully, my ass," said Coach Smith. "You'll be there."

The team, it seemed, was always at different points. One player up, another down. Trost — any of the coaches really — could have been the guy in the circus who spins plates, frantically racing between them, always a plate somewhere that needed a quick, gentle spin so it wouldn't crash to the ground.

Now, it was Maurice Ragsdale's turn to wobble.

For Maurice, it had been a bad day all around. At school, he received a detention for mouthing off, though he told the coaches it was only a misunderstanding with a teacher. He had looked at the game as a chance to turn his day around. Friends had come to see him play. Girls, too. But before the game, Maurice checked the board with the assignments and discovered he wasn't even on the kick return team anymore.

Now, as the others laughed and carried on, a hip-hop CD loud and throbbing in the background, Maurice didn't respond to anything.

This ain't right, he thought.

He had practiced catching punts that week. He had gotten better. But he was only in for a few plays at the end when it didn't matter. Mark? He skipped practice and never apologized. He got to start. Rob had walked off the field. He got to play. Ronell had told Trost to suck his dick. He got to play. It wasn't right. No. Not at all.

Finally, Maurice turned and walked away. Marty Wallner, his locker-mate, watched him cross to Trost's office. Sensing something was wrong, Marty positioned himself outside the door.

In a few minutes, the door opened with a bang against the wall. Maurice, eyes angry, rushed out.

"Be there at noon tomorrow, right?" Trost shouted behind him.

"Naw, man," said Maurice.

"Work your way back."

Maurice brushed past Marty on his way up the back steps.

"Hey, what's going on?" Marty asked, following him.

That day, in his Elements of Persuasion Class, Marty had given a five-minute speech, something he dreaded. The topic: Why you should play football. He worked on the speech the night before with his father, who was good at that sort of thing, and his mother, who listened to him recite it a few times. His younger brother Jack, so precocious his grandfather referred to him as "The Senator," was also part of the willing audience. The coaches had relaxed the jersey-to-school rule since it was red, white and blue day at Messmer, so Marty delivered the speech in the red Shorewood jersey he had always dreamed of wearing. Marty, whose voice often had a stammering quality to it, had delivered the speech so well, he earned an A.

"Ain't nothing going on," Maurice told him.

Now Marty gave an encore performance in his bare feet on the cold sidewalk in the glow of a security light. Trost and Carroll came out and joined the conversation and, in a few minutes, Marty came inside. Marty would say later that his feet didn't feel cold at all. It was kind of nice, actually, they were so sweaty from the game. And Marty would say there was no doubt. Maurice would be back.

"He ain't a quitter," Marty said.

But the coaches, they heard a plate crashing to the ground.

Chapter 9
"A circle is difficult to break."

The team was being lined up carefully, precisely: Carlo Albano, a Shorewood junior in the middle. Drew O'Malley to his right, then Justin Moore, then Evan Rivera. To the left: Jay White, then Ronell Halbert and then Big Nate. That was the back row.

"Coaches here," the photographer said.

It was team picture day, delayed for a week because on the original day the volleyball pictures ran long, so naturally football got postponed. The first bunch of players was standing on two benches dragged over from the softball diamond. They wore the red jerseys, which were bright in the sun, along with the muddy and grassed-up practice pants.

The photographer had the team line up from the tallest to shortest, which caused a little dissension at the end of the ranks, where the players still were sorting out the final spot. Jason Davis, a Messmer sophomore, stood back-to-back with Martin Wallner, the Shorewood sophomore. As Rob Wyatt sized them up, each tried to come off as a little bit taller than they were.

"Marty, you're the smallest," Rob declared finally.

"Yeah, you're the smallest," Jason repeated with a smile.

So Marty was the last to be positioned, on the end of the front row. As they waited, the team looked like a proud bunch, shoulders back, chests out, the sun warm on their faces. The opponent on Friday would be St. Francis, a team Shorewood had some success against last year, going into halftime tied 6-6, before the requisite collapse and a 41-6 final score. It was Monday and the players were still pumped from Friday's showing against Pewaukee, knowing how good it felt — finally — to hit hard. Evan Rivera would miss the game, suspended for throwing the punch, but could practice. Rob, not Nate, was already designated the new fullback, a position Rob last played in eighth grade, where he was a veritable bowling ball coming through the line. "Am I suspended from special teams, too?" Evan had asked Trost earlier. Then, with a wry grin asked: "Can't I be George Lasley this week?"

"OK," the photographer said. "Look over here."

"Wait a minute," Trost snapped. "Who are you, young man?"

There was a new face, down in the front row. Whoever it was, he had picked up a jersey, pulled it on and slid into line undetected.

"Step out of the picture," Trost said, angrier. "What are you doing in there?"

The front line scrunched together to fill the sudden gap.

There were four rows, 22 players in all. A few, including Maurice Ragsdale and Pertell Mallett, were missing, but 22 was the same number Shorewood started with last season, when Trost was so concerned that he pitched the partnership with Messmer. Most of them were the ones who lifted weights all summer, the ones who came twice a week to camp, the ones who played the pickup games in the Messmer gym, the ones who were there from the start. They had more invested. It was harder to walk away, though a few would never have dreamed of it.

They all looked at the camera.

Someday, when a yearbook — the Shorewood "Copperdome" or the Messmer "Capitol" — is pulled from a dusty shelf, the team will be remembered as pioneers. The first public-private football partnership in Wisconsin. The only city-suburban pairing in the nation. The first to carry the combined Shorewood-Messmer banner. The Praying Dogs. The Mighty Bishounds. The Fighting Greyhops. However they'd be tagged for posterity.

But for now, at both schools, whenever a player wore a red jersey on game day, the snide comments following him down the hallways like a stalker, they were labeled as one thing only — a bunch of losers.

"OK," the photographer said again.

Everyone smiled.

Snap.

This week, Micah Moore was in at quarterback from the start, which was fine with Ronell Halbert, who in yet another formation wasn't out at receiver, but lined up at tight end. The new plan was a seven-man front, plus the quarterback and the three in the backfield. It was at least the fourth formation and the third quarterback in six games. If nothing else, the team was becoming adaptable.

With the long, rocky week behind them, the team seemed to have a newfound confidence. Trost ran them through their paces.

"Stretch, Mark, stretch," he called out, as Mark Moore hit the edge of the line. "Good."

Trost wanted Mark to make sharp, decisive cuts up the field. He cringed when Mark would string a run out along the line, rejecting one hole for the potential of another, and that hole for the potential of the next, until he reached the sideline only to be stopped for no gain. Sometimes with Mark it was like watching a kid jumping rope on the playground, waiting and waiting — head bobbing — trying to decide when to jump in.

On the pass plays Trost decided Micah would just roll to one side or the other, usually the right, instead of staying in the pocket. Micah was more comfortable that way and it was a crapshoot as to how long the line could protect him. Micah threw a nice pass to Ronell. Then another, one that glanced off his fingertips.

"That was a beautiful pass," said Drew. "Dang."

"My fault," said Ronell, returning to the huddle.

"Better, better," said Trost, arms crossed.

They ran a pitch to Mark, who casually took it up the sideline, defenders on his tail.

"I can't believe these guys are catching him," Trost said to Coach Trawitzki.

"He's not running hard," Trawitzki said.

Mark jogged back, dropped the ball and headed to the huddle.

"Are you running hard?" Trost asked him.

Mark paused for a moment. If he said yes, he'd have to explain why two of the defenders caught him. If he said no, well, he'd have to explain that, too.

"Naw," Mark said, offering a sheepish smile.

The same play was called, and this time Mark burst past the defenders and through the flailing arms of the secondary.

"What a difference," said Coach Carroll.

Later, after the defensive work — no Oklahomas today — everyone lined up for sprints. As they ran, Trost blew a tune through his whistle: Da da dut, da da duh.

"Charge," he shouted.

He turned to Trawitzki, half amazed.

"Everybody's running."

The story was the same Tuesday, although Mark was missing, having left class and gone home with the flu. "Self-diagnosed," Trost remarked. The practice was crisp, focused. And when they lined up for the sprints, Trost had a better idea.

"Ten good ones," he shouted, then revised his instructions as they began. "Let's hear your school songs while you're running, Shorewood first."

The words, sung after every game and practice, came

back in a mumbled jumble, the team out of breath, mouthguards making it sound as if everyone was chewing on marbles: "U rrr rrrrr rrr, Shhrrrwood red n grey, de schooolz gotta pep'll say."

As the team ran, Trost skittered and bopped across the field, pointing his fingers this way and that in a herky-jerky dance. There were four games left, and the team had to win them all if they were going to somehow make the playoffs, but the pressure was gone, as if the sky had cleared after a relentless storm. The players didn't know about the coaching turmoil, and the coaches didn't tell them. Trost, no longer worrying about next year, about building a program, establishing himself as a turnaround specialist, was much more relaxed.

The players shook their heads at Trost's antics.

But they kept singing. As they grew louder — "Mzzzmr High Skuul, how ve lvvve thee, to ur Bshps" — members of the St. Francis freshman football team walked past, on their way down to the big field for their game. That only provoked the team to sing louder, this time gathered at the center of the field, mouthguards out, helmets raised. Maurice Ragsdale, who had returned to the team, stepped to the front and shouted the words, pumping his helmet toward the perplexed freshmen.

The words came loud and clear.

"Loyal are we. Always firm and strong. Jump for the Blue and White."

A few minutes later, Trost and Trawitzki followed the team down to the locker room.

"We'll turn this thing into a chorus yet," Trost said.

"You oughta hear Pertrell sing," Trawitzki remarked.

To Pertrell's considerable embarrassment, his voice had become a topic of conversation on the team, between the players and any coach that spent any time at Messmer, where Pertrell sometimes sang at assemblies and prayer services. Trawitzki had been at Messmer that day, inter-

viewing for an open social studies job. He arrived at practice looking exceedingly uncomfortable in a suit and tightly-
cinched tie, which drew sarcastic compliments from the
players. His radiation treatments nearly over, Trawitzki was
as free as Trost. All of the coaches were. The week before,
frustrated by the fallout from the Luther Prep locker room
incident, they all told Cindy Wilburth, the Shorewood
athletic director, they wouldn't return. And Trawitzki, tears
welling in his eyes, said he was also resigning as wrestling
coach. Now, in his more comfortable shorts and T-shirt,
he lumbered down the stairs and followed Trost into the
locker room.

"Pertrell, you're gonna sing for us," Trost declared, walking up to him. "You owe us for missing two days."

Pertrell had missed Saturday and Monday. He had
missed so many practices, the team had taken to calling
an unexcused absence "pulling a Pertrell," a joke Trost
didn't exactly appreciate.

"Huh?"

Pertrell looked up, sweat on his forehead, still breathing heavy from the sprints.

"Naw, man," he said. "That's embarrassing."

Pertrell had been put on the spot once before, about a
year earlier in his Oral Communication class at Messmer.
He had been humming absently in the back of the room
during an assignment when Ms. Williams caught him,
called him to the front and demanded he sing for the class.
Pertrell, who liked modern R&B more than the bombas-
tic rap, eventually gave a rendition of Eric Benet's "Spend
My Life With You" that left the girls wide-eyed, hands to
their mouths, smiling at the revelation. Handsome *and* a
killer voice. Later, Pertrell made his formal debut singing
"Silent Night" at a Christmas assembly. He had a dream
of recording a demo tape, maybe cutting a CD. Eric Benet,
from Milwaukee, had made it big, even hooking up with
movie star Halle Berry.

Indeed, Pertrell's football skills emerged the same way
— a couple solid hits out of nowhere one day during the
Oklahoma drills and it was as if he was suddenly fluent in
a new language.

Now, in the locker room, the team jumped in.

"Yeah."

"Let's go."

"C'mon, man."

Finally, Pertrell relented. He stood on a bench, his white
T-shirt soaked with sweat. He paused for a moment, shook
his head, took a deep breath and, looking down at the tile
floor, began to sing in a halting voice: "Amaa-aazing grace,
how swee-eeet the sound that saa-aaved a wretch li-iike
mee." He began over the locker room din and the din
quieted.

Blake Comer, a Messmer junior, began waving an arm
back and forth, picking up the unheard rhythm and the
rest joined in. Trost was up on another bench, watching in
amazement. It was a moment. Definitely.

Pertrell stepped down.

"You've got a good voice, young man," Trost said.

Everyone clapped.

"Hey, he's singing at the homecoming game," declared
Rob and everyone agreed.

"Yeah." "You have to." "Definitely."

"This is embarrassing," Pertrell said again.

"Do you know the Star Spangled Banner?" Trost asked.

Pertrell shook his head.

"How does it start?" he asked.

At that, Trost began singing. His rendition was horrible, off-key, but everyone joined in, a mish-mash of voices
trying to help Pertrell along. Ronell gave an uneven salute. Marty stood near his locker, hair mussed, smiling.
Coach Trawitzki, whose innocent remark started it all, stood
in the doorway, hands in pockets, rocking on the balls of
his feet.

"O'er the laaa-aaand of the freee-eeee."

"Helmets up," someone said, and they raised empty hands instead.

"And the hoo-oome of the braaaaaaave."

Everyone laughed and slapped backs and joked and in a few minutes the locker room had mostly cleared out, leaving Pertrell and Nate and the regular group of stragglers. Trost went to his office, returned and handed another letter to Nate.

A University of Wisconsin logo was on the envelope.

Later, Trost joined some of the other coaches at the freshman game. The freshman team had 28 players, more now than the varsity. But of those, 22 were from Messmer, raising questions among some Shorewood parents about how long the experiment would last if Shorewood didn't bring up its numbers. Though Messmer paid a $300 fee for every player that participated, why would Shorewood operate an all-Messmer team?

On the sideline, Blake Comer and Sebastian Negron, two Messmer players, tossed a football back and forth and Coach Hoagland tried to play matchmaker, calling over a Shorewood girl who had been checking out Sebastian, asking if she was coming to the varsity game and if she had plans afterward. Both turned red. On the field, Shorewood-Messmer led 14-13 at the half, but the game wound up 28-28, which was a victory of sorts.

After the game, Rick Monroe, the Shorewood principal, caught up with Trost as he headed to the parking lot. It had been a week since Trost was supposed to meet with Monroe, that day when Trost figured he'd be fired. Even now, Trost didn't know exactly what had unsealed his fate.

What happened was this: That night when Trost was meeting with Athletic Director Cindy Wilburth, Monroe called Drew O'Malley at home and asked him about the locker room. What happened? What was said? Monroe knew Drew and his family from church. Everything is fine, Drew assured him. They had a meeting. Trost had apologized for calling them cowards. All under the bridge. So the Trost situation was put on hold until after the season. Drew O'Malley, who Trost had nearly kicked off the team a few weeks earlier, never knew the weight his endorsement carried.

That day, the coaches had worried about what would happen to Mark Moore without football. But they could have also worried about Jim Trost.

After finishing high school with no interest in college, Trost went to work for American Bridge and Dismantling, then for a Chicago lumber yard. It was hard, physical work. Brawn over brains. A few years later, he took a job with the gas company, first reading meters and then moving up to collecting overdue bills. It was a good job, good pay, and Trost figured on sticking with it 25 years, then collecting a nice pension. But what he really wanted to do was coach, and the best way to do that was to get into the classroom as a teacher. So, in 1992, seven years after finishing high school, Trost started classes at Cardinal Stritch University near Milwaukee and Moraine Park Technical College in West Bend, driving the more than 100 miles back and forth from Chicago, where he was still living.

He was pushed by his wife, Sheila, who was just his girlfriend at the time. The two met on Milwaukee's Bradford Beach one summer, when Trost was in town to visit his brother, Chris, during Summerfest, a lakefront music festival billed as the world's largest. Trost had gone down to the beach with a couple of buddies to scope out babes. Once married, in 1994, Trost moved to rural Hartford, Wisconsin, where Sheila grew up, and as he worked on his degree he coached in youth sports leagues there. Trost finished his degree in 1999 and that fall joined the Shorewood staff as an assistant. Indeed, as a head football coach, even at lowly Shorewood, Trost was where he always wanted to be.

Trost and Monroe talked for awhile, standing between the buildings as players and families drifted past to the parking lot. It was the first time they had run into each other since the Luther Prep fiasco.

"He wanted to talk me off the ledge," Trost said later.

And, for once, Trost was willing to be convinced.

The new twist with sprints was to line up in the offensive formation and call out a play. The players would execute it and finish off by sprinting all the way down the field, conditioning and repetition all in one. On Wednesday, when running the offensive plays grew stale, they lined up in punt formation to do the same thing. Drew O'Malley was the punter and Mark Moore was in the upback slot, midway between Drew and the center. If there was a bad snap, it was Mark's job to try and hold off the defenders. Now Coach Carroll had them try something different. A fake. The snap would go to Mark, who would loop toward the edge of the line, Drew following behind him. If Mark was going to be tackled, or if the defense bit, he'd pitch the ball to Drew.

"Option!" Trawitzki called out as they ran it.

"Nice," said Trost.

Neither knew it was coming. Carroll had been waiting for weeks to put the play in. The idea for it had come early in the season, when they were practicing point-after attempts, with Drew as the kicker and Dave O'Harrow, then the quarterback, as the holder. On a bad snap, Dave was supposed to call out "Fire" and designated players would run pass routes. At one point, just screwing around, Dave rolled out to the side and pitched the ball to Drew. Coach Carroll buried the idea deep in his bag of tricks. Not that they needed the play. Five games into the season, the team had scored only two touchdowns and had yet to try an extra point. Now Carroll adapted the play for a punt formation — something the team had become all too familiar with.

"We gotta use it," said Trost.

"That may be the greatest play of the year," said Trawitzki.

Indeed, Trost had kicked around running the option in the past, putting Mark in at quarterback to get his best athlete in the most important spot. But last year, Mark wasn't keen on it. And this year there were other athletes that could be plugged in at quarterback. That's why Ronell got the back call when Dave quit.

Now, when the team broke up into units, Trost was ready to keep experimenting.

"Mark, come here," he said. "Switch with your brother."

Mark gave a quizzical look, but lined up in the quarterback slot. Now that Micah, his younger brother, was playing quarterback, it didn't look so hard anymore. In the formation, Micah was slipped into one of the running back slots but mainly would be a blocker. Depending on what the defense did, Mark's pitch would go to Drew at running back, or could go to Rob Wyatt at fullback, or Mark could keep the ball and run. Trost demonstrated a few times, taking the snap from an invisible center. Then Mark tried it.

"Nice," said Trost.

Again.

"Beautiful."

Again.

"Mark, you're a natural."

Finally, Trost called the rest of the team over and they ran the play against a phantom defense. Trost told the team they'd use the option just a few times, to catch St. Francis off guard. During most games, defenders would call out the plays — "Number 22, 22, pitch left, pitch left" — based on the Shorewood-Messmer formation and the odds that Mark would get the ball more than anyone else. They worked the option a few more times, Trost adding new wrinkles as they progressed, including the chance for Mark to throw to Ronell. The passes came out wobbly and short.

"Man, this quarterback stuff," Mark said at one point, shaking his head. "They've got a lot to do."

Trost laughed.

"And you're only running one play."

The atmosphere between the coaches and the players had improved all week, so on Thursday when Rob Wyatt told Coach Trawitzki he wasn't feeling well, the exchange went like this:

"What's the problem?" asked Trawitzki.

"I got a heart murmur," said Rob Wyatt.

He didn't, of course. Rob suffered from asthma, which often left him short of breath and was one reason for the trouble with the sprints, but not a heart murmur. For all Trawitzki knew, it was the topic of the day in science class.

"Heart worm?" Trawitzki asked, raising an eyebrow.

"Heart *murmur*," Rob said, correcting him.

"You do huh? What is it?"

"I don't know."

"Well, you can't have it unless you know what it is," Trawitzki said and waved him away.

But, better relationships or not, Thursday was still a day to be serious.

"It has been a good week of practice," Coach Carroll said, as the team gathered together at the end. "But if we go out tomorrow night and take a step back, it's going to hurt."

James Carroll, 25, was an English teacher in his first year at Bay View High School. The year before, during his student teaching, he was at Custer High School, where teachers said if you can make it, you can make it in any Milwaukee Public Schools building. Friends sometimes questioned why Carroll wasted his time teaching in the public schools — teaching "those kids," meaning the black ones. Carroll didn't see it as a waste at all, since for every difficult case there was a student who tried hard and deserved a full effort from the teacher. He joined the Shorewood staff last year on a volunteer basis, quickly connecting with Trost, a fellow Chicago native. Carroll loved the Chicago Bears and the Notre Dame Fighting Irish, not necessarily in that order, but today had a different team in mind. He had recently read *The Junction Boys,* a book about the 1954 Texas A&M football team.

"Bear Bryant," Carroll said. "Who knows him?"

A few hands went up. Two, then three, then four.

"He used to coach at Alabama," Carroll said. "A legend."

The players nodded.

"Before that, he was at Texas A&M. He took over a team that was 2-7, turned it into a national title contender. That first camp, he took his team to Junction, Texas. This is west Texas. Nothing there but desert, sand and cactus. They went out in two buses. Fifty guys, 60 guys quit. They were dragging guys off the field. This was in the days when it wasn't manly to drink water when it was 110 degrees."

In reality, the attrition was much more severe. It was 115 players who went out on the two buses and 35 who returned on one bus to start the Texas A&M season, which ended 1-9.

"Those guys who came back from Junction eventually won the Southwest Conference Championship," Carroll said. "They called those guys The Junction Boys."

There were about 20 players on the field around him, an especially small number for Holy Thursday. Since the beginning, eight weeks earlier, perhaps 40 others had come and gone, staying for a week, staying a day, trying on football as if it was some kind of new suit, then returning it to the rack. At Carroll's own high school, Maine South in suburban Chicago, the varsity football team was something to aspire to. The school colors were red and black, but only the varsity wore black jerseys. And when the players pulled them on, they knew it meant something to wear them.

No one, of course, would confuse Shorewood, Wisconsin, a well-to-do lakeside suburb, with Junction, Texas. And nobody would confuse Jim Trost with Bear Bryant, though Trost did have a nail-spitting, old-school attitude at times. "The first time you quit, it's hard," Bear Bryant is quoted as saying in the book. "The second time, it gets easier. The third time, you don't even have to think about it." The words fit for this team, too.

If the team could see itself as those players, to see there was something strong about being a survivor, something noble, that would be a good thing.

"You guys are The Junction Boys," Carroll told them.

Milwaukee Journal Sentinel photo by Benny Sieu

Shorewood-Messmer players kneel to pray in the locker room before a game. Early in the season, the coaches were skittish about locker-room prayers, but the players often led them as the season went on.

"You're the ones who made it through the crap. All the physical hardships, all the mental hardships. You came back from the days in the desert. You take that. It bonds you. You take that for the next four games."

The team soaked it in.

"Four games we're gonna win."

Friday night. While the team did its stretches, the bus carrying the St. Francis squad pulled up and, within minutes, the St. Francis players ran onto the field. Twenty-two guys. Twenty-two small guys.

"That's the varsity?" asked Justin Moore, Flex, looking up. "We better win. Dang."

The team had gold helmets, a red "SF" in a circle on the side — just like the San Francisco 49ers of the NFL. Red pants. Black socks. White jerseys. The Shorewood-Messmer players watched as they traced the edge of the field in a single-file run.

"I know that ain't the whole team," said Maurice Ragsdale.

"It ain't the team," chastised Rob. "The linemen ain't even out here yet. Quit ya'll talking."

Sure enough, more guys ran out a few minutes later, larger, stronger. One pushed 300 pounds. The stands were slowly filling. It was Parents Night for Shorewood-Messmer, so family was everywhere. After a day of late-September dreariness, the sun had finally broken through. Overhead, a plane sketched a line from behind the clouds, which were tinted blue and orange. On the track, a reporter from one of the local TV stations waited. The team was still news, or at least a novelty.

As the team returned to the locker room for last-minute instructions, Trost spotted Br. Bob Smith, the president of Messmer High School, talking to Joy Bretsch, the Messmer athletic director. Trost brought Br. Bob into the locker room with him.

As they walked in, the room grew quiet. Micah and Ronell were in the bathroom, both putting the quarterback black under their eyes. They came out and lowered their heads. Br. Bob stood in the middle. From the Messmer kids especially, he commanded respect. A former parole officer in Detroit who grew up in Chicago, Smith sometimes refereed high school basketball games. He also held a bachelor's degree in criminal justice and a master's degree in administrative leadership. He had no tolerance for baseball caps in the classroom, foul language, fighting, or even a hint of disrespect toward a teacher, staff member, or any adult. Smith, 43, belonged to the Capuchin Franciscan order, which includes a focus on urban areas. His regular attire was a shirt with a white collar, not a brown robe. Sometimes players would do Br. Bob impressions — "That's it, yer outta here!" — but they knew to stay in line.

"Grab the hand of the guy next to you," Smith said and everyone did. "Now close your eyes, heads down."

He paused.

Several weeks back, when he came to watch the Red and Blue game, Smith was surprised he couldn't recognize many of the players in their pads, helmets and jerseys. He had figured on easily picking out the Messmer kids. In the 1970s, Smith had played high school football himself — linebacker and halfback — at St. Lawrence Seminary, a rural school of several hundred north of Milwaukee. At the school, Smith was one of seven black students. There was one day when Smith, a freshman, sat in the office and a senior walked in. It was a snowy day. "Why don't you go outside and roll around in the snow?" the senior asked him casually. Smith was puzzled. He didn't know how to respond. "That way you'll look more like the rest of us," the senior said.

White.

Now, looking around the room, Smith could see the

mix of faces — black, white, Hispanic. There were sturdy seniors and slight sophomores, burly linemen and thin receivers. All together. Shorewood, Messmer. Holding hands. One.

"Right now you have a circle," Smith said. "And a circle is difficult to break."

The room was quiet as it had ever been. No shuffling of feet. No nothing. Confidence growing in the calm.

"From this moment on," Smith continued, "remember, it is not 'I.' It is 'We.' For if I do my job, we will do our job. God, we ask you in a special way tonight, use us to do your will. Allow us to give our all. Lord, if we do that, our only result is victory. Amen."

"Amen," came the response.

The coaches offered a few more words, but the words were lost in the moment.

"I'm going to give you two minutes to think about it," Trost said. "Then I'm gonna call you and when I call you, I want you to respond."

The coaches left the room and it was just the players, a wide circle around the edges. The helmets were scuffed now and some grass stains lingered on the gray pants, but in the red jerseys the team somehow always looked more powerful, more unified. Mark Moore, who rarely spoke to anyone on game days, and who had been curled up sick on a locker room bench an hour earlier, shouted almost instantly.

"Ya'll, bring it in."

He was quickly surrounded, helmets raised over his head.

"I hope ya'll ain't scared," Mark shouted. "Let's go out there and bust heads. Let's do this for my mom."

Everyone knew Mark's mother was gone. They could only sense how much it hurt. Mark had a tattoo of a cross on his right arm, "RIP" over the top, "Mom" written underneath. He got it two months after she died, having taken the fight to the cancer, which, in the end, always seems to win. Micah got a similar tattoo. It was on nights like this, Parents Night, that Mark felt his mother's absence the most, felt her absence more than her presence.

"My mother, she would bust heads," Mark shouted. "She was a soldier."

The team shouted — deep whoops and piercing screams — and thrust closer.

"Ain't nobody better be scared," Mark said. "Remember ya'll, we're like a piece of iron and iron don't break. Nobody better be scared."

The team pounded on each other's shoulder pads, screaming in each other's faces, screaming until their voices were raw. Nate Shorter and Mark Moore were in the middle. One Shorewood, the other Messmer. The senior and the junior. The season had not unfolded as either planned. Now the two, chests together, faces close, screamed their emotions loose.

"Let's do this shit. Let's do this shit."

The team sprinted out, across the dark upper field, down the stairs and into the light. The band was lining up on the track. The team waited in the end zone, pacing, fists clenched. Finally, to the blast of trumpets and the pounding of drums, they stormed onto the field, Mark Moore leading the way.

This was it.

This had to be it.

Two plays into the game, Mark took the handoff from his brother, sprinted right, turned up the field and emerged past the line, past one tackler, then another, still another, into the end zone, 75 yards. Touchdown.

This was why he played football — the thrill of spinning out of tackles, the feel of the football tucked in your gut, of hands on your legs, your shoulders, slipping away as you ran, no one able to bring you down. The feeling was as addictive as it was elusive.

Milwaukee Journal Sentinel photo by Benny Sieu

Mark Moore, a senior running back for the Shorewood-Messmer team, tries to escape a tackle during the team's game against Whitefish Bay Dominican High School. Thanks to a strong performance from Mark, the team took the lead in the second half, but could not win the game.

"How many more you want tonight?" Coach Smith asked Mark on the sidelines.

"That's for all the haters out there," Nate shouted, toward the stands, where the fans were cheering wildly, haters no more.

St. Francis scored on a long drive, matching the two-point conversion and an 8-8 score. But seven plays later, it was Drew O'Malley's turn. They ran Roar Back, the play that failed them on the goal line at Lakeside Lutheran, a play they never seemed to get quite right. But this time Drew took the hand off from Micah and slid behind the line to the left. One guard held the defenders off at the line, the other pulled. The blocks were crisp, the assignments sure. Everything, finally, came together for perfection. Drew turned up the field, ducked inside an oncoming defender and, with a few long, easy strides darted into the clear, then, 36 yards later, the end zone. Pandemonium on the sideline.

And, finally, they believed. They believed without question.

But St. Francis answered again.

And then Shorewood-Messmer couldn't.

The score 14-14, the second quarter just underway, they punted. Drew sent the ball aloft and Mark trailed the play down the field, the safety valve in case the returner slipped through. After a moment, when the bodies cleared, Mark was on the ground, staring up at the empty sky. He had been hit in the back, but his heart hurt now, too. And there was the trainer, Steve Wittemann, at his side, carefully sitting him up, lifting him up. And there they were, walking slowly back to the sideline. How quickly things turn. How empty Mark felt.

On the field, St. Francis scored again.

Maurice Ragsdale was sent in for Mark on the kick return squad. Marty replaced him in the backfield and on defense.

And St. Francis scored again.

Mark sat on a bench for a while, deep breaths. He stood and walked, gingerly, like an old man. He tried to run, stopped. The team physician, Todd Swenson, watched, finally slipping a pack of ice under Mark's jersey, in the back of his pants.

"Couple minutes," Swenson said to Trost, who was already pacing nearby.

"Bruise?" Trost asked. "You don't know yet?"

Swenson shook his head.

Trost walked past him, over to Mark. "You all right young man?"

Mark nodded.

A few minutes later, Trost returned.

"When you go back in there, I want you to give me everything you've got, all right?" he said. "You have no apprehension. You're not afraid, right?"

Mark shook his head. No.

At halftime, there was no time to go all the way back to the locker room, because the players were to be introduced with their parents. Trost gathered them under the goal post, talking over the band, which was performing its half-time show, a sampling of songs from "West Side Story," a musical about rival gangs from different racial backgrounds who fight and kill each other, only to come together in the end. The team was behind 42-14, the last score for St. Francis coming 10 seconds before halftime. The team had crumbled as soon as Mark, its leader, went down.

Trost called the hit a cheap shot and shouted across the field at the St. Francis coach, Doug Sarver, who yelled back. The referees ordered both to tone it down. Other players were complaining of cheap shots, too, late hits and facemasks, though the refs hadn't flagged anything — except one call against Shorewood-Messmer.

"We can't have any more 15-yard penalties," said Trost, urging the team to stay focused. "Number 22 is coming back. I think he's going to show them what he's made of."

"Mark's in the locker room," said Micah.

"What?"

Indeed, Mark was in the locker room with Swenson.

He did exercises to try and loosen his back, but his back tightened instead. And when it came time for the players to walk down the track with their parents, Mark was still in the locker room. Micah walked alone with their aunt, their mother's sister, who carried two red carnations, one for each of the brothers. The Shorewood players, by and large, walked with two parents. The Messmer players, often walked with one. Mark Williams pushed his grandmother, the one who told him to stick with football, in her wheelchair. Nate Shorter was with his mother, who rarely made the games, and stepfather. His father didn't make it.

Pertrell Mallett and his father didn't hear their names when they were called, so they were left lingering with Maurice Ragsdale, whose mother worked nights and couldn't come.

"Let's just walk, ya'll," Maurice said. A friend, Kenny Beamon, who Maurice considered like a brother, walked next to him.

Mark Moore returned to the sideline for the second half wearing a dusty old Shorewood Football raincoat, the hood pulled over his head. He watched the team flail away, players shuffling in and out to fill holes, coaches shouting, players trying to turn it up a notch, trying and trying, but stalling out like a flooded engine. He watched it all, hands in the coat pockets, helpless to stop it. They never even got to try the new option play. The team had lined up in the formation once, but as Trost suggested, Mark made a simple hand-off just to get comfortable behind the center.

If life was a movie, Mark would have returned. Mark would have scored the winning touchdown, scored it for his late mother.

Final score: 55-20.

The two teams lined up and shook hands, the Shorewood-Messmer side feeling as if it was ripped off again, all the cheap shots, all the blind referees. Helmets off, steam rose from their heads in the cool night.

"You got one on the ground over here," one of the St. Francis coaches said, nodding toward midfield.

It was Nate, on his back. Not injured so much as wasted and spent. He slowly got up and limped over to the circle, where Trost was more positive than ever.

"Now is when we start getting the wins," Trost said. "No question. You did great things out here tonight. Most points all season."

The coaches had spent the week taking back all the stuff about being cowards. They said it over and over — it took courage to keep coming back. And it did. It took courage to be the first players at Messmer in nearly 20 years to try football. It took courage to come out to the first practices and try drills that left them stumbling over their own feet. It took courage for all of them, Shorewood and Messmer alike, to each day, every week, lace up their cleats and go to the foot of the mountain and try to play a football game while climbing uphill.

Coach Smith had told them, way back on the eve of the first game, they could move a mountain with a mustard seed and, for a moment, they believed him. When they called out the breakdown after practice and before games, they called themselves soldiers, and, at times, they believed it. Or at least wanted to believe it.

But they needed to make the belief permanent. They needed to win.

"What I saw out there tonight was football players," Trost told them. "I'm proud to say I'm your football coach. I'd go into battle with you any time."

But as the team broke up, some of the players were still deflated.

As they walked back to the locker room, Sebastian Negron fell in next to Flex. Both were Messmer seniors. Indeed, of all the classes and splits on the team, the greatest in number was the Messmer seniors — six of the 24 or so guys still on the team. They had waited four long years for football.

"I wish some of the people from Messmer would get out on the field," said Sebastian, streaks of sweat running through the black smudges under each eye.

"They talk shit every week but they ain't out on the field," said Flex.

While the Shorewood seniors were used to the hallway insults, the truth was they heard less of them than at Messmer. At Shorewood, there were no expectations, no high hopes. It was different at Messmer, where the players had talked about achieving big things and their classmates each week held them to it.

They didn't know what it was like, what it took.

A year earlier, Sebastian was on the Messmer cross country team. Though he had confessed at one practice to not watching much football on TV, Sebastian had worked his way up to starting safety. His parents had sent him to Messmer from suburban West Bend High School two years earlier, after he and two friends were caught shoplifting. Sebastian's parents turned him over to the police themselves, after finding a stash of CDs in his bedroom. At Messmer, Sebastian, who was Hispanic, somehow found a way to fit in, though he remembered being uncomfortable when he first heard kids talk of fights in their neighborhood, or when he went up the block to a bus stop, looked down and noticed blood stains on the concrete.

Where Sebastian was quiet, Flex was loud. Though he still wasn't playing much, and hadn't worked his way into the starting lineup, Flex had a boastful streak, always declaring in class that this was the week they would win, most definitely, they had this one in the bag. Hearing the boasts, a theology teacher had taken to writing the final score from all the games on a schedule pinned to the bulletin board, then tallying up points scored and points allowed.

Sebastian and some of the other players were in that class. They tried to laugh it off, but it hurt, especially after hearing all the whispers and wisecracks from classmates: You guys ain't shit. You're gonna get your ass kicked again this week. You couldn't win a game in practice. If during morning announcements students were asked to pray for the football team that night, someone in the classroom was likely to finish the statement with "So they only lose by 30 this week."

It took courage, too, to listen to all that.

"I wish we could take them all out here for one practice," said Sebastian, then revised his statement. "An *easy* practice."

Justin Owen, a Shorewood sophomore, had caught up with them. He would have been a starter, but his back kept acting up.

"It's just like that at Shorewood," Justin offered. He said something about comments made by a soccer player in the training room the other day.

"I used to play soccer," said Sebastian. "Soccer you don't get hit."

"You get tripped," said Flex.

"You skin your elbow," said Sebastian.

He paused. Shook his head.

"I ain't taking no shit, swear to God."

Chapter 10

"You gotta see the bottom to come back to the top."

On the Saturday after the St. Francis loss, the loss that officially ended the dream of making the playoffs — if anyone was still clinging to that tattered old dream — practice was held late so everyone could go watch the game between Whitefish Bay Dominican (0-5) and Brown Deer (2-3), the team's next two opponents. Coaches and players from both schools had been spotted in the stands at Shorewood the night before, and now Shorewood-Messmer would return the favor.

But first Trost had a task for the team.

"We're going to set some goals for the week," he said.

Trost stood in the middle of the locker room, holding a small dry erase board and a green magic marker.

"Who's got one?"

"Score 80 points," offered Rob Wyatt.

"Realistic goals," said Coach Carroll.

"That is realistic, isn't it?" Rob asked.

To be sure, the team would not be facing a machine Friday night. In football, the eight-team Parkland Conference had a line drawn exactly down the middle. The top four teams — Luther Prep, Slinger, Pewaukee and St. Francis — had a combined overall record of 20-4, while the other four teams tallied a mere 2-20. And of those, only Brown Deer had won any games. Thanks to the scheduling gods, Shorewood-Messmer had already played the four powerhouses and now was left with its fellow bottom-feeders.

So, in a strange sense, the team had reached the promised land. Broken and battered, numbers down and tensions still high, they had made it to the point in the season where the victories would come. The night before, standing on a chair at the Parents Night reception, after the team's best performance of the year, Trost told everyone: "I have a good feeling about these last three games." They were the sure things, the gimmies. They were Ws, all of them.

More goals were tossed out.

"Keep them under 100 yards of offense," someone said.

"That is definitely a good goal," said Coach Carroll.

Trost wrote the goals down as they were called out: Have more special teams points than Dominican. No kick returns past the 30. Eliminate penalties. Score on special teams. Get 300 yards of offense. Stop the dive. No turnovers.

"Finish with as many players as we start with," said Drew O'Malley.

"Another good one," said Trost.

Many of the players knew some of the guys from Dominican. Some had played in the St. Bernadette league with Mark and Rob and the rest. Others had gone to grade school with some of the Messmer kids. The two schools, Dominican and Messmer, recruited in many of the same Catholic elementary schools, though Dominican with its suburban location had many more white students than Messmer. In any case, there was no mental block with Dominican. The team knew they could play with them.

"Aggressive on defense."

That made 10.

"Here's one more bonus one," said Trost.

He wrote his goal down, underlined it and held the board up as he read it aloud.

"Best week of practice."

The trip to the Dominican-Brown Deer game wasn't a sanctioned school event, so the players and coaches drove separately.

It was perfect fall evening for football and when the coaches arrived at Whitefish Bay High School, where Dominican played its home games, the sky was already dark, the air was cool and the trees in the distance held more than a hint of fall color. The shouts from the field hung in the air, as fans staked out spots on the bleachers, some arriving with blankets under their arms. The coaches sat in the last row on the Dominican side. Some coaches from Greendale Martin Luther, the last opponent on Shorewood-Messmer's schedule, were a few rows down, doing their own scouting. The two staffs exchanged nods. Trost followed the action on the field with his video camera, delivering a running commentary while the other coaches, each with a clipboard, drew up the formations and plays.

"Here comes a reverse," Trost said at one point.

The play unfolded. A reverse.

"Am I a prophet or what?"

Coach Carroll had already remarked that watching the game was like looking in the mirror. And it was. Like Shorewood-Messmer, the teams down below — Dominican in green and black, Brown Deer in brown and white — were small in number and the players, with few exceptions, were small in stature.

As the coaches watched the game, the players drifted in, most of them dropped off by Mr. Wyatt in the van. Others, like Drew O'Malley and Evan Rivera, came on their own. The coaches couldn't really require them to be there, though about a dozen showed up. The players found their own spot in the first few rows of an otherwise empty section. They talked and joked as much as watched the game, reliving their own highlights from the night before — Mark Moore's great runs, Micah Moore's passing. Ronell Halbert, with 143 yards receiving, had made it in

the morning newspaper as one of Friday night's top per-
formers. On one of his catches, the ball had hung up in
the air, but Ronell came back to get it, leaping between
two St. Francis players before racing up the field. Ronell
demonstrated how he did it for the others, miming the
catch and exaggerating his triumphant run to the end zone.

The game itself was slow and the crowd was quiet, so
quiet you could hear the plays called out on the field.
Dominican led 7-6 at the half, but by the start of the
third quarter its own fans were growing impatient. Lots of
predictable plays, lots of punting.

"They know what we're doing," a Dominican fan
shouted, throwing up her arms. The woman turned to a
friend and declared: "I don't know anything about football and I know what we're doing next."

Nearby, the players swallowed their grins.

"Man, this is boring," Drew O'Malley said a few minutes later, hands in pockets, then shouted: "Somebody do
something."

Brown Deer eventually scored twice, both times after
getting turnovers deep in Dominican territory, so they
never had to mount a sustained drive. With a few minutes
left on the clock, the players wandered out to wait for Mr.
Wyatt and the van. As they did, they walked under the
scoreboard.

"Looks like it's 21-7," one player said sarcastically. He
said it loudly, though no Dominican fan was near enough
to hear the remark, let alone take offense.

"Yeah," another said. "Look at that."

**On Tuesday, after a typical lackluster Monday prac-
tice** and the standard late start, only 16 guys in uniform
ready to go, Trost went to the locker room and returned
with the board that listed the 11 goals for the Dominican
game.

"Best week of practice," he read aloud, the players

stretching around him on the grass. "That's a good one."

Nobody looked up.

"Aggressive on defense. That's a good one. Remember that one."

When they began the customary sprints, Trost assigned the board to Blake Comer, a Messmer junior who had injured his knee the week before. Blake was to carry the board around and whenever a player passed him, whether it was while running a play or going for a drink of water, that player had to shout out one of the goals. Blake stood in the middle of the field, holding the board aloft like a ring-girl marking the rounds in a boxing match. As the team ran sprints past him, the goals came back in a garbled mess: "Aggressive on no run past turnovers defense 300 yards of special teams week of returns past the offense best no scores on practice eliminate penalties."

Once they got organized, the goals came back cleaner, shouted in unison.

"Eliminate penalties!"

"Aggressive on defense!"

"Stop the dive!"

Trost and Trawitzki stood together. There were 23 guys running now, everyone having made it out of the locker room and the trainer's room. Trost long ago had abandoned his down-to-the-minute practice schedule, mostly winging it instead. Every day was an adventure. One player, back at the start, quit after being put on the line with the scout offense, declaring: "I ain't *about* playing guard." Another didn't show up on the day coaches called his name as a first-string safety. He was never seen again. Still another, a huge Shorewood sophomore, lasted about a week, as soft as the coaches predicted.

The shouts continued.

"No turnovers!"

"Score on special teams!"

"I wish I had a guitar," Trost said. "If I had a guitar I

could make this thing into a song."

He started playing air guitar and singing. Even now, decades removed from his brief TV commercial career, Trost was a first-class ham.

"Goals for Dominican," Trost sang and began bouncing in and out of thoughts as if he was going up and down a radio dial. "Da dun dun da, aggressive on defense. God Bless America, my home sweet — eliminate penalties — home, put your hands in the air, stop the dive, throw your hands in the air."

Trost wore a pair of red shorts, which he playfully hiked halfway to his chest, and a plaid shirt from his day in the classroom, a blue slip of paper sticking out of the pocket. Trost had picked up the message slip in the school office on his way to the locker room. It was from a coach at North Dakota State University inquiring again about Mark Moore. Though Mark was getting down on his chances of playing in college, the school remained interested. Over the years, North Dakota State, located in Fargo, had created a pipeline to southeastern Wisconsin and now eight of the 102 players on its roster were from the Milwaukee area. The school was a Division II power, sometimes leading the nation in attendance, and was planning a move up to Division I-AA.

Trost had been in contact with the coach and sent him a tape of the Slinger game, in which Mark racked up 129 yards and made some nice plays on defense. That game, though, was stopped at the half because of rain. And this time Johnny Cox, who coordinated the Milwaukee area recruiting, wanted a complete game. But there wasn't much else that could be sent. Not the Whitefish Bay carnage, or Luther Prep, or even Friday's St. Francis game. In that one, Mark was amazing early on, but once he was leveled on the punt coverage, he never returned.

The knock on Mark Moore had always been he turned it on and off. He'd have a few great runs, then give up if a block wasn't there. He'd be determined one minute, drifting the next. The other coaches in the conference knew it and, in truth, Trost would sometimes say the same thing when the office door was closed and true feelings could be laid out. For Trost, it was a reward to watch Mark's growth from a timid freshman to the sort of leader who could shout out demands in the locker room and lead the team into battle, as he had against St. Francis. But it was a frustration that he never seemed to put it all together.

Trost figured he could stall the North Dakota State coach until after Friday's game against Dominican, but that meant the pressure was on for a good performance from Mark. At the end of practice, Trost stepped to the middle of the team.

"Who thinks the team we're playing is horrible?" he asked.

The players were unsure how to react. Finally, Maurice Ragsdale tentatively raised a hand. So did Coach Trawitzki.

"But so are we," Trost said.

His voice was loud and urgent.

The game was winnable, he said, but they had to focus. That was the message from the moment the St. Francis game ended. Focus, focus, focus. Of the remaining three teams, Dominican easily had the most explosive athletes. One receiver was the state 100-meter track champion. There were also a couple lanky basketball players, one at tight end and the other at receiver. And the game was Dominican's homecoming, which meant they'd have a big crowd and the team would be more fired up.

The coaches could sense their own team was looser and cockier, but too loose and too cocky. They weren't just confident. They were overconfident. They were 0-6, yet to win anything, and somehow overconfident.

"I'm really concerned about Friday night," Trost told them

As the other coaches talked, Trost pulled Mark aside

and showed him the message slip. No one else noticed —
all eyes were on Coach Carroll, intense as ever. Mark looked
at the message sheet, listened as Trost talked, and nodded.

"Why do you think you're the homecoming game?"
Carroll asked the team.

He was always the walking reality check.

"They have no respect for you and they think they're
going to win," he said. "What's going through their heads
is, 'We're going to win our game against Shorewood-
Messmer, because whatever is wrong over here, it's worse
over there.'"

**Although the season was two-thirds over and they had
worked** on kick coverage for the past eight weeks, the team
still couldn't master who did what. It was like dealing
with a group of amnesia patients. Every day the mental
chalkboard was wiped clean. On Wednesday, Coach Carroll
changed the approach. He walked along the line and assigned each player a specific guy on the return team to hit
and take out of the play.

Ronell Halbert was assigned Flex.

Drew O'Malley sent the ball through the air and the
two sides raced toward each other, like the charge of the
cavalry. No worries about who was supposed to bust the
wedge and who had to contain the outside, all that mumbo
jumbo. Just take a guy. One guy. Knock him out. And
then get the returner.

Ronell leveled Flex.

Coach Trawitzki doubled over in laughter. Flex had
waited to be hit, not taking on the block at all, and wound
up bounced to the ground.

A quick look at Flex and it was clear he had the body to
be a football player. But he missed many of the critical
early practices with a twisted ankle, suffered while playing
basketball in the final days of a summer youth camp, where
he was a counselor along with Nate Shorter. Some days,

Flex would wear a wooden cross around his neck and a T-shirt from the camp that read: "Ask me about non-violence." Flex was one of those in tears after sitting during the Lakeside Lutheran game. He fought back in the Oklahoma drills, only to struggle the next week with the tackling dummy, unable to wrest it to the ground. His season had been up and down.

Today was a deep gully.

"Good block Justin," Trawitzki said, still laughing.

"He got *run* over," said Coach Carroll, more proud of the hit than worried about any bruise to Flex's ego.

"Wow," said Trost. "I wish I had seen it."

"Watch, here it comes again," said Trawitzki.

All season, the coaches had urged the team, pleaded with them, to treat the players in practice like the enemy. And the coaches pleaded with the team to show some excitement, to let loose after a solid hit, even strut a little.

The ball was kicked again and the two ran toward each other — Ronell, the lanky receiver, and Flex, the big lineman. Flex desperately wanted to do well, but whenever the coaches were watching the closest, he always seemed to be on the wrong end of things. This time, Ronell hit Flex so hard he went airborne, spinning around like a helicopter before crashing to the ground. If it was the movies, the hit would have come in slow motion. Instead, it was quick and hard. Flex slowly stood up, glowering at the coaches.

"Get pissed off, man," Coach Hoagland said to Flex. "Run *him* over."

"Hey Ronell, you gonna hit Demi like that?" Trost asked. He meant Demi Omole, the Dominican kick returner and state sprint champ.

"Hell yeah," Ronell said.

They did it again. And again Flex was on the ground.

But a new tone had been set. Soon everybody was hitting. Hard hits. Monster hits. Nobody got hurt. No one cared. Instead, they lined up to do it again.

As the players ran toward each other, Coach Carroll stood in the middle.

"Why did it take so long to figure out this is fun?" he asked.

Thursday now. Once again the last chance before Friday to get things right. The week had been different, the ups and downs higher and lower than usual.

The team was down on the big field, the sky heavy and gray, the wind blowing hard, like a slap to the face. They ran through the plays: Option left, Option right, Roar Back. Mark was practicing again, after sitting out a few days with the sore back from the St. Francis hit. So the option formation made its return, too. Mark kept alternating with his brother, Micah, the regular quarterback, as they ran through the week's playbook.

The practice was slow, sluggish, a bit rough.

Fumble. Whistle.

"Micah, I knew you were going to fumble that," said Trost. "You're walking around out here, mouthguard out, thinking you're Michael Vick or something. C'mon, put the mouthguard in."

Micah had left his mouthguard on the side of his helmet, wedged inside the frame of the face mask.

"My teeth hurt," Micah said.

"Your teeth hurt?"

Micah waved an arm, a dismissive wave, and mumbled.

It was a replay, a near carbon copy, of Trost and Ronell Halbert two weeks earlier, on the eve of the Pewaukee game, the dispute that moved Micah — nervous and shaking — into the starting spot.

Uh oh, Ronell thought, as he watched.

There had already been too many moments like this one, moments when things teetered between blowing over and blowing up. The first time it was Drew O'Malley, tired of his assignments, feeling picked on by the coaches. The next it was Ronell, feeling singled out for discipline after helping orchestrate the locker-room meeting. Now Micah. Some of the players had jokingly started calling him "Micah Vick," after the scrambling rookie quarterback for the Atlanta Falcons. Micah didn't like it. He never pretended he could play like Michael Vick. And his teeth really did hurt. His wisdom teeth were growing in.

Micah stared at Trost for a second or two and then slowly put his mouthguard in and called the next play.

Disaster averted.

But a few plays later, Micah went out to receiver, while his brother stepped in to run the option. The play was choppy. Sloppy and choppy.

"Micah, that was a pathetic route," Trost said as the team gathered in the huddle. "I'm going to give you a choice right now. Run the pattern or step off the field. I don't need an attitude out here. Let's do it again."

Photo courtesy of Michael Tucker

Nate Shorter, a Messmer junior, concentrates on his stance. Nate, who battled a nagging knee injury, was an anchor on the offensive and defensive lines.

Micah turned and walked toward his spot on the line. He walked and kept on walking. His helmet hit the ground. Then his shoulder pads. He tossed the wristband, the one with the plays on it. Lost the mouthguard.

"Not again," said Pertrell Mallett, hands to helmet.

"Are you kidding me?" said Coach Carroll.

"Micah!" Flex shouted.

Micah shouted something over his shoulder, your basic fuck off message, and continued the walk to the locker room, a trail of equipment on the grass behind him. At that moment, the team on the verge of crumbling, Mark Moore made his own choice. There were three games left in his senior year. A college scholarship on the line. The taste of victory so near, oh so near.

"Marty, get over at receiver," Mark said and tried to line the team up again himself.

As the team stretched on the field Friday night, its white road jerseys glowing under the lights, there was a quiet clamor in the distance, a vague honking and shouting and singing, punctuated by the occasional whoop-whoop of a police siren. The team tried to ignore it, but the noise grew louder and louder, closer and closer, until a parade of Dominican students rounded the corner. There were dozens of them, hundreds. Students mixed in with cars pulling floats, the pep band leading the way, loudly playing some oldies tune. It was Dominican's homecoming game and the group had paraded from the school to the stadium at Whitefish Bay High School. The lights on the police cars flashed red and blue.

Again the siren: Whoop-whoop brrrraaaappp.

As the team warmed up, Micah Moore stood on one of the benches on the Shorewood-Messmer sideline, hands in his pockets, a smug look on his face.

The night before, after the blowup on the field, Coach Carroll followed Micah into the locker room, where Micah cursed at him, a withering string of obscenities. Micah left without his brother, though when he got home his aunt made him call Trost and leave a message of apology. Micah apologized again that afternoon, just as Ronell had after his meltdown. Trost had worked with kids for years. Sometimes, he thought, they just snapped. Who knew why? Trost left the punishment up to Coach Carroll, who decided Micah should sit out the game. But in a season built on second chances, like Ronell before him, and Drew before that, Micah would get another chance.

The Dominican fans, almost all outfitted in green, were still passing through the gate, walking across the field and climbing the steps to the bleachers. The crowd was double, triple, the week before. Micah watched it all, a few players from the freshman team standing nearby. Across the way, Coach Hoagland and Coach Larsen, who was missing more and more practices himself, were getting set up in the press box, hooking up the connection with the sideline headsets.

"Hurts them more than it hurts me," Micah said casually, nodding toward the field.

Warmups complete, the team ran to the locker room, past the Dominican student section. There was a rain of boos from the stands. One student, face red, ran down to the railing and shouted: "You suck ass. You suck ass." Mark Moore offered a mock salute as he ran. The other players were stunned.

"No respect, no respect," Rob Wyatt shouted in the locker room.

"I want a victory," screamed Drew, his voice high and piercing. "I want a victory."

The team listened to the coaches, scowls deep on their faces, seething. They had found anger. They had found, somewhere, rage. It demanded a release. They listened to the coaches but the words were a blur, a blur that was lost in the humming of the florescent lights. They pulled helmets on, banged heads, pounded chests, ready to burst. They shouted out their breakdown — "What time is it?" "*Game* time." — and gathered themselves in. A year ago, in the last game of the season, Shorewood led Dominican at the half, 19-6, but the coaches still lit into them in the locker room, telling the team to stay focused. But, confidence sapped, the team wilted instead and lost 41-27.

Tonight, tonight would be different.

Trost looked at his watch and told the team to wait a few minutes.

He went outside and talked with the other coaches, their shadows long on the sidewalk. To them, the banging and shouting that echoed from the locker room was the most beautiful sound of the season. For the players, the rage was simmering.

"They kept me out of that school," said Flex.

"They never accepted me," said Maurice Ragsdale.

"Actions speak louder than words," Rob reminded them.

Nate Shorter paced in a small circle, like a bull finding its footing in the dusty ring.

At the overnight session in the Shorewood gym, when the players had all declared who they were playing for this season, they listed mothers and fathers, aunts and grand-mothers, teachers and teammates. It may have seemed self-ish to say they were playing for themselves, but now they were. They had to play for themselves.

The team had lost the coin toss, so it would kick off. All week, they had practiced variations of a short kick to limit Dominican's chance at a big return. Instead, Coach Carroll told them to kick it deep, letting the team run down and bust somebody from the start.

"You motherfuckers on the kickoff team," Ronell shouted over the din. "You better hit some mother-fucking somebody."

Since Ronell had been moved back to quarterback, he was off the kick off squad, even though his hits had won the most raves in practice. Now the coaches told the team it was time.

They pulled on their helmets as they ran to the field.

The Dominican students had formed a line on the field to welcome out their team. The Shorewood-Messmer players ran past, focused. The fans shouted, held out hands for mock handshakes, then pulled them back. It was a blur of letter jackets, sweatshirts, blue jeans. A jumble of shouts. "Lose a few pounds No. 72," someone shouted. That was Nate.

The team lined up on its sideline and waited.

The crowd for Shorewood-Messmer was somewhat sparse, so one could easily pick out the faces. There were Marty's parents, in the middle, with Jack, his brother, and an aunt. There was a group of Messmer teachers. A clutch of Shorewood students. Drew's parents. Evan's parents. And, near the railing, Matt Moore, Mark's twin brother. He was a somewhat slighter version of Mark, who technically was three minutes older.

"Tonight's the night Shorewood," came a shout. It was Marty's dad.

Br. Bob Smith, the Messmer president, stood nearby on the sideline.

The first time Trost went to Messmer after the merger was approved, Smith met him on the stairs inside the front door. "If you only win one game this year," Smith told Trost, before shaking his hand and finishing, "it better be Dominican." The two schools were longtime rivals from back in the old Metro Conference, particularly in basketball. Even now, though they rarely matched up in sports, the blood remained so bad that when the idea of exploring a football partnership with Dominican was broached, the Messmer graduates on the school's board of directors shot it down immediately.

Smith had met the team at Shorewood, where he again led them in prayer. This time, instead of a talk about the strength of a circle, he delivered a stemwinder. "They don't like Messmer," Smith told the players. "They've seen our trophy cases. They know they're on the other end of a lot of those trophies. We've gone through them over and over. When you hit a man, put him down." He pounded a fist into his palm for emphasis. "They are not going to give you the game. You have to go out and take it, play by play, quarter by quarter, half by half."

Now Smith stood watching the warm ups, arms crossed.

The victory would mean something for him, of course. But he wanted it for the team. Everyone did. Nothing resolves problems like a winning. And one victory could set up two more. It would generate headlines, create a hallway buzz, get more players interested for next year. It would be something to remember. Not just for now, but forever.

Several Messmer players sought out Br. Bob, giving him hugs, patting him on the back.

"We're gonna take this one to the house," promised Montreal Miller, a seldom-used senior. "This is our game."

The two teams lined up for the kickoff, but before the Shorewood-Messmer team was entirely set, Drew O'Malley raised his arm, dropped it to his side, and ran forward, kicking the ball. He was off and running, the ball twisting and tumbling through the air, the team following him down the field, the ball landing in the arms of Demi Omole, the Dominican return man and state 100-meter sprint champ, who raced 90 yards up the field, untouched, slicing into the end zone.

"What happened?" Pertrell Mallett asked, coming off the field.

Marty Wallner, who had been flattened on the play, followed Pertrell.

"Did you like that?" Coach Carroll asked him. "That wasn't good, was it?"

Dominican missed the extra point, but lead 6-0.

The game was 10 seconds old.

"Keep it positive," said Coach Trawitzki.

"Get it back," said Coach Smith.

The two teams shoved back and forth for a while, one

possession, then another, up and down, no scoring. A
Shorewood-Messmer fumble was lost, but the team held
and forced a punt. At one point, Nate's helmet was busted.
He came out, ripped the mouthguard from Pertrell's helmet, put it on and returned to the fray. Series to series,
quarter to quarter it went, evenly matched. Finally, on a
pass play, Jonathan Williams burst through the Dominican line and smashed into the quarterback. The ball
tumbled from his hands and Rob scooped it up and ran.
Rob tried to distance himself, but was caught from behind and knocked to the ground.

Shorewood-Messmer ball.

On offense now, Ronell lined up the team, shouted
out the count and took the snap. A pitch to Mark, who
caught it smoothly, in stride, slipped the football under
his arm and darted toward the left side of the line. He
disappeared into the bodies, white pushing forward, green
driving back, and then shot through the other side, feet
pumping effortlessly as he raced to the end zone. Thirty-
five yards. Touchdown. This was for college. Micah followed it all with Trost's video camera. The team jumped
and screamed. The two-point conversion was good and
Shorewood-Messmer had a lead, 8-6.

Matt Moore leaned down from the bleachers as his
brother reached the sideline. "Mark, can I get four more?"
he shouted. "Four of those."

Mark nodded.

They kicked off again. And again the ball went to Demi
Omole, who banged up the field, past the 50, tackler after
tackler falling away, until Jerrel Jackson dragged him to
the ground at the Shorewood-Messmer 38-yard line.

"Why do we keep kicking to him?" Trost shouted.

Four plays later, after a short Dominican touchdown
run, the score was 12-8. It stayed that way until half time.
So close. In the balance. In the locker room, Drew sought
out the trainer. His right hand was bloodied, knuckles

red, scrapes up and down his arms. Many of the others
had scratches and bruises on elbows and knees. The team
sat on tables and chairs, the floor, chests heaving.

"Relax for a couple minutes," Trost said. "Relax."

He said it for himself as much as the team.

"We're gonna win the football game," Trost said finally.
"If you keep the faith."

There it was again. Faith. They had to believe. Not
one, not two of them. Everyone. In theology class, faith
might be defined as "believing without seeing." All season
long, this team operated in reverse. It had to see. Sure,
they got the mustard seeds before the Whitefish Bay game.
Some of the players still had them, tucked in desks or
their lockers. They took the seeds, but six games later,
they had yet to move a mountain. If Jesus Christ himself
stepped in at quarterback, they'd ask if he knew the plays.

For this team, winning was believing.

"We get the ball," Trost said. "We score and we stop
them, that will be it."

Two steps.

"That will be it," he said again.

Trost had saved his mustard seed. It was at home in his
dresser drawer.

"You guys want to win a football game?" he asked.
"There you are."

They talked about adjustments, more passes to counter
the blitz, but no more of the Roar Back play to Drew,
which kept getting blown up on the penetration. Even
with Ronell at quarterback, they were running the "trips"
formation, but Trost put the three running backs — Mark,
Drew and Evan — out there. They were the most trusted.
Not Marty Wallner or Maurice Ragsdale, who had competed for a starting receiver position all season long. With
so few chances, neither had caught a single pass.

"Can me and Evan switch?" Drew asked. "So Evan is
next to Mark and I can be spread out?"

"Why?" Trost asked.

"So I can catch the ball," Drew said confidently.

The sky was dark as they returned to the field, though the trees beyond the bleachers seemed to shine from the glow of the streetlights, like matches, red and yellow, against the night sky. Beyond the clouds, the moon was muffled. It was full, or nearly so, just like on the night of the breakthrough Brown Deer victory the year before.

"You're getting 25 carries this half, young man," Trost said to Mark on the sideline.

Shorewood-Messmer took the kickoff, but had to fall on the ball at the 10 yard line. No return. First play: A pitch to Mark, out to the 26. Then a short gain for Mark. Then a penalty dropped them back five yards. Everyone tensed on the sideline. Another pitch to Mark. Then Evan ground it out to the 35 yard line. Third and one. The possession felt like a bumpy old road, all jostled and unsettled.

"C'mon, Shorewood," came a shout from the stands.

And the response: "C'mon, Messmer."

Evan bulled forward for the first down and away they went. Not in a quick, high-speed fashion. But methodically, confidently. At one point, Evan plunged up the middle again, to be tackled after 10 yards, dragging several Dominican players with him.

"They needed like six guys to bring him down," marveled Sebastian Negron on the sideline.

Now the team lined up in the "trips" formation. Drew took the outside spot, as discussed in the locker room, and as the blitz came, he drifted to the center of the field, caught Ronell's pass and raced toward the end zone, finally tackled at the six, no the four, no the two yard line. The Dominican stands were quiet now, while the Shorewood-Messmer side was crackling with excitement. The last time they had been in this position was week two against Lakeside Lutheran, when the play resulted in a disastrous fumble. This time it was a pitch to Mark, on the left side.

Untouched. Touchdown.

They had scored: 14-12.

Step one.

On the next kickoff, a carefully placed shorter kick, Drew was again the first one down the field, but this time he leveled the receiver. On the sideline, the players slapped hands and hugged. Drew leaped to his feet, hunched his shoulders in a show of strength and clenched his fists at his side. A few plays later, Dominican punted.

Now they had stopped them.

Step two.

This was it.

This had to be it.

The mountain. Moved.

But then they started going backwards. Mark was caught from behind on a play, one that could have gotten him around the end and into the clear for a first down. There was a bad snap on the punt, the ball slipping from Drew's hands as he was about to kick it. The ball sailed low, hitting Pertrell in the back, less than 10 yards downfield. Dominican scored on the next play, a 50-yard pass.

"What happened?" Trost asked Mark, who was covering the receiver.

"I got burned," Mark said.

At least it was honest.

A few plays later, Evan was injured while blocking for Mark, twisting an ankle as he wound up on the bottom of a pile, screaming "Get off. Get off. Get off." His leg was folded under him. "You can do it," Sebastian told Evan on the sideline. "We're soldiers." But Evan watched the remainder of the game from the sideline, sitting on the bench, a bag of ice on his foot, his foot on top of his helmet.

Confidence back, Dominican soon was hitting harder,

striking faster. Sharp runs to the outside. Quick passes over the middle. Slashing tackles that sent the ball tumbling loose. At one point, a referee walked Drew O'Malley over to the sideline and demanded the trainer look him over. "He's hanging his head down awful low," the referee said. Drew protested: "I'm fine. I swear. I'm fine." It was difficult, of course, to separate the physical head-hanging from the mental. Even Br. Bob Smith, hands in pockets, quietly stared at the ground.

Final score: 39-14.

After the Whitefish Bay game, on the day the coaches sprinted the team half-way to death in the baking sun, Coach Smith — always prone to quote the Bible — had told the team that the Good Book says the righteous man must fall seven times. The measure of success, then, is not in never falling. It is in always getting back up.

This made seven.

And it hurt worse than the rest. Nate Shorter was completely muddied. He finished with 15 tackles — down the field, at the line, behind the line. It was an amazing number for a lineman. He pulled off his pads and jersey at midfield, the dirt-brown sleeves emphasizing how white his T-shirt had been. Others were just as sapped, faces red, or covered in sweat. Jerseys torn. Pants stained green from the grass and brown from the mud.

"I say as long as we had fun," said Maurice Ragsdale, who had not played much and who was positively leveled on a late kick return.

"Fuck that," came the response. Several players offered it.

"Don't let it get you down, guys," said Coach Smith. "You gotta see the bottom to come back to the top."

The sky was clear now and the moon was bright. But the moon was not full, after all. A sliver was missing.

The players made their way back to the bus. There

were two buses, actually, one for each team. The first was happy and light, laughter through the open windows. A homecoming bonfire awaited Dominican back at the high school. The second bus was sullen and heavy. Players from the two teams passed on the sidewalk, some exchanging greetings.

"We had this bitch won," Micah told a Dominican player.

"You owe me 20 bucks," a Dominican player said to Maurice. It was the one who had tackled him on the kick return.

Finally, Trost climbed on the bus, his son Bryce with him. Bryce carried a football. His eyes were sleepy.

"I know everybody is down," Trost said. "I'm down."

How many times could he make this speech?

"We're all down," Trost said.

At least once more.

"I really thought we'd win a football game," Trost said. "I thought we'd get there. We had a lead in the third quarter. We moved the ball effectively. We've got trying times. We'll be better for it."

The words seemed hollow now.

"We'll be better for it."

The windows fogged up with frustration.

Chapter 11
"Ain't no turning back"

At the start of practice on Monday, Coach Trost and Mark Moore stood on the sidewalk at the edge of the field. Players drifted past, or just leaned against the fence under the tree, which had already changed from green to brown. It was a flashback of sorts, back to the beginning. To the first day, but with all the promise gone, blown away like so many dry and wrinkled leaves.

"I'm starting to think last year's team was better than this one," Mark said.

"More experienced," Trost agreed. "Two games left. We'll see."

The two hadn't talked this way for a while, casually and evenly, coach and star player assessing the team. Trost had been miffed about Mark not signing the clipboard on the bus back from Luther Prep. And Mark was irritated his commitment had been questioned at all. But on Saturday, after the post-Dominican practice, Trost called Mark into the office and the two talked for about 10 minutes. This is it, Trost told him. This is your team. You have to carry us. It was something the coaches had resisted telling Mark all season, for fear he wasn't ready to meet the challenge. But there was no more time to wait.

Mark lifted his practice jersey and buckled the pads across his chest.

"How many times do you think we've led in a game this year?" Trost asked.

"Two," Mark guessed, looking up.

Trost shook his head.

"One?" Mark tried again.

"Three," said Trost.

In seven games, the team had, in fact, led in three — Lakeside Lutheran, St. Francis, Dominican. That was one more than last year.

"Doesn't matter much," Mark said after a moment. "In the end."

Indeed, that was true as well. They had led in three. But in each, they gave up the lead in spectacular fashion and, in the end, they had lost. There was no credit for leading. Of course, one could argue the journey was the reward and there was meaning to be found in the struggle, in surviving all the adversity. But that didn't help now, everything fast slipping away. The coaches were still talking with Mark about the Shorewood rushing record, but he would need to put up something like 330 yards in each of the last two games to reach it. Last year, against Brown Deer, in that glorious 51-19 victory, Mark ran for 242 yards and three touchdowns. It was his 17th birthday and the day he and Leslie officially started dating. With Brown Deer on tap again Friday, it meant almost a year had passed. And it meant that Mark was now almost 18. Another line to be crossed, another demarcation between youth and adulthood.

Mark mentioned Valparaiso University. Someone he knew might go there.

"You want to go to Valparaiso?" Trost asked. "I can get you in at Valparaiso."

He knew one of the coaches.

"I don't know," Mark said, shaking his head. The test scores were still a concern. "It may have to be junior college."

His voice was one of regret and resignation, as if there was no choice for him in the matter, no role to play in the outcome. As if it was all over, already decided for him.

Regret.

It was the emotion the coaches felt every Friday night when they stepped onto the football field. It was the voice that whispered all of the things they could never change. Coach Carroll could not go back and change the second half of that playoff game. For Coach Smith, that last-second field goal would always sail through the uprights, costing his team the state championship. Coach Trawitzki couldn't go back and get treatment before his condition was so far along. And Trost would never have the athletic body that, with his grit and determination, would have given him a shot at college.

Coach Carroll would often tell the team regret was the worst emotion of all, because there is nothing you can do to make it go away. The players felt it now, too. They had lost to Dominican. They had lost seven times. They couldn't go back and set everything right. They couldn't go back to August. They couldn't go back to the moment before morning, when all was possible and everything new.

Trost looked over at Mark. The video from the Dominican game was ready to go in the mail to the North Dakota State University coach. There were still two games left. Hadn't they talked about it? Two more games.

It was too early for never.

Trost blew his whistle.

"Let's go," he called out.

At the end of practice the next day, Tuesday, 20 guys stood around Trost and the rest of the coaches. As usual, the team had a sluggish start, but things picked up.

"Much better today," said Trost. "Much better."

The group, ever smaller, seemed tired and weary.

At Messmer, first quarter grades were out so a few players were suddenly ineligible. Sebastian Negron was among the missing, off running in a cross country meet for Messmer, his first of the season. He had been on the cross country squad last year. Even now, so far along, Sebastian was having second thoughts about choosing football. By now, there was gallows humor everywhere. At one point, Coach Carroll finished explaining an assignment to Pertrell Mallett by saying: "You block the end right there." Pertrell looked at the line opposite him. "Nobody's there," he said. Indeed, the team was back to air blocking. "Well," Carroll said, "in imaginary fantasy world."

"Want to guess how long it's been since Shorewood won a homecoming game?" Trost asked.

"1730s?" joked Mark Moore.

Evan Rivera, who was still sidelined with the gimpy ankle, had overheard the coaches talking about it, so he knew.

"Um, 18 years?" he offered casually.

Yes, 18 years. For Messmer, it had been at least that long, since the school hadn't had a football team since 1983, and nobody knew for sure how the soccer team fared for all those years when the school tied homecoming to soccer. Or how the basketball team did, when Messmer tried a basketball homecoming.

"Eighteen years," Trost repeated.

Of the players around him, only two or three had even been born.

"Seniors, you have eight days left," said Coach Trawitzki. "All you should be thinking about in those eight days is two wins."

Brown Deer on Friday, the homecoming game for both Shorewood and Messmer, then Martin Luther on Wednesday — a short week to help set up the post season for the teams that made the state tournament.

"You've gotta play iron man football out there," said Coach Carroll, who noted the players shouldn't get too caught up in any homecoming hoopla.

"We don't need bonfires, balloons, anything else," he said. "We're gonna win this game for the people standing here. And we're going to celebrate with the people standing here, because the people standing here are the people who wanted to be here all along."

On Wednesday, as the team stretched out on the grass under a dreary sky, there was a clap of thunder in the distance, one that rumbled and echoed closer.

"Hey, it starts lightning, no practice," declared Flex, who after the Dominican game threatened to quit, but came back.

Coach Carroll was walking past. He stopped, astonished.

"We've got a game Friday we can win and you don't want to practice?" he said and shook his head.

At the front of the group, up by the captains, Trost was teasing Drew O'Malley about whether he was going to the homecoming dance. Trost waltzed around with an imaginary girl, while humming some mystery song.

"Mark, who're you taking to the dance?" Trost asked.

It had to be Leslie.

"I ain't going," Mark replied.

"Why not?"

Mark just shook his head. A few weeks back, he and some of the others had talked in the locker room about which school would have a better dance and who planned to go. Mark said he'd only go if he was named king. It would fit, of course. At most high schools, the football star is the homecoming king. But not at Shorewood.

"We're gonna party," Mark offered.

"Practice Saturday night," Trost shouted. "We'll go to the dance as a team."

As they finished stretching, the rain began to fall, slowly at first, a drizzle, then faster, harder, until the drops pelted the helmets and the patch where the grass was worn bare became a puddle, and, once the rain slowed, the puddle became mud.

They practiced kickoffs and punts, mud splattering on their pants as they ran down the field. The players only shouted and ran harder. The ball skittered in the mud and soaked up the water until it was heavy and hard to throw.

"Let's do Okies in the mud," said Jay White, a Shorewood senior.

No one ever volunteered for Oklahoma. The coaches watched, bemused and encouraged. The call had gone out that lighting had been spotted. The soccer team ran past, back into the building. Then the girls cross country team. The football team stayed put.

"It's a beautiful day in the neighborhood," Trost sang, off key as usual.

After a quick, spirited practice, the rain disappearing as fast as it came, Trost sent the running backs and receivers over to the chutes, where the linemen were doing their drills. The chutes were a deeply hated contraption. They consisted of a piece of metal mesh maybe four feet above the ground, suspended on a slight angle. The chutes were designed to force the linemen to stay low. If they broke their stance or came up too soon, they'd bang their heads. As the backs and receivers — the small guys — wandered over, everyone knew what would happen next. The linemen rubbed their hands. Fresh meat.

"My guys vs. your guys," Trost announced.

The newcomers sized up the chutes.

"I have a hard time taking a dump," Micah Moore observed to no one in particular. "I can't get down that low."

It was a mismatch, of course, the one-on-one competition, big guys on one side, small guys on the other. First it was Nate Shorter vs. Mark Moore. No contest. Nate pushed forward, quickly dumping Mark and pressing him to the ground. Then Rob Wyatt vs. Drew O'Malley. Although Drew had played line early on, Rob quickly took him out. Tim Lathrop, the all-purpose lineman, matched up against Sebastian Negron — "Pretend you're at a cross country meet," Trost called out, sarcastically — and Timmy won. But then Ronell Halbert, a receiver, pushed past Jay White and Micah rocked Flex back on his heels. And then Marty Wallner, the undersized receiver, lined up against Mark Williams.

Both sides were into it now.

"Yeah, Marty."

"C'mon, Mark."

"You lose this one, you're not a lineman anymore," Rob said loudly.

Mark Williams didn't laugh.

The whistle blew and, as they crashed together, Marty almost slipped to his knees. But that won him some leverage and then Mark Williams was sliding back, as if he was on skates, and Marty was up on his feet, legs pumping in the mud. Victory. After two more match ups, the two sides wound up tied 4-4. It was Drew against Rob in a tiebreaker, with Rob notching the easy win.

"I need the backs," announced Coach Hoagland. "Updowns."

There was a loud groan.

"We came over here and won four," Trost said. "You should be doing updowns."

He was right. What self-respecting group of linemen would allow themselves to be pushed around by the running backs and receivers?

"Running backs, c'mon," said Coach Hoagland.

He offered them a choice.

"You can either bear crawl across the field, or run and slide in the mud."

"Mud," came several responses at once.

"I'll do the bear crawls," said Mark Moore.

The bear crawls were another dreaded exercise for linemen. They consisted of walking across the field on all fours without anyone's knees touching the ground. Bear crawls hurt. But if you did them, at least you stayed clean.

Then Sebastian ran and dove, sliding across the mud, standing up, his jersey wet and brown. Then Drew, then Marty, then Ronell with a belly flop, and Micah spinning across the ground like a top. Finally, Mark Moore ran and tip-toed past the mud, laughing at everyone.

"Pretty boy," Nate said, and ran toward him.

So did the rest, lifting Mark and dropping him in the mud, rolling him around until everyone was laughing. Mark stood up, the familiar No. 22 on his jersey smothered in mud. The others got up, too, everyone looking the same. Differences disappear in the mud, if they were ever there at all. The pack soon fixed on its next target.

"OK," said Trost, backing up quickly. "I'm outta here."

He ran toward the gate, whistle in his mouth, the team behind him. He turned right, then left. An 8th grade football game was being played down on the big field, so Trost circled back on the track, finally blowing his whistle and waving the team off.

"On the goal line," Trost said.

Time for sprints.

The players returned to the field, frustrated. Trost was like the fox who ran up a tree and, once cornered, discovered he had the power to call off the hunt. But then Drew swept in from behind and Trost was in his arms, then on the ground in the sandy mud of the softball diamond. The team dropped handfuls of mud on his back, rolled him over, laughing. Then it was Coach Carroll's turn. Then Coach Hoagland. And then Coach Trawitzki. Into the mud. All of them. The whistles wound up filled with dirt. Clothes were soaked and muddy. Trost wore a splatter of mud on his head like a bad toupee.

They all laughed and shouted. They sounded like kids.

It was like finding a football in the park, or under the tree on Christmas morning. It was football under the street lights or on the playground during recess. It was catching

Milwaukee Journal Sentinel photo by Benny Sieu

Messmer senior George Lasley, who quit the team early in the season, is the center of attention at a pep rally before the homecoming game. The next night, Lasley was named homecoming king at Messmer.

passes from your father or running into his arms across the living room floor. It was childhood pure and simple.

If only it could last.

On one side of the Shorewood gym, the band was squeezed into a section of the bleachers. It played so loud and so strong the notes bounced and echoed off the walls. The students flowed in, quickly filling in the bleachers on the opposite side. Just the freshmen, sophomores and juniors first. Finally, once they were all situated, there was a loud chant from the hallway.

"We!"

Louder now.

"We are!"

Louder still.

"We are the mighty seniors!"

And the mass squeezed through the door, arms raised, calling down respect, lording their advanced status over the rest of the student body: "We ... we are ... we are the mighty seniors!" Many of the seniors wore the traditional Shorewood "dink," a small red and gray beanie-type cap, marked with a red "S" on the front. The dinks were in their 51st year at the school and carried the legend that any underclassman who wore one would lose his or her hair. A few weeks earlier, there had been a temporary crisis when Shorewood learned the Milwaukee company that made the dinks had closed. They got by with the existing stash this year, but for the future, dinks were in doubt. Wearing them was a tradition for the pep rally, which capped a week of the sort of days that turn high schools around the country into places where not much learning gets done. Among the days at Shorewood: Opposite Sex Day, Flashback Day and Big Hound-Little Hound Day, in which seniors and juniors selected an outrageous outfit their designated sophomore or freshman victim had to wear.

For a single week of the year, Shorewood was — almost — the kind of high school that Evan Rivera and some of the other players wanted, the kind from the movies, where football players walk with pride and the hallways buzz with talk of the big game. Even Homecoming Week, though, couldn't turn the clock back 15 years, to a time when the school had a pompon squad and cheerleaders, who'd wear their sweaters and skirts to school, ribbons in their perfect hair.

At Shorewood, the pep rally ordinarily would be in the stadium, followed by the powder puff football game, pitting the senior girls vs. the junior girls. But it had rained steadily, if not hard, for most of the morning, so the game was postponed until Monday, lest anyone slip and get hurt. Everything else was moved to the gym.

The coaches had again allowed the players to wear their

jerseys to school, but in the crowd the players were still hard to pick out and the format didn't make it any easier. At Shorewood, where the valedictorian doesn't necessarily speak at graduation, where cheerleaders are nonexistent, and the football team has been horrible for two generations, there should probably be little surprise the players don't get to charge through a giant paper sign and strut around the floor. Instead, only the seniors were introduced. For all the fall sports, not just football. And they simply stood up in the bleachers. When the names were called — Timmy Lathrop, Mark Moore, Drew O'Malley, Evan Rivera and Jay White — they could barely be heard over the chatter. Even Brandon Blanke, who quit the team a few weeks earlier without explanation, was introduced, though he didn't stand.

Once that formality was taken care of, it was on to more important things.

Like the pickle-eating contest between the class officers. And the student and teacher who had to take baseball bats, put their foreheads to the handles and the tips to the floor, and then run in circles before dizzily trying to catch mini Butterfinger bars that were thrown in the air. And, of course, mud wrestling, in which two seniors and two juniors climbed into a blue plastic wading pool and fumbled around in the slop to see who could find a quarter first.

If Trost or any of the other coaches had walked in, they would have been appalled. They knew football didn't receive much respect at Shorewood and never would until they put together some wins. But it still turned the world of high school upside down, as if Shorewood held homecoming despite the game, not because of it.

Messmer staged its own pep rally in the afternoon. The coaches had talked about getting the players from both teams together for one of the two events — "If we have to take the 62 bus down Capitol Drive we'll do it," Trost had declared. But if anyone had pursued it, that option had fallen through. In the gym, the Messmer band, a group of maybe 20, played as the students arrived. Nearly everyone wore blue or white, except the players who stood out in the red jerseys. Some students had their faces painted. A few teachers had dyed their hair blue.

From each corner of the gym there was a different shout, each class attempting to drown out the others, until it was a cacophony of screams and music.

"Oh-2, Oh-2"

"Oh-4, Oh-4."

Everyone held up the accompanying number of fingers, as they shouted out the prominence and dominance of their class year.

"Oh 3, Oh-3"

"Oh-5, Oh-5."

The pep band played the school song, the one sung each day after practice, and the players heard it with music for the first time. It was livelier, peppier. Each class sang it, then the teachers and then everybody at once — "Messmer High School, how we love thee, to our Bishops so we can't be beat." Then the fall sport teams were called down to the floor, first cross country, then girl's volleyball, then the football squad. There was a resounding cheer, even though most of the students had not been to any of the games. The players gathered in and jumped together and relished the moment, at last at the center of attention

At last, if only for a few minutes, hallway heroes.

Some of the former players, the ones who had quit, watched the hoopla from the bleachers, mixed in with the rest of the students. George Lasley, who had quit after the Whitefish Bay game, was in the band, playing baritone because the tuba was broken. Back at Bay View High School, when he walked into music class on the first day, a teacher said, "You look like you want a big instrument." George nodded, but quickly rejected the xylophone as too sissy. So it was the tuba.

He watched as the team crowded onto the floor.

George was comfortable with his decision to quit the team. His "auntie" was still alive, alive but slipping. She would be moved home soon, the seizures having turned into something more severe, maybe Alzheimer's, she seemed so confused. There had been days when George was at practice and his auntie would call out, "Where's George? Is George here?" Those days were the longest days.

No regrets.

At Shorewood, before the game, Coach Smith told the other coaches he had subbed for one of the teachers that day and before one class, when he and Nate talked about the game, a girl piped up and said, "Who cares? Ya'll ain't gonna win anyway." Smith then told Nate to stand and told the girl to look at him. He told the whole class to look at Nate, who shuffled his feet in embarrassment. Smith told them how Nate had a bad knee and yet always got up, how the team went up every week against bigger and stronger opponents, but kept fighting, how difficult it was to try so hard and get so little support. "You want to talk crap?" Coach Smith said to the class. "Then talk it to the guys who quit." Indeed, a few more had quit after the Dominican loss, with only two games and 12 days left in the season. After having to double up on lockers at the start of the season, nearly every player now had one to himself.

"They were all saying, 'Yeah, you're right,'" Smith said.

Coach Carroll wasn't buying it.

"They were just patronizing you," he said.

On that, the two schools were connected.

On the football field, it was as if backgrounds didn't matter. A Shorewood player didn't get a head start because his family was wealthy, because he had two parents, or the promise of a college education, safe and secure. A

Messmer player couldn't rely solely on athletic ability, or street smarts, or even the kind of determination instilled as the only way to get ahead in life when you start behind. Smith would often tell the team that it was all really simple when it came to dealing with differences, dealing with life: "If you're good enough to block for me, you're good enough to be my friend."

Opponents, when they scoffed at the team lined up across from them, surely didn't make any such distinctions. White, black. Rich, poor. Suburb, city. Public, private.

Shorewood, Messmer.

All wore red. All were the same.

At Shorewood, the parking lot was lined with pickups and floats for the homecoming parade, which would wind down the streets of the village, arriving back at the stadium in time for kickoff. The theme for Homecoming Week was "Disco Inferno." One float had a "Disco Wrecking Ball" sign and a mirrored ball that hung suspended above a crushed Falcon, representing Brown Deer. Another had several well-dressed mannequins, each with a hand in the air, striking a "Saturday Night Fever" pose.

In the locker room, Timmy Lathrop told of finding a sign hung over a water fountain that read: "Falcons will beat Shorewood." He ripped it down and tossed it in the trash. Hearing about it brought some scowls.

Others were in their own conversations.

"You gonna run?" Rob asked Mark Moore.

"You gonna block?" Mark asked.

"If you're gonna run, I'm blocking."

Pertrell Mallett seemed a little nervous, taking longer to pull on his pads. He was starting on both offense and defense.

"Make sure to block the end," Trost said as reminder, while walking through the room.

"Is he big?" Pertrell asked, looking up.

"Not as big as you."

Trost continued to his office. There were more people drifting in and out of the locker room, more people already out in the stands. As the homecoming game, the crowd would be bigger, of course. And after Shorewood's victory over Brown Deer last year there was a rising hope for a repeat.

Rob Wyatt broke away from his conversation and addressed the whole room.

"After we win tonight, everyone here is going to start seeing new friends," he said.

That night last year, as word spread by cell phone that Shorewood was winning, actually winning, the stands grew more crowded as the clock ticked away, fans rushing out to catch history in action. Instant bandwagon.

"Those people who talk about you when you're losing, they ain't your friends," Rob said. "Your friends are right here. Don't play for anybody in the crowd. Play for us in here."

As the team gathered outside before heading down to the big field for warmups, the Messmer players were videotaped by Michael Tucker, a Messmer teacher who put together elaborate videos to commemorate each sports season. Each player had to run to a spot in front of the camera, turn, and then announce his name, position and year in school. Some had a ball tossed to them from off camera. It was just like on *Monday Night Football.* The star treatment for everyone.

Nate Shorter stepped outside, scooped up a glop of mud and wiped streaks under both eyes — his version of the quarterback black.

"Why you using mud?" asked Maurice Ragsdale.

Maurice had missed the pep rally at Messmer. He had missed practice the night before. He was missing a lot of practices, without explanation. And his grades, always borderline, were teetering the wrong way. The day before, Maurice had argued at school with Coach Smith, who sent him to Joy Bretsch, the athletic director, who told him if he quit now, the school would charge him the $300 it paid Shorewood so he could play. "You're an adult," she told him. "Make an adult decision." His adult decision was to come to the game, knowing he wouldn't be allowed to play. He apologized to the coaches and took a jersey so he could wear it and stand on the sideline with the team.

"Natural," Nate replied, the mud already drying.

He jogged into the frame, turned — "Nathan Shorter, Class of Oh-Three, defensive tackle." First take. Perfect. Others took a few attempts, fumbling over the words, or purposefully taking extra chances just to enjoy the moment.

"I want to get in the Messmer video," said Drew O'Malley, a Shorewood senior.

"You can be like, 'Drew O'Malley, just hanging out with the niggas,'" said Flex, one of the Messmer seniors.

Flex was black. Drew was white.

Drew repeated it and laughed. They both did. Easily.

It was an exchange, filled with acceptance, no one could have imagined just 10 weeks ago.

"Yeah," said Tucker. "That'll go over big."

When the team was back in the locker room, awaiting the final words from the coaches, everyone sat quietly. It was hard to tell if they were businesslike or nervous.

"Let's go," Drew shouted, attempting to bring some fire with him into the room. "Let's do this. Homecoming. That's what it's all about."

Unlike two weeks ago, the last time they were in the locker room before a home game, when Mark called down the football gods and asked the team to play for his late mother, there was no response.

Photo courtesy of Michael Tucker

Rob Wyatt, a Messmer junior, comes out of his stance during warmups. He constantly urged the team to put internal squabbles aside and have fun.

Just the shifting of feet.

Nate sat on a bench, eyes distant. A leg bounced with anticipation, nerves. His right shoe was wrapped with tape, a makeshift solution to hold the shoe together. The shoe was coming apart at the sole. Nate was a long way from July, when on the last day of summer camp he didn't bring any cleats and kept slipping on the grass when the camp coach, Greg Flint, timed players in the 420-yard shuttle, which required players to sprint back and forth over ever longer distances. Flint had told the players that college coaches had contacted him about three of them. He wouldn't say which three, but everyone knew it had to be Mark, Nate and Rob. So, when Nate ran and slipped, borrowed a pair of cleats from Mark and slipped again, finally rumbling through the drill at 1:09.99 seconds, nowhere near the top, everyone cringed. Nate had to be one of the three.

But he wasn't.

The three were Mark, Rob and Ronell.

By now, though, Nate was getting more college mail than the others. He ranked third in the conference in tackles, 46 through five conference games. And though he sometimes had second thoughts about having stayed at Messmer — Vincent High School, where he once considered transferring, was ranked third in the area — Nate was playing high school football. Even if the enthusiasm from the students that day so long ago in the auditorium had disappeared amid the losses, it hadn't for Nate. No. Never.

The coaches gave their speeches, but the words were old and familiar.

The team prayed, holding hands in an uneven circle.

"Everything we do, we do for you," Coach Smith said, head bowed. "Everything we breathe, we breathe for you."

They broke and the team walked toward the door. Nate lingered near the back.

"We did not come this far," he said to himself. "We did not come this far."

He never finished the sentence: "To lose."

On the sideline, they listened to the national anthem, sung by a Shorewood graduate. Pertrell Mallett, the Messmer senior who wowed the team that day in the locker room, would sing it Wednesday at the last home game. Maurice Ragsdale, a red jersey pulled over his shirt, walked along the line, pounding a fist onto each player's shoulder pads.

There were a mere 21 guys in uniform, not even enough
for the team to play a game against itself. Their helmets
were marked with the dried mud from a few days earlier.
There were tears and rips on some of the jerseys. The pants
had grass stains that wouldn't come out. It was a long way
from July for everyone.

"Ain't no turning back now," Nate shouted, and issued
a primal scream, then yelled: "Whoooo-oooh. Let's go,
men."

The team got the ball first and slowly, methodically,
drove down the field. Two yards. Then six more. Then six
and another four. A little Mark to the outside. A little
Evan up the middle. One first down and then another. It
was all very businesslike. On the opposite side, the Brown
Deer team watched helplessly, everyone clapping in unison, a rhythmic clap, trying to boost the guys on the field.
Another run. Another. Then Evan took a handoff and
crashed through the middle of the line, dragging defenders to the 16 yard line.

The end zone was close now, within reach. To score
first? It would be huge. To manhandle Brown Deer down
the field? What a message. Trost sent in the play: Roar
Back. It was the play that had failed at the goal line against
Lakeside Lutheran, but worked beautifully against St.
Francis. Could the team find perfection again?

They broke the huddle, a loud clap, and Micah Moore,
back at quarterback after his one game suspension, took
them to the line.

"9-9-9, 9-9-9."

Micah shouted out the count.

"Set Red Hit."

And took the snap.

Micah faked to his brother, but Brown Deer didn't
bite. Drew O'Malley said "Mississippi" in his head and
crossed behind the line looking for the ball, but ... but ...
Brown Deer came on a blitz, three guys, and one of them

muscled through the line and then Micah held the ball
out for the hand-off and he and Drew both slowed, unsure how to complete it, and then — just like that — the
Brown Deer player sliced past, ripping the ball free. Micah
gave chase, tackling him after about 20 yards.

The damage was done.

Final score: 36-0.

In the office, the coaches slumped into chairs and
against the walls. As Coach Groser called in the statistics
to the newspaper, the others winced with each brutal detail: Four interceptions. Three fumbles. Six penalties. A
safety. Only 102 yards of offense, less than 50 for Mark
Moore. The school rushing record was long gone.

In the locker room, some players packed up quickly
and left. Others were slow. There was the pounding of
cleats on the floor, clumps of dirt bouncing free. Nate
shuffled in. The streaks of mud from under his eyes had
been sweated away long ago. Timmy Lathrop, a Shorewood
senior, leaned against the wall in the corner behind the
office door, slid absently to the floor and looked up, dazed.

"I really don't want to be the one 0-9 team," said Jay
White, a Shorewood senior.

He wasn't talking to anyone in particular.

"Man, we got our ass busted," said Mark Moore.

Where do you turn for solace when there is no hope to
be found? How much more hurt before you cannot stand
anymore? How many more tears until you drown?

Lockers were banged shut. Jerseys stuffed into the yellow laundry basket. Shoulder pads tossed on top of the
lockers.

Some grumbled about the play calling. Run, run, run.
They remembered the three passes caught by Ronell for
55 yards, but — selective memory — not Micah's four
interceptions. It was the kind of performance that drove
Dave O'Harrow from football.

"Do the coaches even want to win?" Flex asked.

"I don't think they believe," said Pertrell. "They didn't believe in me,"

Pertrell, the project from the beginning, had started both ways — offense and defense. But he got the hook on defense almost immediately and was taken out several times on offense, too.

Maurice Ragsdale stood near his locker. He had taken the jersey so he could stand on the sideline, but as the score grew worse and worse, he took it off and slipped into the stands instead. Maurice walked up to Marty Wallner, shook his hand. There was an air of finality to it. It seemed like goodbye.

"See you Monday," Marty said, loudly, as if saying it in a determined fashion meant Maurice would be there.

Maurice left without another word.

Soon, the locker room was nearly empty. Timmy and Nate were the only ones left, then Nate left and it was only Timmy.

He had wanted the game. Desperately wanted it. Despite all the shuffling during the season at quarterback, Timmy never got the chance he wanted there, the chance he prepared for over the summer. But he never complained about it either. Now he pulled on his letter jacket. He was the only Shorewood player to wear one. A year earlier, against Brown Deer, he and the rest had posed for victory photos in front of the scoreboard. A picture of Timmy, beaming, made the front page of the school newspaper. Now his face was red, hair wet and tussled into an imprint from the inside of his helmet. A couple players from last year's team, ones who had graduated, wandered in, in search of Trost.

"How ya doing, Timmy?" one asked.

Timmy paused to consider the question, as if it was deeper than it was.

"I hurt," Timmy said.

His body was sore, too.

At Messmer, the homecoming dance was held Saturday night in the student commons area in the basement.
The gym floor was too new to risk all sorts of scuffs, so the
DJ set up at the end of a hallway and the students jammed
in, a giant fan offering little relief from the heat. Most
dances were held at a nearby National Guard Armory, with
members of the Guard serving as uniformed chaperones,
so no one stepped out of line. But the impending war in
Afghanistan meant the troops were gone and the building
was off limits.

It was the school's first football homecoming in almost
two decades.

No varsity players attended.

But no one seemed to notice. The music blared and
the lights flashed and the dance floor pulsated, everybody
dancing with everybody and everybody dancing with nobody, a mass of people. Chaperones watched for kids dancing too close, which earned an old-fashioned "timeout"
spent standing in a corner. In the middle of it all was
George Lasley, wearing a bright orange sweater, a helium
balloon tied around his neck, the balloon wiggling and
bobbing above the crowd. George was up for Homecoming King, but figured he wouldn't get it because the other
guy was more popular.

When George was a freshman at Bay View High School,
he had been voted to the homecoming court. He remembered running out onto the muddy field when his name
was called at half time, wearing his red, white and black
band uniform, amazed to discover he was popular. He was
only starting to sell drugs and didn't expect such a reaction. Like Nate, thankfully, blissfully, he was a long way
from there.

When the music stopped and the announcement came,
George's name was called. And there he was, king, the

crown tilted on his head, a wide smile on his face. He had come to the dance alone, but had already spotted a girl he wanted to take home.

None of the football players made the homecoming court. None even made the voting. Not at Messmer. Not at Shorewood. On that, too, the two schools were the same.

At Shorewood, the homecoming dance was more traditional.

It was held in the gym, strings of Christmas lights strung from the basketball hoops to the middle. The bleachers were pushed back, with dozens of colorful construction paper cut-outs of bell-bottom pants taped to them, the names of couples printed out in magic marker on each. A series of tables circled the dance floor, colorful balloons floating above the chairs. Some students had grumbled about the rule changes — no more dirty dancing, all songs pre-approved by student council and the principal — but the gym was still crowded. With the "Disco Inferno" theme, music alternated between "Super Freak" and "Smells Like Teen Spirit," the couples getting down one minute and moshing the next.

At Shorewood, homecoming was definitely a date dance, an event. Guys looked awkward with boutonnieres in their lapels, girls had corsages slipped onto their wrists or pinned — oh so carefully — on strapless dresses. And when the music slowed, and those who came to the dance alone slipped out to the hallway for a soda, the rest made it to the dance floor, the girls closing their eyes and the guys measuring how close they should dance, how tightly they should hold onto the moment.

A few of the Shorewood players went to the dance, some with dates and some without. But most of the team had decided to boycott the festivities.

Instead, a group got together at the Hyatt Regency Hotel in downtown Milwaukee. Stories varied on whose

idea it was, who got the room, whether alcohol was involved, and if so, how much. Some high school secrets are
held tighter than others.

Mark was there with Leslie. It was his birthday, 18
now. Micah was there, so was their brother, Matt. So
were Rob Wyatt and Ronell Halbert from Messmer, along
with Flex. And the trio of Shorewood seniors — Drew,
Evan and Jay. Evan had told his girlfriend he'd meet her
after the dance. They all had invited Nate, but Nate never
much went to parties and didn't want to go to one where
people might be doing things he wouldn't do. He stayed
home and watched college football by himself.

At the hotel, they cranked up the music — old-school
rap from Too Short — but soon the police arrived and
they were kicked out of the room. The group wound up
across the street at George Webb's, a 24-hour hamburger
joint, where they crowded around tables, the street outside so dark that everything was reflected in the glass. They
teased each other about bad plays from the night before,
asked Micah what he was throwing at, rehashing the loss
and vowing it wouldn't happen in the last game. No. Never.

Nothing else to do, at around 10 p.m. they piled in
cars and drove to Shorewood to crash the dance. Most
snuck in, though some were kicked out a few minutes
later.

No one stayed long. It was mostly over anyway.

They cruised around Shorewood for a while, amid the
quiet streets and the giant houses. But the Shorewood police
were out in force, so it was no time to be cruising and no
time to be on the wrong side of the river.

They may have become one team.

But their worlds were still different.

Chapter 12
"To us, it can mean the world."

The final game. For some teams in the Milwaukee area, it marked a chance to complete a perfect season. For others it was a game for the conference championship or had a playoff berth on the line or at least was a chance to notch a winning record. For Shorewood-Messmer it was, well, what? An ending, certainly. Survival, of course. The whole season had been about survival. Validation? Redemption?

They would know soon enough.

The game would be played Wednesday, which meant a mere two days of practice. Fortunately, Greendale Martin Luther was nearly as bad as they were. The school had dropped its freshman squad for lack of players and the varsity boasted only 35 guys. Martin Luther had gone into its Friday game against Dominican without a victory, but managed to win. So instead of a matchup between two winless squads, Martin Luther was already one up on the mighty Bishounds of Shorewood-Messmer. And in the cruel world of sports math, in which one can usually line up any sequence of past games to allow for an upset, in this case it was all too clear: Martin Luther had beaten Dominican and Dominican had beaten Shorewood-Messmer. There wasn't a player on the team that hadn't done the calculation.

It was Monday, exactly 10 weeks since the team held its first official meeting, everyone crowded into the "S" Room at Shorewood, players wandering in even after the meeting had started, until they leaned against the walls and sat on the floor, players everywhere. That day, Trost told them he was so excited he called up Coach Smith the night before, put the phone to his stereo speaker and cranked up "Ain't No Mountain High Enough" — the theme song from the football movie *Remember the Titans*. Back then, the talk was of a championship. Back then, it was easy to think so.

Even just a few weeks ago, Trost would have said his team should destroy Martin Luther. Now, he would settle for a win, any kind of win. He had promised them a win.

Right on schedule, Trost walked out to the practice field and didn't stop until he reached a spot where a few orange cones were set up. The team barely had a chance to warm up. Some players hadn't stretched at all.

"Over here, let's go," Trost said, impatient. "Oklahomas."

"What?" Ronell Halbert exclaimed. "We ain't done Oklahomas in centuries."

Indeed, the team hadn't done the dreaded drill since the Luther Prep game, when they came out during warm ups and started hitting, to the bemusement of the Luther Prep players. With the last game coming, Trost wanted one final focus.

"Jay White, you want to play defensive line this week, get in there," he said.

Trost considered Jay softer than butter, but as a senior, he would get a last chance to show he deserved to start. The team, 19 players today, was split into two groups, based more on convenience than ability. Some cautiously pulled on their helmets, others hung near the back of the line. There was a whistle. One group went. Another whistle. The next.

"Hit 'em," yelled Trost. "Attaboy."

Two guys locked up. A timid clack of pads.

"C'mon, we're kissing," Trost said. "We've got to hit."

The October sky was overcast and it was downright cold when the sun slipped behind the frequent cloud. The tree beyond the fence was nearly bare now, shedding more leaves with every gust of wind. The leaves on the ground crackled underfoot.

The Oklahomas continued. Micah Moore stepped in at running back, his brother, Mark, in at linebacker, and the two literally stood and waited as the linemen bumped up against each other, hands clasped to shoulders, feet barely moving.

"Hey," Trost shouted, "the homecoming dance was Saturday."

He checked his watch. Another group went.

Then there was a loud scream — "Aaaaaaahhh" — and a player fell to the ground, clutching his left knee, eyes closed, teeth gritted. It was Drew O'Malley. The punter. The kicker. The running back. The linebacker. The return man. The captain. The senior, with only 48 hours remaining in his high school football career.

"Stay down," Trost said, instantly at his side.

In football, coaches will tell you, there are many ways to measure success.

There are the statistics, of course, numbers neat and clean. But when lined up on a sheet of paper, numbers can often obscure a season more than capture it. They don't measure the obstacles, how far the team came, how far behind it started. They don't measure fear or courage, heart or pride. They don't cover any of that, none of that at all.

For some teams, success is about never falling.

For others it is about always getting back up.

Drew looked over at Trost. He had tried to stand up, but now rolled back and was on the ground, his left leg flat on the grass. Drew had locked up in the drill with

Milwaukee Journal Sentinel photo by Benny Sieu

Tired Shorewood-Messmer players — (from left) Mark Moore, Ronell Halbert and Torry Spencer — at half-time of one of the team's games.

Nate Shorter, the biggest and strongest player on the team. Drew had braced his leg for leverage, but instead he was twisted to the side, the knee giving a quick awkward bend.

"Did you hear anything pop?" Trost asked.

"No," Drew said, shaking his head furiously. "I didn't hear anything."

The trainer, Steve Wittemann, was found, and as he examined Drew's knee, the coaches told the team to take a lap around the field. It had begun to rain. Light drops. The team jogged, players looking back at Drew.

This is how it all can end. In an instant.

The coaches gathered together.

"We have to rally the troops," said Trost.

"More like a resurrection," said Coach Carroll, discouraged.

In the last regular season game of his own senior year, Trost injured his right ankle. It hurt like hell and a doctor quickly delivered the news: Broken bone. But with a playoff game the following week, the first ever for St. Pat's,

Trost went home, threw away the walking cast that was to be slipped in the bottom of his shoe, and told his coach it was just a bad sprain. He played the game. His team lost, but he played.

Trost had come to see himself in Drew.

"You'll see," said Trost. "When Drew is out there running this week."

Wittemann examined Drew's knee, testing it, measuring the pain in Drew's eyes with each bend. Drew was helped to his feet and guided into the hallway, where he sat on a chair, his leg stretched out, a bag of ice on his knee. Wittemann looked over the knee again and though Drew protested — "I can go. It doesn't hurt. I can go." — Wittemann walked out and told Coach Trawitzki that Drew was done. A partially torn ligament. It would take a month to safely heal. Why risk it now, with so little left?

Wittemann turned to go back inside, but Trost called him over. The two were no longer on good terms and kept a wide distance between themselves. Trost had long suspected Wittemann was the one who complained to Rick Monroe, the Shorewood principal, about the locker room incident at Luther Prep, all the coward stuff. And, when confronted now, Wittemann acknowledged it. Why not? Nothing to hide. It was the right thing to do. Wittemann thought Trost pushed the players too hard and too fast.

Trost thought Wittemann worried too much — kids knew when they were really hurt — and was full of medical mumbo jumbo. At one point, early in the season, there was a concern about Rob's health, but it turned out his sluggishness was due to a change in his asthma medicine. There had been all the worries about Nate's knee, but Nate was always out there. Evan Rivera hurt his ankle in the Dominican game, but was back dragging would-be tacklers through the line against Brown Deer.

Now Drew.

After a few minutes, Drew walked out to the field, all

gimpy, wearing a flannel shirt, his practice pants still in place, his knee still wrapped. Drew's eyes were red.

"It doesn't even hurt," he said and shrugged.

Drew took a few steps, jogged gingerly, tried to make a cut, then just stood and watched the rest of the team.

At the end of practice, the team gathered around the coaches. It was downright cold, the wind whipping through the mesh jerseys, all the way to the bone.

"It's very easy — *very easy* — to kind of pack it in and quit," Trost told them. "But there's no quit in me and I know there's no quit in you."

The coaches talked about how the game could be won. It could be taken over by one player. By Mark. By Nate. Or by both. The two, one Shorewood and one Messmer, had become close. As always, the game — the season — was on them.

"To a lot of people this game means nothing," said Coach Trawitzki. "To us, it can mean a lot. To us, it can mean the world."

The next day, Drew arrived at practice with a note from a doctor — James Langenkamp, the orthopedic surgeon for the Marquette University men's basketball team. The night before, Drew's mother had called Langenkamp, who lived nearby in Shorewood, and practically begged for a quick appointment. Drew went in that morning and brought a medical clearance note with him to practice.

Trost was beaming as the other coaches arrived, showing each the piece of paper, which read: "Strained MCL. Knee is stable."

Drew sat in the locker room, slapping hands with the other players as they arrived. He had braces on both knees and a bag of ice on the strained one.

In the office, Trost joked about the diagnosis and how Wittemann might explain the overnight recovery: "And then the Virgin Mary came down ... and ... and touched his knee ... which was encapsulated ... and ..."

The coaches laughed. It was a laugh of relief.

"Pin it on the board," Coach Hoagland said, nodding toward the wall.

"No," said Trost. "That one's going on my bedroom wall."

It was the last practice of the season and there was an easiness about the locker room — players and coaches alike. As if they had rounded the last corner of a marathon, or reached the end of a long tunnel and now were bathed in the warm light.

Mark Moore was among the missing. Some of the players asked where he was.

"He's getting tatted," Rob Wyatt reminded them.

Mark already had a set of praying hands tattooed on one arm, a cross and his mother's initials on the other. No one knew what he was getting tattooed today, but he and Leslie had just marked their one-year anniversary and she might be coming to the game.

When practice began, Drew was out there on kickoffs, and after a few tentative attempts was driving the ball deep. He was booming punts. Running the ball around the corner of the line. Trying to forget the injury, swallow down the pain.

"Hey Micah, where's Mark?" Coach Trawitzki asked at one point.

"He's at a doctor's appointment," Micah said, shrugging.

Trawitzki shook his head.

"Star running back misses last day of practice," he said, as if reading a headline.

It was a fitting footnote for the season.

As a joke, Trawitzki and the other assistants wore plaid shirts and red shorts, hiked way up over their waist. The Jim Trost school of fashion. Coach Hoagland walked around blowing his whistle wildly, shouting out Trost's catch phrase: "Let's go, let's go, let's go." One day early in the season, Coach Carroll tried to count how many times Trost said it in a day, but stopped somewhere past 30. And that was just in the first hour of practice.

When the offense lined up again, Trost called out for Pertrell Mallett, who would be singing the national anthem before the game. Trost had talked with the band director, and the consensus was if Pertrell couldn't practice with the band, both he and the band would be embarrassed if they tried it together, so Pertrell would have to do it alone. Trost and the others loved the idea of the band standing silent on the field, instruments lowered, while a football player commanded the attention. Today was Pertrell's only chance to practice at the stadium, but he didn't want to do it with all the guys listening.

"It's OK, we'll pray over it," Coach Smith said as they walked toward the press box.

Once it had become clear Trost wasn't joking about him singing, Pertrell found the words to the national anthem and practiced singing them over and over. Sometimes, he sang the words in his head, other times out loud at home, with one of his younger brothers declaring, "That was horrible," before allowing it was really pretty good.

After a few long moments, there was a scratchy tap, tap, tap over the loud speakers. Then Pertrell's voice, slow at first, then building in strength and momentum.

"Oh-OH, say can you SEE."

"Everybody stop," Trost said.

And the team stood and listened. A few players took off their helmets. Down on the big field, the 7th and 8th grade football teams were practicing. They stopped, too, surprised at the smooth and strong voice that drifted out across the field, twisting and echoing in the stiff wind. When Pertrell came to "and the home of the brave," someone shouted out "Helmets up," and then there were helmets in the air. Pertrell cut off the last word a bit too soon, but there were cheers from his teammates.

"Whooooh!" Trost shouted.

Pertrell's head popped out of the booth. Trost gave a thumbs up.

"Offense, in the huddle," he said. Back to business. "That was all right."

A second attempt sounded even better and then Pertrell ran across the field and back to the team, picking up his helmet and taking his place with the offense as a starting tight end. The team applauded as he arrived. Pertrell shook his head, eager to slip into the anonymity of a guy on the line.

Trost shook Pertrell's hand, then slapped him on the butt.

"We love you Pertrell," said Torry Spencer, a Messmer sophomore.

Trost called out another play, and then another.

The pass was dropped, so they ran it again. Catch. Whistle.

"That is the last play you'll run in practice this year," Trost said.

The team formed a circle around the coaches again. The sun was out, but low in the sky. The sun was setting. The entire season was. The wind had blown much of the sky gray with clouds, so it was only blue on the horizon, at the edges all around.

"What you take from this practice," Trost told them, "what you take from the game, that will be the last thing you leave with."

He meant they should leave with effort, with their best shot.

They should leave with pride.

"This is a clip from my senior year in high school," said Trost. "It stays with me."

He held up his key chain. It included a metal clip,

taken from his shoulder pads after his final game, the playoff game in which he played on a broken foot, fighting the pain the whole time, the only game his father ever saw him play. The team lost 13-7. Trost's senior year in high school was 1986, a full 15 years ago.

The clip stayed with him.

Other coaches talked about the start of the partnership, how there were probably 80 guys who at one time or another expressed an interest in football. Some never even tried. Others did and gave up. Now it was just them, 20 in uniform today and the absent Mark Moore. It had been stripped back to the core, to the group that lifted weights all summer, the group that sweated into the grass during the camp drills. They were the ones still standing.

"Without a team, there are no coaches," said Coach Carroll. "Without a team, I'm just some loser who wishes he was still playing high school football."

Players looked at the ground or at Carroll. Some chewed on their mouthguards, or crossed their arms, the sky above them now spitting rain, though the sun still was bright in the distance. It was cold, too. It was as if everything was mixed into that single moment.

"You guys do have courage for being here," Carroll said, then talked again about regret, about his own last game, the one he still ached over.

The players were silent.

"People may say that was years ago, why don't you just let go," Carroll said. "But I still hold onto it. I still dream about it. I wish I could go back and do something different. We can't change the past weeks. The only thing you can do is make your final statement tomorrow."

The wind blew hard.

"It's cold," Drew said. He smiled wryly.

"It's not cold," said Trost, falling into the familiar lines, as if he had been handed a script. Trost would never concede it was cold. He wore shorts for every practice and game.

"It's *brisk*," said Carroll, correcting Drew and hitting his own line.

Everyone grinned.

And then it was Coach Smith's turn. At one point, he had planned to ask his girlfriend to marry him at halftime of the homecoming game, but did it a few weeks before that. Smith always talked of family. This team, he said, is a family — his family.

"Get a sleeping bag, ya'll," joked Flex, as Smith continued on.

Everyone was standing now, pressed in close. The wind blew cold again. The shadows were long and deep. It began to sleet, but only for the briefest of moments. And with the sun slicing in, a few players looked up, searching the sky for a rainbow.

It had to be there somewhere.

The final game didn't start off as planned. The scoreboard read 10-0 as the team headed to the locker room at halftime, but the game was still in the balance. Martin Luther wasn't overpowering. Far from it. They had scored a touchdown early on and got a field goal with two seconds left. As Mark jogged off the field, he saw a familiar face at the fence and slowed.

"You OK?"

It was Leslie. She had been on the visitor's side of the field, with Mark's aunt, who was videotaping the game. Mark had gone down, briefly, in the first quarter, but after a few minutes on the sideline put himself back in the game.

Mark nodded.

"Have fun," Leslie said. "It's your last game, senior."

The whole day had roiled with emotion. For the coin toss, Trost sent all nine seniors out as captains. Jay White had shown enough to get a start on the offensive line, his first, so the season ended with seven starters from

Shorewood and four from Messmer. Pertrell Mallett sang the National Anthem, taking the bleacher stairs two at a time to get back to the sideline when he was done. Helmet on, Pertrell snuck a peak back at the stands. Neither of his parents had made it. Work interfered. His shoulders sank. Mark, meanwhile, had his new tattoo. He showed it off in the locker room before the game — his mother's smiling face on his left shoulder, drawn out like the tattoo Coach Smith had of his brother and himself.

In the locker room, the team sat on the benches. Players tried to catch their breath. Nate Shorter was bent over, hugging his stomach.

"I'm all right," he said, waving off the coaches.

Trost and Coach Hoagland, who from the press box had the best view of the field, ducked into the bathroom and drew up a play for the second half while the other coaches offered words of encouragement.

Trawitzki: "We're a second away from an interception on defense."

Carroll: "We can't give up anything on the return. We have to fly down the field and show them we're gonna win the second half."

Trost came out with the board, climbed on a bench and held it up for all to see. There was the I-formation, with arrows right up the middle, showing Evan Rivera, the fullback, and Mark, at running back, going through the same hole, both behind the center, Timmy Lathrop, who would smash forward first. Martin Luther was worried about Mark on the edges, Trost said. No one — not a single player — was watching the middle.

"It's wide open, Mark," Trost said. "You follow Evan, you hit the hole, you're going to the house."

As Trost spoke, he used the marker to draw a new line over the arrows, emphasizing how easy it would be, over and over until the lines were thick.

"Timmy, you gotta get out there. This is a touchdown."

He drew another line.

"Mark, you want to run through the line, it's a touchdown. You do it a second time, another touchdown. You run hard through this hole, it'll be nothing but daylight."

By the time Shorewood-Messmer got the ball in the second half, though, the scoreboard read 17-0. They couldn't stop Martin Luther, which took the kickoff and marched down the field. But now Shorewood-Messmer was ready to pound the middle. The first time, Mark got five yards, not a touchdown. The second time, even less. One yard. Trost raked his scalp and paced the sideline. He sent in a different play: Roar Back. The play, always executed either perfectly or poorly, had come to define the season.

The handoff went to Drew O'Malley, coming across from the right. He hit the outside and was bumped back, but he kept his balance, then ducked and dodged forward until he was tackled, the ball inches from the 30-yard line and a first down.

The ball sat on the dirt.

"Measurement, measurement," Coach Trawitzki called out.

The nearest referee shook his head.

"Our lines are crooked," Trawitzki said.

Not even a chuckle.

Fourth and short. They had to go for it.

This time, the ball went to Evan Rivera, the fullback. He plunged forward. The ball slipped from his hands and he reached down, plucked it from the ground and pushed forward again, but he didn't make it.

Martin Luther ball.

There was little left now, the last gasps of the season coming short and shallow. Shorewood-Messmer got the ball back. Mark fumbled. The quarter ended and the band played "La Bamba." There was a bad pass. Another inter-

ception. The sideline was quiet. Br. Bob Smith, the
Messmer president, was down at the edge of the field,
calling out support. The team may not have gotten any
victories, the players may not have even completely crossed
the racial bridge, but they had tried. That, he thought,
was something in itself. Joy Bretsch, the Messmer athletic
director stood nearby. They both knew this project would
be a long one, maybe years until the team was solid. So
did Cindy Wilburth, the Shorewood athletic director, who
watched from the stands, leaning on the railing. They were
now, officially, playing for next year.

Trost, headset off, called plays from the top of his head.
He hadn't decided if he would be back next season, but he
was leaning toward staying. He was too proud to go out
0-9. How many times had he said he wasn't a quitter?

On the field, Nate Shorter continued to make tackles.
So many, that after one brutal stop, stuffing a guy at the
line of scrimmage, the referee returned to his spot at the
edge of the field and looked over at Br. Bob Smith.

"Number 72 is a good ball player," he said. "A real
good ball player."

"Thank you," said Smith.

"Is that your guy?" the referee asked. "He's a keeper."

Nate was the future, and it was his team now, if it
really belonged to anybody. He was the future and Rob
Wyatt was the future and Ronell Halbert, and even Martin Wallner, who had some of the best skills of all. They
would get a do-over, a mulligan, another chance. In some
cases, they had two seasons more.

The seniors?

They had less than 5 minutes.

The team stood in the huddle, pants muddied, shirts
stained with sweat. The clock read 4:49. The end zone
was 69 yards away. With a loud clap, they turned and
lined up, fists pressed into the cold grass, cleats dug into

the dirt, eyes wide with expectation. This was it. The last drive. They had to have it. No doubt.

Mark Moore, the senior, was in at quarterback now. Option football. He stepped behind the center, paused for a moment to survey the defense, then barked out the play. The linemen tensed before the snap. It came and the fullback, Evan Rivera, crashed into the line. But it was a fake and the defense bought it, all of it. Mark slipped out to the right, feet pumping, arm cocked, eyes scanning the bright field. He spotted Ronell Halbert two steps, maybe three, past the defenders and catching steam. Mark slammed to a stop, caught his balance and launched the ball. It sailed into the cold air and hung there, hung there for the longest time, as if the season had been put on pause. Then the ball wobbled down from the sky, down, down. Ronell saw it all. He doubled back, lept over two defenders and pulled the ball in, clutching it to his chest as he tumbled to the ground.

There was a ripple of excitement in the stands.

It was the whisper of what might have been.

The ball was at midfield. The clock ticked faster. Hearts pumped harder. The huddle broke quicker. This time, Mark dropped back, pumped the ball, another fake, and stole to his left, past one defender and another, then another, feet slicing up the sideline. To the 40, the 30, the 20, the 15, now the 13, where he was knocked out of bounds.

There was another burst of cheers and the chant came: "We ... we are ... we are the mighty Greyhounds."

The band played, loud and brassy, the notes lingering in the night.

And, just like that, the whole team was back in the mud. They were back to a time before airplanes were missiles and cities were targets, back to that last day of summer camp, the evening shadows scraping across the grass, the season not yet begun, the record perfect, everything pure and full of promise.

Everyone kids again.

The team lined up, quickly. Mark took the snap, dropped back and looked for a pass. And again he pulled the ball down and ran left, dodging past the line, past one linebacker, then another, dragged down finally at the two yard line. The clock read 3:44. They could feel it now. It was so little, the distance from here to there. Almost nothing.

Was even that too much to ask?

The play came in from the sideline and Trost crossed his arms. The players stood, some with hands on their knees, and shouted out encouragement. "C'mon. We need this." The crowd cheered. Mark walked to the line, slowly, confidently. He looked at Ronell, spread out to the right, and seemed to nod. He shouted out the count.

"9-9-9, 9-9-9, Set-Red-Hit."

And the ball was snapped.

After the game, the team gathered at midfield one last time, at the same spot where they had collected the mustard seeds so many nights and so many dreams ago. Timmy Lathrop knelt off to one side, tears spilling from his eyes. Mark stood, helmet off, a tear mixing with the sweat on his cheek. If life was a movie, the tears would have been tears of joy. If life was a movie, they would have won this game.

"You gave it your best," Trost said, his glasses up on his forehead. "All you can say."

Players looked up. There was nothing more.

Life is not a movie.

"I need the seniors right by me," Trost said.

Singing the school songs after each game was one Trost tradition. For the end of the season, he had another. The seniors would be carried off the field. So the sophomores and juniors came over and, two-by-two, lifted the seniors up and carried them from midfield to the sideline, now empty except for the stray water bottle or helmet.

First Drew. Later, Evan and Jay. Flex.

Mark Moore.

The rest.

Photos were snapped and parents applauded and shoulders shook and tears fell and the band slowly marched away, the rattle-tap of drums disappearing into the night.

The team came back to midfield and sang the school songs, helmets raised. And then they broke it down — "What time is it?" "Game time!" — everyone dancing and jumping and shouting like there was still something left, one more chance to shake down a victory, one more game, one more chance to bring back the day.

The team walked back to the locker room and the field went dark behind them, the stars gone from the sky.

Epilogue
"Now you've got to expect to win."

 The last drive, the one that took Shorewood-Messmer down to the two yard line, a breath away from a touchdown and some measure — however small — of redemption, ended instead in one final disaster.

 When the team lined up, the clock read 3:44. And, though Mark Moore had moved the team down the field while running the option, Coach Trost put Micah Moore, Mark's younger brother, back at quarterback, then spread out the offense — Drew O'Malley and Ronell Halbert off to the right as receivers, Pertrell Mallett and Mark Moore to the left. The idea was to leave the middle soft for fullback Evan Rivera, who was alone in the backfield. It was a formation they hadn't worked on much, if at all. Trost had called Micah to the sideline and explained the play to him.

 The clock ticking, now at 3:29, Micah took the snap and pitched the ball back to Evan. But Evan bobbled it and, as he reached out to pull the ball in, a Martin Luther player burst through the line, clutched the ball to his chest and raced down the open field, Evan and Drew chasing close behind. They caught him, finally, at about the three yard line, though Martin Luther was backed up on a clipping call. Four plays later, Shorewood-Messmer got the ball back. With time nearly gone, the team made another desperate run down the field, but the season ended with the ball on the 16 yard line, the band already lined up on the track and set to march away. Final score, 24-0.

Final record: 0-9. The wins would have to wait.

Two days later, the coaches and players had a final meeting in the Shorewood locker room. The room was clean again, the lockers washed out and the floor mopped, ready for the varsity basketball team, which would start practice in a few days.

"In order to be successful in life," Coach Trost told them, again standing in the middle of the room, "you have to have an opportunity."

So they talked about opportunity.

The merged team, Trost said, was an opportunity for everyone. A chance for the Messmer kids to try football. A chance for the Shorewood players, especially the seniors, to have a team. They talked about the unknown. How no one, back in August, knew just how the season would end up, how sometimes no one knew who would be there at the start of practice, or if everyone who was there at the start would still be on the field at the end. The coaches had believed the wins would come. They had promised the team success. Now, with the season over, only words could put it right.

So, they talked about brotherhood, how on the field everyone had to protect each other, fight side by side and stick together when things went bad. They had to sweat with their teammates, ache with them and, yes, bleed with them.

White, black. Red, blue.

One.

"Remember the people who you thought were cool, who you thought were your friends?" asked Coach Smith. "They're not in this room right now. How many of them would take on a 300-pound lineman, a defender, coming right at you? I know Nate would. I know Drew would. I know Pertrell would. I know Rob would."

He looked around the room as he talked.

The faces were familiar now. Who could forget Mark bursting into the open field, or Nate slicing through the line and bringing a runner down? Who could forget Drew, fingers twitching with anticipation on defense, or Evan dragging tacklers down the field? Or Pertrell singing the national anthem? Or Rob calling out the breakdown, the team pressed in around him, jumping and shouting, helmets raised? Who could forget the locker rooms or the bus rides, those first tense meetings or the sleepover in the gym?

"If I see one of you guys on the street or in the hallways," Smith said, "I'm going to say, 'There goes a football player.'"

It was a high compliment.

Finally, Trost talked about the expectations. How high they had been and how far from them the team had finished. He talked about the losses.

"When you're talking football 20 years from now, you don't have to say you were 0-9," he said. "I take the responsibility for that. I'm 0-9. It's on my record. Not yours. I accept all the responsibility for what happened this year."

A final pause.

"I accept everything."

At the team banquet the following week, the coaches huddled to decide who should get the team awards. The biggest question was the "Hardest Hit" award. To be sure, the hit everyone remembered was Ronell Halbert knocking Justin Moore — J-Flex — through the air while practicing kick coverage during Dominican week. But they decided it would be wrong to pick a practice hit. Instead, the award went to Drew O'Malley, the Shorewood senior, for his hit on a Dominican player who had fielded his kickoff after Shorewood-Messmer's go-ahead touchdown.

Nate Shorter, the Messmer junior, was named the defensive Most Valuable Player. Mark Moore, of course, offensive MVP. Evan Rivera received the Coaches Award, for every-day effort. Timmy Lathrop the Heart Award — an award Trost noted he received himself back in high school. Finally, the overall MVP award went not to Mark Moore, the team's established star, but to Drew, whose season almost ended in a practice-field dispute with Trost. Of the players who finished the season, Drew was the first to turn back from quitting and become a leader instead.

"Two years ago, Drew was kind of floundering on the soccer team," Trost told the players and parents. "That was good for us. You other players, you should ask him what I mean by, 'The light goes on.' He started for us last year, but didn't make the same impact. Then the light went on."

Mark Moore, who struggled to meet sky-high expectations all season, didn't attend the banquet. With a long weekend ahead, he went to visit Leslie at college.

Throughout much of the second half of the season, after the loss to Watertown Luther Prep and the fallout from the coward comments in the locker room, Coach Trost wrestled with whether or not he should come back for another season. Initially, he was set against it, but by the time the season ended, he vowed to return and get the wins that had eluded them all.

"How do I walk away 0-9?" Trost said one day. "How do I walk away like that and say I'm not a quitter?"

A few days later, he resigned.

Officials from both schools said Trost was simply trying to save face, that a decision already had been made to fire him.

The dispute played out in the daily newspaper and on local sports talk radio. Trost said he quit because he thought it was too dangerous for Shorewood to continue with a varsity program, since the kids were so inexperienced and would end up hurt. He said he had made the case to Shorewood administrators before the start of the season,

Milwaukee Journal Sentinel photo by Benny Sieu

Messmer senior Justin Moore wears a long face on the sideline during one of the team's games. He and others, though, learned valuable lessons about teamwork and togetherness.

something Rick Monroe, the principal, denied. Trost complained of being ordered to play each player in every game and argued Shorewood only kept the team at the varsity level so the band had somewhere to play. This, too, was — vehemently — denied.

It was, of course, a game of spin from both sides. Trost complained of the "revolving door" of players, including some who came for the first time during the fourth week of the season. Yet he let those kids play. He complained of players getting hurt during games, yet most of the more serious injuries happened in practice, several during the controversial Oklahoma drills. The administration, meanwhile, said Trost wasn't respected by the players, though when examples were offered, most were from a season or two earlier. They could have acted sooner. And they said Trost and the coaches got plenty of support, but it wasn't until the second season that the combined team got new uniforms.

The divorce was best for both sides. But it was messy.

The season may have ended, but high school was not over for the players. There were still tests and homework, dates and dances, basketball and baseball and track and, of course, graduation day, which truly sent the players their separate ways.

After the last game, **Mark Moore,** the Shorewood senior, sat at his locker for a long time, finally removing a clip from his shoulder pads — the same thing Trost did at the end of his high school career. Around him, others exchanged promises to stay in touch and pealed the blue Ms off their helmets, the decals destined for scrapbooks or lockers. A few weeks after the season, Mark retook the ACT exam and passed.

In Fargo, North Dakota, the coaches at North Dakota State University, which was planning a jump from Division II to Division I-AA, evaluated the game tapes Trost had sent and asked for more. Mark's aunt, Sandra Tomlinson, sent some of her own tapes, along with a copy of Mr. Wallner's tape from the Lakeside Lutheran game. On the tapes, the coaches saw the flashes of excellence from Mark that punctuated the season, paying closest attention to what Mark did when the rest of the play unfolded right — when fakes were executed and blockers picked up their assignments, when Mark had an opportunity to run well, not just a chance to carry the ball.

On Feb. 6, 2002, Mark Moore signed a national letter of intent to play football for the North Dakota State University Bison, though the news got only a small newspaper mention amid all the local players going Division I, including Whitefish Bay's Booker Stanley to the University of Wisconsin. In August, Mark and his aunt drove the 575 miles from Milwaukee to Fargo, the biggest move of Mark's life. Mark redshirted his freshman season, though he practiced with the team, where the coaches raved about his skills and attitude. During one fall practice, a line-backer blasted through the line and tackled Mark hard in the backfield. The coaches told him not to worry, they would get the problem with the blocking scheme fixed. "Don't worry," Mark told them wryly. "I'm used to it." He was expected to play in the fall of 2003.

While Mark was in North Dakota, calling home frequently, his brother, **Micah**, worked out at running back — not quarterback — for the Shorewood-Messmer team. But Micah injured his knee during the first game, on a Mark-like run to the outside, and missed the rest of his junior season. His friend and classmate, **Curtis Jeffries**, missed several early games recovering from a broken hip suffered during summer baseball. Curtis came back against Luther Prep, notching 10 solo tackles from the linebacker slot. He eventually moved to running back on offense, scoring his first varsity touchdown in the seventh game, against Dominican. He wound up with five. A few months later, his father was transferred to a job in Chicago. Curtis would miss season three.

After the season, **Nate Shorter,** the Messmer junior, thought about transferring to another school, but remained at Messmer and was the anchor of the team his senior year. He also continued as a junior deacon at his church. During his junior season, the team's first, Nate finished third in the Parkland Conference in tackles, with 79 in seven games, but made only honorable mention all-conference. After his senior season, Nate was named first-team all-conference on both offense and defense, as well as first-team all-region. Soon after, his phone began ringing in the evenings, college coaches interrupting his homework: St. Cloud State and Winona State, both in Minnesota, along with Northern Iowa, South Dakota, North Dakota, North Dakota State, Northern Illinois, Miami of Ohio and others — a mix of small Division I schools, along with Division I-AA teams. After graduating in 2003, Nate wrestled with whether he wanted to leave the state or not and, ultimately, enrolled at the University of Wisconsin-Whitewater, which has a Division 3 program.

At the team banquet, Nate shared the MVP award with classmate **Rob Wyatt**, who also thought about transferring over the summer, but instead lined up next to Nate on offense and defense. He liked the new coaching staff better, reveling in game plans he said left the players feeling like they always knew what would happen next. Meanwhile, **Ronell Halbert**, Rob's nephew, caught three touchdown passes from quarterback **Teddy Hanrahan**, the Shorewood player he admired from the freshman team the year before. But, fighting off several nagging injuries, it was a disappointing season for Ronell when it came to individual goals and his oft-stated aspiration of "going D-One." Rob registered an honorable mention all-conference spot, for both offensive and defensive line. Ronell did not. Both received some interest from Winona State, though only Rob wound up with an offer to play college football. He would join Nate at Whitewater.

Pertrell Mallett, the Messmer junior who sang the National Anthem before the final game, wanted to play again as a senior but could not. His father, the divorce now final, needed Pertrell to work to help pay the bills. So, a summer job in the packaging department at Howard Precision Metals, where his father worked, became an after-school job in the fall. After graduation, Pertrell planned to go to a nearby technical college to learn computer programming. He still dreamed of recording a demo for a CD, though at $300 to $400 he deemed it too expensive.

In the winter, Messmer senior **George Lasley**, who had quit after the first football game, tried out for basketball, his favored sport. He made the squad, but quit after a few games, never feeling he was really a part of the team. His "auntie," Allee Potts, died at age 92, shortly before Christmas. George would say when he was growing up that she was the only one who would tell him he would be something someday. "I'm going to be OK," he assured her before she died. In the spring, George graduated and, like many from Messmer, went to Marian College in Fond du Lac, Wisconsin, where he was studying in hopes of one day becoming a principal. The college is predominantly white, a sharp reversal from Messmer. George and the other Messmer students were able to attend through a scholarship fund at the school set up in the name of Messmer President Br. Bob Smith.

In spring 2003, though, George was arrested on a charge of possession of marijuana. An agreement was reached that deferred prosecution, dropping the charge completely if he shaped up.

Seniors **Montreal Miller**, who played sparingly in the final game and broke his wrist on the last play, and **Justin Moore**, Flex, who nearly skipped the last two games, also went to Marian College. Meanwhile, **Sebastian Negron**, who left the football squad to run in Messmer's final cross country meets, considered the military, but instead went to the University of Wisconsin-Milwaukee, through its Navy ROTC program. Of all the football players, the only one not to graduate with his class was **Mark Williams**. He completed his final semester at North Division High School, a Milwaukee public school.

Before the final game, Messmer senior **Maurice Ragsdale** hung out in the locker room. He couldn't suit up because he had again missed practice. At the pre-game meeting, when Trost asked the players if they had anything to say, only Maurice spoke up, saying, "I want all ya'll phone numbers." Trost hushed him immediately. Maurice watched the final game from the stands. Afterwards, he was back in the locker room, looking for a ride home. Maurice and Martin Wallner, the Shorewood sophomore who was his lockermate, exchanged phone numbers. They talked once, after an extensive article about the season appeared in the *Milwaukee Journal Sentinel*, but didn't stay in touch. Maurice did not respond to numerous attempts to be interviewed for this book project.

The article about the team, which ran in the Nov. 25, 2001, edition of the newspaper, received mixed reviews from the players, some of whom thought it delved too deeply into their personal lives or, in the words of Messmer Principal Jeff Monday, wished they had been "more heroically portrayed." Others, though, said it was an honest, unvarnished look at a difficult time and a difficult season. The article appeared in the newspaper's sports section, instead of the front section, as originally intended, prompting some to question why a losing team had gotten so much coverage. Others saw it as a story more about life than about football. Many community leaders said it spoke deeply about the area's racial divide and the differences that mark growing up in Milwaukee and its suburbs.

Dave O'Harrow, the Messmer quarterback who quit after the second game, graduated in the spring from Milwaukee School of Languages, his original school. He planned to attend college somewhere in Illinois in the fall. He and his family did not respond to requests for a follow-up interview for the book project. Likewise, **Drew O'Malley**, the Shorewood senior, declined initial attempts at being interviewed. Finally, a day before he left for Spring Hill College in Alabama, Drew agreed to be be interviewed, but only on football-related matters. When asked about going to the City Conference football game between Marshall High School and Rufus King High School, a statement that spurred a locker-room discussion that touched on race, Drew said he was never at that game. Over the summer, Drew had finished a firefighter training course, but still needed additional classes before he could take a full-time job as a firefighter.

His friend, **Evan Rivera**, went to the University of Wisconsin-Milwaukee, though he talked about eventually transferring to a school somewhere in the south. **Jay White**, the third member of the trio, also went to UWM. **Timmy Lathrop**, the other Shorewood senior to complete the season, competed on the wrestling team, losing his last match in the regional finals to a wrestler from Thomas More, where Coach Trawitzki wound up coaching. Timmy went to North Central College in Naperville, Illinois, planning to major in religious studies and psychology.

Marty Wallner, the Shorewood receiver, returned for his junior season a few inches taller, a few pounds heavier and no longer the smallest guy on the team. He started every game at wide receiver on offense and caught a touchdown pass in the team's first game, though his father was so excited he neglected to snap a picture. Marty also returned punts and kickoffs and started at safety, where he was in charge of calling out the defensive adjustments. Marty, who didn't miss a practice, became an all-conference honorable mention selection and won the Coaches Award. He tried out for the varsity basketball team and made the squad, in no small part due to working on his ball handling skills in the basement every night after finishing his homework during football season.

Indeed, it was at a basketball game the previous spring, a game in the first round of the state tournament, that Messmer president **Br. Bob Smith** knew he could declare the experiment a success. The game matched Shorewood against North Division, with Messmer to play the winner in the second round. Some Messmer students went to Shorewood to watch the game, and as it went on, Smith noticed a group of racially mixed kids talking as if they were old friends. Some were from Messmer, but he didn't recognize the others. When he asked who they were, Smith was told they were mostly football players. Having seen so much of the team in their helmets, he didn't recognize them now.

That, he thought, is how it is supposed to be.

On Aug. 13, 2002, practice began for the second edition of the Shorewood-Messmer football team. The team had a new coaching staff, led by Ron Davies, a 1960 Messmer graduate who left coaching 10 years earlier after a career that included three state championships and two second-place finishes at Kenosha Tremper High School, a powerhouse in Wisconsin high school football. Davies, 59, had already been inducted into the Wisconsin Football Coaches Association Hall of Fame, as well as the athletic hall of fame at both Messmer and Tremper. Davies retired from teaching at the end of the 2000-01 school year, but took the job at Messmer in hopes of rebuilding the program, admitting at the time to being "scared to death."

Davies quickly vowed he wouldn't become a team nanny over the summer, hounding kids to get to the weight room or get in shape. And there would be no joining the team after the season started. Davies, a notoriously detail-minded person, had attended two of the Shorewood-Messmer games the year before and couldn't believe players who had quit the team were still included on the printed roster and, in some cases, the jersey numbers in the program didn't match the players on the field.

When the players arrived for practice, they found the old banged up lockers had been painted a bright red, courtesy of Davies and Coach Groser, the longtime Shorewood assistant. On the first day, there were 24 guys on the field, about an even split between the two schools. Trost's departure brought back three Shorewood seniors who had played football as freshmen. All had been in the band the year before. There also was a TV crew and a local filmmaker, who was planning to follow the team's second season for a documentary project. The Shorewood-Messmer partnership, which would be renewed for another two years after the season, still carried great local interest as the underdog that never had its day.

The traditional rivalry game against Whitefish Bay had been dropped from the schedule, something Coach Trost had long advocated. Instead, the team opened on a Saturday afternoon against Winnebago Lutheran Academy, a small school in Fond du Lac, about 70 miles north of Milwaukee.

The team made its debut in new uniforms — still the red and gray of Shorewood, though the school name was no longer on the front and blue trim was added on the sleeves and around the numbers to signify Messmer. The team fell behind early, rallied in the second half, but lost 14-6 before a crowd of about 50 parents and boosters.

On the opposite side of the field, **Coach Jim Trost**, **Coach Joe Trawitzki** and **Coach Stanley Smith** did their best to blend in with the home crowd. The three, along with the other former coaches, followed the new team closely throughout the season, but mostly from afar. They figured the new season would reflect on them as much as the last season had and were torn between wanting the players to have success, but not so much success it would justify the switch to a new staff. After the season, Trost had applied for an open head coaching job at Grafton High School, a rural town north of Milwaukee, but didn't get it. Instead, he completed his master's degree and, in the fall of 2003, became coach at Horicon High School. The other assistants, including **Coach Jim Carroll** and **Coach Steve Hoagland**, all found jobs as assistant coaches at area high schools. **Coach Herb Larsen**, the assistant from Messmer, left the school for another job — teaching in the science department at Shorewood. **Coach Luke Groser**, still planning to have his ashes sprinkled on the Shorewood football field someday, was back coaching the freshman team and on the varsity sideline keeping statistics, despite an off-season heart attack and bout with pneumonia.

When the team had its first home game a week later, there were 28 players on the sideline. The game was against Lakeside Lutheran, the team Shorewood-Messmer had almost beaten the year before, the game with all the questionable calls. Several former players were there, all a few days away from the start of college classes. Coach Smith watched as well, giving Trost the play-by-play by cell phone. The team lost 42-18.

Nevertheless, as the team went through the brutal opening stretch of its conference schedule, there were signs of progress. The defense gave up fewer big plays and forced more punts. The offense mixed in more passing and seemed to come through more often in key situations. In the game against Watertown Luther Prep, which had crushed them a year earlier, Shorewood-Messmer stopped Prep four times on fourth down inside the 10-yard-line, once from about a foot away from the end zone. The result, however, was still a 27-0 loss. There were also losses to Slinger (42-7), Pewaukee (42-7) and St. Francis (42-0).

On Oct. 11, 2002, the team played host to Dominican High School, which entered the game with a matching 0-6 record. It was homecoming for both Shorewood and Messmer, which was a longtime Dominican rival.

Shorewood-Messmer scored first. And second. And third.

The team held a 21-0 lead late in the first half, when Dominican scored on a 78-yard pass over the middle. But with 22 seconds left, Messmer sophomore Joshua Jackson took the kick off and raced up the middle of the field, ripping his jersey free from a final would-be tackler, and completed an 86-yard run to the end zone, dropping the ball behind him, the stands erupting in cheers that carried as much release as excitement.

A half remained, but the game was over.

It was a perfect night, the sky clear and the air crisp. Br. Bob Smith, the Messmer president, watched from the sideline, along with athletic director Joy Bretsch, who waited until after the start of the fourth quarter before, finally confident of victory, she frantically called TV stations in hopes of getting cameras to the field. Shorewood principal Rick Monroe was in the stands, along with athletic director Cindy Wilburth. So was Messmer principal Jeff Monday — everyone who had a hand in putting it all together. Even Coach Trost, who first pitched the merger, was spotted during the first half watching from outside the fence along Capitol Drive.

The team would go on to lose to Brown Deer, 42-7, but would defeat Greendale Martin Luther, 21-14, and Milwaukee Juneau, 48-6, in an extra non-conference game, to notch a 3-7 record. It was the most wins for a Shorewood team since 1988, the year before the long slide began.

Br. Bob Smith would later say in those final weeks he could see the players growing up before his eyes, finding a fight that had been forgotten, a confidence they could carry with them to the classroom, to college, into life.

Although the team tasted victory three times, none could compare to the first win.

That night, the stands nearly full and the crowd crackling with excitement, the team forced fumbles and interceptions. It clicked on offense and dominated on defense. There were crushing sacks and fingertip catches, perfect field goals and bone-jarring tackles. During the second half, once the lead stretched past 35, the game went to a running clock, and though the clock raced along, it couldn't get to zero fast enough.

2:55. A TV camera crew arrived, turning its spotlight first toward the stands, where students raced to the fence, surounding a Greyhound mascot, screaming and shouting, raising their fingers in the No. 1 sign. Then the camera caught the sideline, where the team chanted — "De-fense, De-fense" — and punctuated it with claps.

1:37. The players formed a wall behind Coach Davies, who was still shouting out instructions and directions, making sure everyone had gotten in. The scoreboard read 42-13. The players blocked Nate and Rob and Ronell, who had located the requisite container of ice water. They hoisted it overhead and dumped it on an unsuspecting Davies.

Zero.

Students ran from the stands and the team raced onto the field, jumping and laughing and shouting and hugging and screaming and basking in the moment that would never come. Blake Comer, a Messmer senior, slid to his knees, fists raised in triumph, he could be labeled a loser no more. "That's for all the haters," he shouted. In the stands, the parents stood and cheered, pumping fists and hugging each other. In North Dakota, Mark Moore's cell phone soon was ringing, courtesy of his aunt, who handed the phone to Rob Wyatt to deliver the news.

Coach Davies herded the team over to shake hands with the Dominican squad, then sent them to the sideline, where they raised their helmets to thank the crowd. But Davies had to wait until the locker room to deliver his message: "You guys responded great. Now you've got to expect to win. This has to be where it's not such a big deal to win." On the field, the team was lost in the moment, gathering behind Nate Shorter and Teddy Hanrahan, one Messmer and one Shorewood, as they talked into the TV camera, to any and all who were watching. Teddy said it was a message game for teams in the conference: Shorewood-Messmer would no longer be a doormat.

"We worked hard," Nate said, when it was his turn. "We had limited numbers, but we did it."

The words could have been scripted, read by any player from any team standing before any TV camera. But this team was not any team.

"Now we're gonna keep doing this," Nate said, not knowing how right he was. "We're gonna keep doing it."

Yes, things were different. Finally, they were different.

The lights on the field didn't stay on all night.

But they should have.

Index

H

Halbert, Ronell 31, 41, 85,
101, 108, 139, 164, 174,
175, 193, 208, 227, 231,
236, 239, 241, 250, 252,
277, 282, 284, 303, 320,
322, 334, 335, 338, 340, 345
Haley, Charles 21
Hallmark Hall of Fame 25
Hanrahan, Teddy
182, 240, 345
Hansen Stadium
26, 132, 240
Hartford, Wis. 16, 172, 258
Heller, Lonnie 69
Herman, Lonnie 9
Hines Community College
233
Hoagland, Steve 35, 36,
257, 283, 287, 303,
304, 327, 332, 350
Holiday Bowl 65
Homestead High School 211
Honeymooners, The 25
Hooper City High School 170
Huston, Kate 9
Hutcherson, Carlton 69
Hyatt Regency Hotel 319
Hyche, Aaron 70

I

Illinois 347
Indian Trails Conference 185
Indiana 223
Irvin, Michael 21

J

Jackson, Jerrel 212, 291
Jackson, Joshua 351
Jackson, Miss. 233
Jackson State University
124, 233
Jallings, Jessica 190
Jeffries, Curtis 186, 221, 344
Jersey City, N.J. 60
Jones, Greg 65
Junction, Texas 263

K

Kansas 196
Kansas State University 233
Kenosha, Wis. 147
Kenosha Tremper High
School 349
Kentucky Fried Chicken 25
Kertscher, Tom 11
Keystone Kops 122
King, Dr. Martin Luther, Jr.
170
Koczela, Emily 73
Koss Corp. 66

L

Lake Leelanau St. Mary High
School 75
Lake Michigan 83
Lake Mills, Wis.
157, 159, 189
Lakeland College 36
Lakeside Lutheran High
School 101, 137, 142,
157, 165, 166, 172,
173, 174, 180, 189,